Transcendence and Film

Transcendence and Film

Cinematic Encounters with the Real

Edited by David P. Nichols

LEXINGTON BOOKS
Lanham • Boulder • New York • London

Published by Lexington Books
An imprint of The Rowman & Littlefield Publishing Group, Inc.
4501 Forbes Boulevard, Suite 200, Lanham, Maryland 20706
www.rowman.com

6 Tinworth Street, London SE11 5AL

Copyright © 2019 by The Rowman & Littlefield Publishing Group, Inc.

All rights reserved. No part of this book may be reproduced in any form or by any electronic or mechanical means, including information storage and retrieval systems, without written permission from the publisher, except by a reviewer who may quote passages in a review.

British Library Cataloguing in Publication Information Available

Library of Congress Cataloging-in-Publication Data Is Available

ISBN 9781498579995 (cloth)
ISBN 9781498580014 (pbk)
ISBN 9781498580007 (electronic)

Contents

List of Illustrations		vii
Introduction		1
	David P. Nichols	
1	The Dream of Anxiety in David Lynch's *Mulholland Drive*	15
	Dylan Trigg	
2	Transcendence and Tragedy in *My Son, My Son, What Have Ye Done*	29
	Herbert Golder	
3	*eXistenZ* or *Existenz:* Transcendence in the Early Twenty-First Century	47
	K. Malcolm Richards	
4	Earth and World: Malick's *Badlands*	63
	Jason M. Wirth	
5	Pointing Toward Transcendence: When Film Becomes Art	77
	Frédéric Seyler	
6	Transcendence in Phenomenology and Film: Ozu's Still Lives	87
	Allan Casebier	
7	ASA NISI MASA: Kierkegaardian Repetition in Fellini's *8 1/2*	99
	Joseph Westfall	
8	Transcendence and the Ineffable in Scorsese's *Silence*	121
	David P. Nichols	
9	*La Passion de Jeanne d'Arc* and the Cadence of Images	137
	John B. Brough	
10	Ciphers of Transcendence in *2001: A Space Odyssey*	147
	Kevin L. Stoehr	
Index		163
About the Contributors		167

List of Illustrations

Fig. 4.1	Badlands.	72
Fig. 6.1	Late Spring.	94
Fig. 7.1	8 1/2.	114
Fig. 8.1	Silence.	131
Fig. 9.1	La Passion de Joanne d'Arc.	139
Fig. 10.1	2001: A Space Odyssey.	157

Introduction

David P. Nichols

The *Transcendence and Film* project arises out of a concern that philosophy of film all too frequently falls short of addressing questions about the essence of cinema itself. When philosophers of film use movies to illustrate problems, whether moral, metaphysical, or epistemic in nature, they are borrowing from the art form in much the same way that they might borrow from a lived experience altogether outside of it. We have borrowed philosophical dilemmas from works of literature in much the same way, and for many centuries longer. It is quite a different matter, however, to interrogate film (or literature) for what it is, and what it alone can do. We immediately suspect that such an interrogation must lead us through what it means for film to be art, and not only that, but art of a specific kind.

The moving picture is a relatively recent innovation in the history of art, its birth a somewhat untimely one. It enters history in a postmodern era, when already the "death of art" has become a theme. Yet most of us feel compelled to include film as an artistic mode, alongside ancient forms like music and the plastic arts, and despite its specifically technological character—for it is, after all, art from the machine. The traditional art mediums emerged largely from the cradles of civilization, long before passing under the purview of the philosophical critic or submitting to the collective self-consciousness of "art." What is it about film—or at least great film—that evokes in us a sense of presence like unto standing before a sculpture or viewing a drama? The authors in this book have decided to take the term "transcendence" as a starting point for making sense of this experience of art, and to approach cinema as having its own mode for facilitating it.

Then there are questions about the proximity of film to the other artistic modes. Does film resemble the drama most closely because of its narrative whole and its motion? Perhaps music is a better candidate, especially given that both drama and film so readily make use of it. Maybe Tarkovsky has good reasons for thinking that film resembles sculpting, both in the director's work and also in the final product.[1] Danto raises the point, albeit briefly, that film facilitates an experience akin to that of architecture—"not something merely to be looked at but moved through."[2] Or, might we not make headway by tracing the motion picture back to the history of photography which *in*-forms it, and then to painting as what informs the photo? Suddenly we feel as though we are at the Henry Ford Museum at precisely that place where the horse and carriage displays give way to the remarkably similar look of the first automobiles. When it comes to forging bridges to the other artistic modes, philosophers of film have offered no small number of thoughtful observations, although they have obtained precious little agreement. It may be just as well to admit that the motion picture resembles each of the traditional art forms in some way or other, but that the more interesting reality is to be found in what it has in common with none of them.

At the same time, the *Transcendence and Film* project steers clear of the traditional essentialism whereby one might assign a fixed, timeless definition to what constitutes film as an art form. Instead, we recognize a more dynamic expression whereby a great motion picture can defy and surpass our expectations for what the art form can do. The medium may expand its technical capabilities, as when the silent film gave way to sound, or the silver screen to color. Or the medium may surprise us simply by way of its content, as when it explores unchartered thematic frontiers. New genres will emerge: action, adventure, drama, western, science fiction, and horror. We can now speak intelligently and comparatively of whole production centers for film—e.g., American, European, Bollywood, and Chinese—and the way they become crucibles for stylistic difference. Where transcendence is concerned, the dynamism for any art form is found in its ability to crack open the sky of our world—to upset an established order for how everything hangs together. To do this the medium must summon us to an original experience of how the world is at work, an experience which usually eludes us. The rejection of fixed essences for the arts, or a metaphysical taxonomy of medium types, does not however require of us a wholesale abandonment of the "what" of each artistic mode. No matter how plastic the medium of cinema might become, no matter how much it might expand and stretch its own possibilities, it will retain a distinctive way about itself. It will facilitate transcendence in its own peculiar way too.

The contributors to this volume have drawn upon continental philosophers of various stripes, and of phenomenology and existentialism camps most prominently, for the sake of bringing crucial concepts of transcendence to bear upon the work of leading film directors. The philosophers most at stake: Søren Kierkegaard, Friedrich Nietzsche, Edmund Husserl, Karl Jaspers, Martin Heidegger, Jean-Paul Sartre, Maurice Merleau-Ponty, Gilles Deleuze, Michel Henry, and Alain Badiou. The directors under analysis: David Cronenberg, Karl Theodor Dreyer, Federico Fellini, Werner Herzog, Stanley Kubrick, David Lynch, Terrence Malick, Yasujiro Ozu, and Martin Scorsese. What is most attractive about these applications for the contributors is best summed up by way of the juxtaposition, among phenomenologists and existentialist philosophers, of "seeming and being." From the outset, our experience of a movie requires something akin to a suspension, so that instead of merely seeing a series of variegated colors projected onto a flat, white wall, we allow for the images to come alive, with what Derrida identifies as their spectral quality.[3] Like ghosts, the characters speak to us with a presence and vibrancy that is real and yet of course not real at all, three dimensional and yet of course flat. In truth our orientation is one so convinced of the reality of these ghosts, so taken into their "galaxy, far, far away," that the experience of color projections or the flat screen now requires the abstraction.

Here already the cinema speaks to a crucial divergence about reality pervasive through the history of philosophy as well as everyday life. If we choose to understand it in terms of a "projection," so that how the machine casts forward its images in the theater becomes metaphor for a similar casting in human consciousness, then we might stand in the good company of Plato's cave allegory or a Kantian *a posteriori* synthesis. From a classic phenomenological viewpoint, we might draw conclusions about how phenomena show themselves within a wider horizon of meaning, so that the unfolding of the film sequence opens for us a world without which its individual objects could not meaningfully arise. Or with the existentialists we might insist that film resembles a basic "ecstatic" condition of human existence whereby we inhabit a world whose making we are largely responsible for, and to which we have fallen from the zero of our original selves. Moreover, even within our galaxy far, far away the difference between seeming and being speaks to us—e.g., in symbolic and otherwise vivid images, surprisingly astute thematic realizations, or the ironic plot twist of a suspense thriller. The possibilities for summoning us to greater realities are just as many in film as they are in life, the difference between seeming and being every bit as significant. Yet art has a way of framing reality before our eyes so that the great ontological truths we so readily take for granted step forward to demand attention by way of the medium.

The ten chapters in this volume can be rather disparate with respect to working out what transcendence means and how it opens to us for cinema. Yet several threads emerge through the collection, four of which I anticipate will be particularly helpful to the reader. I will refer to these four threads as the limits of existence, the immanence of transcendence, rhythm or cadence, and ciphers of transcendence. In the first thread, film sometimes opens us to transcendence by heightening our awareness of the limits of consciousness, if not human existence itself. Examples include the dream world sequence of David Lynch's *Mulholland Drive* (2001), where according to Dylan Trigg, the very logic of the film's sequence breaks down around the anxiety of the characters.[4] For Trigg, the film obeys "hypnagogic" and "hypnopompic" patterns that vacillate between dreaming and wakefulness, not unlike the sometimes marginal state of the sleeper. This scheme allows Lynch to place characters in suspension rather than any fixed state about their identity, and to come to terms with themselves amidst a sea of groundless anxiety. Terrence Malick's *Badlands* (1973) impresses upon us the significance of our finitude by way of characters that are oblivious to it.[5] Nothing seems all that real to them on their murderous spree, which leads Jason Wirth to observe that life, like a bad film, typically conceals our existential limits, and with that, our means for transcendence. Stanley Kubrick's *2001: A Space Odyssey* (1968) keeps moving the viewer toward states of disembodiment according to Kevin Stoehr.[6] It does this through various means, including groundless, seemingly nowhere vantage points for viewing heavenly bodies, zero gravity living spaces, the mysteriously self-directed artificial intelligence of HAL, and ultimately the eclipse of human existence by an extraterrestrial race that, with the exception of the reborn Star Child, remains removed from sensible contact. Transcendence in *2001*, while attractively progressive in many ways, also has the unsavory characteristic of tearing us from all things familiar—and really, from every grounding for who we are.

Some of the films under analysis expose the limits for human thought by way of a mythological or fictional consciousness. Herbert Golder describes how the protagonist in *My Son, My Son, What Have Ye Done* (2009), which he cowrote with Werner Herzog, displays a mythical thinking unbefitting the modern era.[7] Brad is completely out of joint in the contemporary world, mentally deranged by our standards. Yet within the logic of the ancient Greek tragedy his pursuits make plenty of sense. What ought to bring him deliverance according to that logic actually results in his ruin. This opens a storehouse of difficult questions for the viewer about what the modern age has lost with regard to mythological consciousness, what film has to do with myth, and what film has to offer as the locus for a new mythology. David Cronenberg's *eXistenZ* (1999), with its fictional game world motif, challenges our capacity to distinguish what makes one phenomenal semblance any more "real" than another.[8] By the end of the film we can no longer determine with any credibility whether the characters reside within a game world or not. Kevin Richards shows that the film destabilizes us in a manner that challenges our most treasured assumptions about how to ground reality. In these sorts of films—by Lynch, Malick, Herzog, Cronenberg, and others—we feel transcendence at those moments that cause us to brush up against the margins of the real, and sometimes to see one world crumbling before another. Allan Casebier captures the existentialist approach to this well when he says in his chapter that "transcendence is a condition wherein horizons are in abeyance."

In our second thread, the immanence of transcendence, we find examples for the nearness of being communicated through cinema. Casebier reviews the Husserlian concept of "transcendence-within-immanence," which lands us, through eidetic reduction, at the givenness of phenomena more so than an overcoming of world. Film has a way of letting the appearances show themselves more fully, argues Casebier. To such moments of being wholly present he would apply the Zen aphorism, "When I eat, I eat; when I sleep, I sleep." We find a use of immanence not altogether different in Michel Henry, for whom "transcendence in immanence" describes art as a radical intensification of life. Frédéric Seyler explores this in his chapter for the sake of contrasting film, as an artwork, with television. Art must work from a fundamental unity underlying the artwork—an origin that nonetheless escapes every attempt to objectify it. This unity makes it possible for the artwork to give rise to a lived context with its own constancy, weight, and coherent totality. Jason Wirth recognizes in Malick's films the immanent quality of the artwork standing as its own original event, not as a device for peddling theoretical concepts. "To be clear: the film does not have a particular philosophical position but rather evokes the space of thinking itself," says Wirth. In all of these approaches to immanence, the authors explore the propensity of film to place us within a horizon of its own immediate and original experience, made possible by the power of the phenomena to show itself. These concepts of immanence may dislodge traditional notions about transcendence, and yet, despite that, we ought not to think of them as replacements. Rather, immanence and transcendence are conjoined in the sense that the nearness of being—so very near to us—is precisely what makes it seem so far away from us.

In our third thread, the rhythm or cadence of film, we encounter transcendence in relation to time, which is, no doubt, key to film as an art medium. Joseph Westfall borrows from Kierkegaard's theory of "repetition" for the sake of tracing the cinematic movement. With Kierkegaard the past is always experienced from within a present moment that must transform the meaning of that past. Likewise for film, argues Westfall, the first scene of a motion picture, and the successive scenes as well, change in meaning as the film progresses. But this repetition of the past amounts to more than a mere recollection or a carrying of memory; it is instead the dynamic repeatability of time itself—the existential repeat, so to speak—whereby each moment presents itself anew. Federico Fellini's *8 1/2* (1963) displays a similar sense of repetition by way of particular repetitious phenomena, so that the viewer comes to realize what is transcendent from within the order.[9] John Brough's analysis of Karl Theodor Dryer's *La Passion de Jeanne d'Arc* (1928) identifies a rhythmic sequence to the series of close-up portraits for characters' faces, especially for Joan of Arc herself.[10] The alternation of these portraits between characters makes for an "oscillation of moods," says Brough, whereby the viewer experiences contrasting relationships to being. The agony of Joan's portraits shows her struggle to remain a responsible spokesperson for the transcendence that she cannot easily explain or defend. Meanwhile the portraits of her judges show their ineptitude to think beyond the simple systematic workings of their rational investigation.

In some cases, the rhythm or cadence of a film invites us to a particular attunement. I attempt to capture this in my own chapter about Scorsese's *Silence* (2016) by drawing upon parallel phenomenological concepts in Merleau-Ponty.[11] The world speaks to us with a "gesture" that precedes our linguistic possibilities and yet pokes through our meaning structures, says Merleau-Ponty. The motion picture has an ontological fabric or "flesh" just as much as the world does, and similarly submerges its own gesture. Scorsese exposes this ineffability through what I call a "monastic attunement": he allows the typically muted natural surroundings of characters to beckon the viewer at every turn. Casebier develops the notion of a "transcendental style" to explain particular types of nonconventional cinematic cadences that open the viewer to the possibilities of transcendence. He uses the minimalistic techniques of film director Yasujiro Ozu to illustrate the effectiveness. Ozu stingily restricts the conventional techniques of dissolves, fades, emotional direction, etc., in exchange for more focused, if not stationary, imagery. The simplified rhythm allows Ozu his signature "still lives" scenes, which focus momentarily but poignantly on simple objects—such as a vase or tatami mat—for a film space emptied of characters and ordinary use. Consequently, Ozu becomes the director of *mono no aware*, the experience of large impressions derived from small things.

In our fourth thread, ciphers of transcendence, we recognize the power of symbolism to open the viewer to deeper experiences of being. Several contributors decided to apply Karl Jaspers' highly influential theory of ciphers to film images. For Jaspers, human beings have no direct experiences of being; we process transcendence primarily through the mediation of ciphers.[12] As the intimate presence of the encompassing of being, and the stuff of art and religion, their truths afford no objective proof or verification—only a flood of meaning possibilities pouring through the image. Stoehr recognizes ciphers as such in *2001*: black monoliths; the colorful, almost birth canal tunnel of the Star Gate journey; the mysterious Star Child; even the vast interstellar shots that punctuate scenes. They are sometimes disturbing, sometimes majestic—but always they threaten to uproot us from our familiar physical reality. Golder observes how *My Son, My Son, What Have Ye Done* bursts with ciphers, from the God-face on the Quaker Oats label in the cupboard to a pride of ostriches, or "dinosaurs in drag," running through the desert. No matter how much those ciphers may glow with being for Brad, they have little currency in the plastic pink flamingo world of his modern neighborhood. Brough's interpretation of Dryer's *La Passion de Jeanne d'Arc* provides a few excellent examples of the cipher, and not only in the troubled visage of Joan, whose face speaks to us as a surface with infinite depth. Joan's oppressors offer her the communion host as a kind of bribe, thus reducing the cipher to a mere thing. Other examples of the cipher in this film capitalize on death and its anguish, including a crown of straw, an unearthed skull, and birds fluttering above her burning body. In much the same manner, when Casebier observes Ozu's ciphers of the vase and tatami mat, or when I interpret Scorsese's ciphers of *fumie*, crosses, rosary beads, and other relics, we are a long way from the symbol as mere one-to-one metaphor.

Now I offer a brief synopsis for each of the ten chapters. The book leads with a chapter by Dylan Trigg who argues that David Lynch's *Mulholland Drive* is more than just a love story gone wrong. It is a film where the border between reality and dream weakens, leaving the protagonist, Diane, to face the anxiety of an awful truth, that far from being a successful actor, she is in fact a murderer. Trigg forges connections between anxiety and dreaming for *Mulholland Drive*. He begins by considering how anxiety is dreamlike for the film and decides that the "dream logic" at work is predicated on the fragmentation and alienation of Diane's own sense of self. Then Trigg makes the case that Lynch's treatment of anxiety is transcendental, in the sense that the anxiety confronting Diane outstrips her subjectivity and ultimately the framework of the film itself.

Herbert Golder comments on his film, *My Son, My Son, What Have Ye Done*, with its conflict of ancient and modern modes of existence. It was directed by Werner Herzog, with whom Golder has worked extensively; it was executive-produced by David Lynch. The storyline for the film is that its protagonist, Brad, acts out the murder that he was cast to play in a Greek tragedy. When he kills his own mother, the mythic and the real become one for him. Instead of achieving some sort of apotheosis through the former, he falls tragically between the cracks of both. Yet between the ancient myth and modern reality Golder pinpoints a great paradox. On the one hand, the modern world rids itself of the mythical consciousness, to the extent that it would be nothing short of madness to live it out in a contemporary setting. On the other hand, a touch of madness might be just what the modern world calls for now that its reigning semblance of meaning seems to have come out of joint. Golder borrows from Karl Jaspers' interpretation of Shakespeare, which imputes to Hamlet a "mask of madness" for the sake of owning up to a crumbling world. Ever the insightful classicist, Golder wrote into the screenplay various images and sequences reminiscent of Homeric similes—dreamy invocations of an alternate, fundamental reality that Brad alone comes to know.

Kevin Richards analyzes David Cronenberg's *eXistenZ*, a film which contrasts and obfuscates technological and natural realms of existence. A virtual reality programmer, Allegra, leads her volunteer gamer, Pikul, through her latest game system, with all sorts of discomforting results. Richards observes multiple examples for how phenomena are uneasily conjoined within the fictional constructs of game world, film world, or natural world. The technological reconstructions of reality can in fact turn grotesque. But even before and after Allegra and Pikul have played the game, appearances have uncanny ways of fitting but not fitting, simultaneously real and unreal. A trademark of Cronenberg films is the failure to reach ultimate ground—that the closer we come to reality, the more elusive, amorphous, and groundless it becomes for us. At the end of the film, just when Allegra, Pikul, and other volunteers seem to have emerged from the game sequence, Cronenberg disrupts any possibility of finding *terra firma*. Instead of redeeming the "real world" from the virtual reality, he leaves the viewer lost in thought about what virtual reality the characters now belong to—or if any at all. Of course these issues about the real come with implications for what separates or connects the world of film and the so-called real world.

Jason Wirth supplies us with yet another example of a crumbling world in Terrence Malick's *Badlands*, even if the characters do not realize it. Wirth notices that despite Malick's strong background in philosophy, he refuses to succumb to the temptation of reducing film to a mere vehicle for philosophical ideas. Instead, Malick wants his films to "think" in their own ways, flawed though that may be. Wirth employs Heideggerian concepts of "world" and "earth" to explain a fundamental tension out of which this "thinking" arises. By world Heidegger indicates a structure of meaning that holds sway over and all around us; by earth he means a concealed ground underlying all of our attempts at meaning, sheltered, and stubbornly resistant to our attempts to understand. Put crudely, it is an ontological distinction between that in which we move and that which we bring with us into those surroundings. Wirth argues that in *Badlands*, characters Kit and Holly inhabit a world that is oblivious to an underlying reality of death. Deleuze has commented that "It is not we who make cinema; it is the world which looks to us like a bad film."[13] The irony about *Badlands*, says Wirth, is that Kit and Holly are actually movie characters who illustrate for us life being like a bad film.

Frédéric Seyler seeks philosophical justification for understanding film as art. He arrives at an answer through a discussion about Michel Henry's concept of art as "intensification of life." Henry opposes the immanence of life to the transcendence of the world, with the end result of a concept of absolute life that he calls "transcendence in immanence." Seyler explores the possibility that film could qualify as art under the condition that it is pointing toward Henry's transcendence in immanence. It would have to distinguish itself, however, from television, which Henry critiques as a "practice of barbarism," and whereby it fails to create the rhythmic whole of such a lived experience. Unlike works of art, television fails to pull a thread that returns us to continuous existence. Seyler uses films like Louis Malle's *My Dinner with André* (1981) and Paul Verhoeven's *Hollow Man* (2000) to make points about the film continuity needed for transcendence in immanence.[14] He closes with some additional thoughts from Henri Bergson about the singularity of narrative purpose accomplished by film.

Allan Casebier explores the notion of a "transcendental style" which occurs to greater and lesser degrees among films. He traces this concept's early elucidation in Paul Schrader's book, *The Transcendental Style in Film*.[15] For Schrader the transcendent style invokes something greater for the viewer than the ordinary sense experience. It runs as deep as the rhythm of the film because it invokes an almost sacred moment worthy of repeatability, somewhat akin to a liturgical experience. Casebier further develops the meaning of the transcendent style by drawing upon phenomenological concepts of transcendence in Edmund Husserl and Karl Jaspers. An important difference between the two philosophers for Casebier is that Jaspers is more open to transcendence as an interruption of horizons. In order to illustrate such phenomenological possibilities for a transcendent style, Casebier describes the "still lives" technique of Yasujiro Ozu, director of Japanese classics like *Late Spring* (1949) and *Tokyo Story* (1953).[16] Ozu's films exemplify traditional themes of Japanese minimalism, such as the restrained or modest suggestiveness that is *shibui*, the deep but subtle impressions of fragile beauty that constitute *mono no aware*, and the pervasive emptiness of *mu*. He allows these themes to show themselves in the lingering presences, and absences, of otherwise unnoticed objects, so as to lend these objects a newly found transcendent power.

Joseph Westfall borrows from Kierkegaard's notion of repetition for the sake of explaining time as well as the rhythmic ability of cinema to obey and convey it. He begins by contrasting Kierkegaardian repetition with Platonic recollection, the latter which, in large measure, we have come to take for granted. "One cannot take one's first trip to Berlin a second time," says Westfall as he recounts an experiment by Kierkegaard. The theater will be playing a different show; the food might not taste the same. The point is that although we experience repetition of the past, even a repetition of world at each moment, the repetition itself must always be, by its very nature, different. Nor can we help but keep reconstituting, reinterpreting, or transfiguring the past in our present moment. On this view of time, the past is not something constant and distant for which we strive to accomplish the correct retrieval. Instead we keep experiencing an unsettling of that past, an opening up of its possibilities, within our present moment. Westfall argues that film is a medium well adapted to these temporal realities about the repetition. Yet, ironically, the history of film has gravitated far more often to narratives that assume the recollection motif.

Fellini's *8 1/2* is one of those cinematic exceptions that gets it right according to Westfall. The film has a peculiar way of creating false repetitions, if not recollections, only to turn them monstrous—e.g., the way that the protagonist, Guido, remembers all of the women in his life simultaneously, as though in a harem; or the way that Fellini clearly borrows images from recently cast popular movies. Guido is a film director who fails to repeat his prior successes, or even to get his next film started, although not for lack of script or crew. He finally attempts to do so by magically incanting a cryptic nonsense phrase, as he once superstitiously did in his youth for the sake of making pictures move: "Asa Nisi Masa." The ritual allows him to establish a seamless continuity from his childhood to his present. Westfall observes that Fellini's *8 1/2* does not end with a conventional resolution of Guido's problem, so much as the self-transcendence of a character whose own moving picture remains, as before, at its "time to begin."

In my own chapter, I describe Martin Scorsese's *Silence* as a masterful demonstration of the power of film to bring to the fore what is ordinarily elusive to our human perception. Scorsese does this by way of a cinematic rhythm that attunes the viewer to background sounds and visual horizons. He also uses religious symbols to convey ontological truths deeper than what we can communicate by linguistic signs alone. In sum, the world so typically muted to us suddenly becomes loud. I form a phenomenological analysis of the film that borrows from Merleau-Ponty's own use of "silence," in which he ascribes to the world a primary rhythm, or a natural structure of phenomena in motion. On this view the original gesture of the world gets buried beneath, and yet embedded within, human language. Merleau-Ponty likewise argues for a silence at work in the rhythm of film, so as to make possible the "flesh" of that film's world. I show that Scorsese's film conveys a similar sense of silence, one that draws upon possibilities from within the film's rhythm, and that, as illustrated by the film's iconography, opens into a kind of face of the world or "Eye of God" before whose transformative power we stand as viewers. The crowning moment of the film, at least for our purposes of grasping what film itself does, occurs when the Jesuit missionary Rodrigues stares at his own reflection in a stream, only to see that image suddenly transform into the face of God looking back at him.

John Brough takes a much more dialectical approach to explaining the possibilities of rhythm, one for which multiple conflicting rhythms may pervade a film and yet flow together. He analyzes Karl Theodor Dryer's *La Passion de Jeanne d'Arc*, situated almost entirely around Joan's trial. Dryer's depiction of this legal proceeding quickly turns personal: It is a trial focused more upon who Joan is than what she has done. The film oscillates in a remarkable series of close-ups, back and forth between Joan's face and the faces of her judges. Strangely, Dryer's classic consists almost entirely of the close-up camera shot. He causes the oppositional sets of images to share a single rhythm, for a disturbing confluence of two streams, each stubbornly maintaining a motion of its own. Brough also identifies the trickle of a rhythm of empathy for Joan among some characters, albeit one that just as repetitively negates its offers. He locates a Eucharistic rhythm too, where the host is presented to her coercively and then freely.

Joan finds herself caught in an existential struggle whereby her faith in transcendence is tested by a seemingly impossible situation. She can condemn herself with the words provided by her accusers or else she can invite condemnation by speaking for an inexpressible mystical experience. Dryer had commented that the facial close-ups had a way of capturing mood, and along with that, meanings inexpressible with words. Brough recognizes various ciphers for transcendence, not only in the faces, but also in twisted images, like that of the Eucharistic host used as an object of manipulation, a crown of straw swept away on a floor, and a worm-ridden skull unearthed accidentally. In the end, the cadence of Joan's portraits, full of anxiety, isolation, and bewilderment, give way to images of strength and integrity, and finally to a death befitting a true heroine. She accomplishes her heroism through a victory of silence, the language that speaks loudest for mystical experiences, if not for the rhythm of motion picture.

In the final chapter of the collection, Kevin Stoehr mines Stanley Kubrick's *2001: A Space Odyssey* for ciphers of transcendence. The film illustrates three modes of transcendence, he says, often conveyed through the cipher: disembodied presence; higher forms of intelligence, machine-based or extraterrestrial; and moments of metaphysical insight. The ciphers have a tragic element about them in that they never take us to their higher level without at the same time uprooting us from where and who we are. The vast interplanetary images that punctuate scenes, as in the "Waltz of the Spaceships" sequence, have a way of removing us from ordinary, grounded perspectives, for the sake of catapulting the viewer into a mental existence far adrift. The use of technology and tool-thinking permeates the film, from the Dawn of Man opening, to various spaceship life scenes, to the destruction of HAL, but always with losses to self, not only for gain. The narrative culminates in the highly enigmatic cipher of the Star Child, which Stoehr likens to a synthesis of the immanent and the transcendent, the earthly and the beyond. Yet this embryonic arrival is no less threatening in its possibilities for human existence. In the end, Kubric's masterpiece facilitates a sober warning about the costs of transcendence in the disembodiment, detachment, and dehumanization that unravels us.

Finally, I would like to express my gratitude to the larger band of participants who made this project possible. This includes Alan M. Olson, Boston University, and Gregory J. Walters, Saint Paul University Ottawa, for their scholarly advice, brainstorming, and organizational assistance. Much of what appears in this volume had its origin in panel meetings for the American Philosophical Association, with a wider crew of speakers, respondents, and dialogue partners. It was there that, in some ways, Robert Pippen, University of Chicago, Shai Biderman, Tel Aviv University, and Kevin Stoehr, Boston University, were catalysts for the *Transcendence and Film* project without even knowing it. Other participants included Alina N. Feld, Hofstra University, Gerard Kuperus, University of San Francisco, Tom Leddy, San Jose State University, Amanda Parris, San Francisco University, Robert Ribera, Portland State University, and Martin Schwab, University of California Irvine.

The *Transcendence and Film* project began as an attempt to revisit what is most at stake for art, ontologically speaking. It resulted in some important realizations about how film allows us to brush up against the boundaries of our existence. At the same time, the pursuit of transcendence also had a way of pulling us inward, back to what is most inherent within film. By and large this is its rhythmic motion, which flows through shifting camera shots like a steady stream among rocks, simultaneously giving shape to a narrative, in a world of its own. I am convinced that the motion picture, through this narrative formation, opens contemporary possibilities for us to have mythology. Herein lies at least the beginning of an antidote to what Nietzsche bemoans as modernity's "mythless man," who "stands eternally hungry, surrounded by all past ages, and digs and grubs for roots, even if he has to dig for them among the remotest antiquities."[17] For the sake of understanding the new mythology, I hope that the exploration of "ciphers of transcendence," a theme pervasive in this collection, will also open some avenues for thought. Finally, should anyone come to these pages too hardened to appreciate what is meant by the experience of transcendence, I would only remind that same person of the first time that he or she sat, with the wonder and awe befitting a child, in a dark movie theater, enraptured by the light that pours forth to us another world. That world did not constitute an "escape" from reality as so many movie-goers like to say. It was instead a more original experience—however brief, however much *felt*—of being in the world.

NOTES

1. Andrey Tarkovsky, *Sculpting in Time: The Great Russian Filmmaker Discusses His Art*, trans. Kitty Hunter-Blair (Austin: University of Texas Press, 2016).

2. Arthur C. Danto, "Moving Pictures," *Quarterly Review of Film Studies*, Vol. 4:1 (1979): 116.

3. Jacques Derrida, "Cinema and Its Ghosts," in *The Continental Philosophy of Film Reader*, ed. Joseph Westfall, trans. Peggy Kamuf, interviewed Antoine de Baecque and Thierry Jousse (New York: Bloomsbury Academic, 2018), 603-13.

4. David Lynch (Producer), and David Lynch (Director). *Mulholland Drive*, United States: Universal Studios Home Entertainment, 2001.

5. Warner Brothers (Producer), Terrence Malick (Director), *Badlands*. USA: 1973.

6. Metro-Goldwyn-Mayer (Producer), Stanley Kubrick (Director), *2001: A Space Odyssey*. United Kingdom: 1968.

7. Bassett, E. (Producer), & Herzog, W. (Director). *My Son, My Son, What Have Ye Done?* United States: Industrial Entertainment, 2009.
8. David Cronenberg (Producer), David Cronenberg (Director), *eXistenZ*. Canada, 1999.
9. Angelo Rizzoli (Producer), Federico Fellini (Director), *8 1/2*. Italy: Cineriz, 1963.
10. La Société générale (Producer), Karl Theodor Dreyer (Director), *La Passion de Jeanne d'Arc*. Paris, France, 1928.
11. Irwin Winkler, Randall Emmett, George Furla (Producers). Martin Scorsese (Director). *Silence*. Los Angelos: Paramount Pictures, 2016.
12. Leonard H. Ehrlich, "Tillich's 'Symbol' vis-à-vis Jaspers' 'Cipher,'" *Harvard Theological Review*, 66:1 (Cambridge University Press, 1973), 153-156.
13. Gilles Deleuze, *Cinema 2: The Time-Image* (Minneapolis: University of Minnesota Press, 1989), 171.
14. Saga Productions Inc., The Andre Company (Producers), Louis Malle (Director), *My Dinner with André*. USA, 1981. Columbia Pictures (Producer), Paul Verhoeven (Director), *Hollow Man* Los Angeles: USA, 2000.
15. Paul Schrader, *The Transcendental Style in Film* (Berkeley: UC Press. 1972).
16. Shochiku Eiga (Producer), Yasujiro Ozu (Director), *Tokyo Story*. Japan, 1953. Shochiku Eiga (Producer), Yasujiro Ozu (Director), *Late Spring*. Japan, 1949.
17. Friedrich Nietzsche, *The Birth of Tragedy*, trans. Walter Kaufmann (New York: Vintage Books, 1967), 136.

BIBLIOGRAPHY

Bassett, Eric. (Producer). Werner Herzog (Director). *My Son, My Son, What Have Ye Done?* United States: Industrial Entertainment, 2009.
Columbia Pictures (Producer). Paul Verhoeven (Director). *Hollow Man*. Los Angeles: USA, 2000.
Cronenberg, David (Producer). David Cronenberg (Director). *eXistenZ*. Canada, 1999.
Danto, Arthur C. "Moving Pictures." *Quarterly Review of Film Studies*, Vol. 4:1 (1979): 1-21.
Deleuze, Gilles. *Cinema 2: The Time-Image*. Minneapolis: University of Minnesota Press, 1989.
Derrida, Jacques. "Cinema and Its Ghosts." In *The Continental Philosophy of Film Reader*, edited by Joseph Westfall, translated by Peggy Kamuf, interviewed by Antoine de Baecque and Thierry Jousse, 603-13. New York: Bloomsbury Academic, 2018.
Lynch, David (Producer). Lynch, David (Director). *Mulholland Drive*. United States: Universal Studios Home Entertainment, 2001.
Metro-Goldwyn-Mayer (Producer). Stanley Kubrick (Director). *2001: A Space Odyssey*. United Kingdom: 1968.
Nietzsche, Friedrich. *The Birth of Tragedy*. Translated by Walter Kaufmann. New York: Vintage Books, 1967.
Rizzoli, Angelo (Producer). Federico Fellini (Director). *8 1/2*. Italy: Cineriz, 1963.
La Société générale (Producer). Karl Theodor Dreyer (Director). *La Passion de Jeanne d'Arc*. Paris, France, 1928.
Saga Productions Inc., The Andre Company (Producers). Louis Malle (Director). *My Dinner with André*. USA, 1981.
Schrader, Paul. *The Transcendental Style in Film*. Berkeley: UC Press, 1972.
Shochiku Eiga (Producer). Yasujiro Ozu (Director). *Late Spring*. Japan, 1949.
Shochiku Eiga (Producer). Yasujiro Ozu (Director). *Tokyo Story*. Japan, 1953.
Tarkovsky, Andrey. *Sculpting in Time: The Great Russian Filmmaker Discusses His Art*. Translated by Kitty Hunter-Blair. Austin: University of Texas Press, 2016.
Warner Brothers (Producer). Terrence Malick (Director). *Badlands*. USA, 1973.
Winkler, Irwin, Randall Emmett, George Furla (Producers). Martin Scorsese (Director). *Silence*. Los Angeles: Paramount Pictures, 2016.

ONE

The Dream of Anxiety in David Lynch's *Mulholland Drive*

Dylan Trigg

MYSTERY, ILLUSION, LOVE

"Part one: she found herself inside the perfect mystery. Part two: a sad illusion. Part three: love."[1] Such is how David Lynch describes the narrative of *Mulholland Drive*.[2] The appeal of the synopsis resides in its enigmatic clarity. Lynch provides us with a schematic of the film's essential structure, offering us the barest outline, which is at once crystal clear and irreducibly murky. But these terms are also misleading. After all, Lynch's film is far from a conventional narrative, in which each part can be considered as a discrete cell. This is a film in which the boundaries between space and time, reality and dream, and memory and imagination dissolve. Furthermore, it is a film, in which the viewers themselves are confronted with their own desires and anxieties in the face of a narrative that is both disintegrating and integrated.

In this chapter, I reflect on the anxiety central to *Mulholland Drive*, and in particular to how this anxiety is peculiar to a hypnagogic state between dreaming and wakefulness. Lynch's films are often thought as belonging to a dreamy space, a kind of alternative universe with a logic of its own, and which is separate from what we term "reality." This view would find evidence in Lynch's usage of dream portals, boxes, keys, and other such everyday objects, which signal the transition from one realm to another. Yet what is overlooked in this formulation is the very transition itself. My thesis in this chapter is that this transition between dreaming and reality is significant, not least because it is the site where Lynch's exploration of anxiety takes place. From the outset, I undertake these reflections in a cautious and compressed way, knowing in advance how broad the theme of dreaming in Lynch is. Moreover, part of the challenge inherent in this undertaking involves an analysis of a phenomenon that is manifestly non-cognitive in structure and nature. Attempting to tie down anxiety and dreaming by way of philosophical reflection may be destined to fail, not least if we take Lynch's own dismissal of such an approach. Indeed, thinking alongside David Lynch—rather than using Lynch as a mere illustration of an already existing thought—means honing in on one issue and leaving several more on the margins, and therefore means necessarily doing an injustice to him. Lynch is not a director who makes films in lieu of a philosophical voice; rather, his philosophical voice is indistinguishable from that of his films, such that the task falls to philosophers to meet Lynch on his terms rather than vice versa.

To begin this necessary injustice, let us turn to the mystery. Two characters occupy a central place in *Mulholland Drive*, each of them having a double identity in their respective dream world. The mystery of *Mulholland Drive* consists of a dream undergone by the central protagonist Diane Selwyn. In the dream, she is not Diane Selwyn but Betty Elms, a successful actor and lover, charismatic and attractive. Betty's lover also assumes a parallel role: she is both Rita, a distressed *femme fatale*, who, having lost her memory, comes to Betty for help, and Camilla Rhodes, a successful actress and lover of Diane's who betrays her. Four selves, two bodies: these are the basic ingredients of Lynch's tale of anxiety. As understood in the convention of the narrative, the "perfect mystery" concerns Rita's missing identity. Together, Betty and Rita set about unraveling the pieces of the mystery. Beyond this mystery, Diane's dream serves another function: to create an enigma, into which the truth of Diane's situation can be obscured; namely, that alongside being an unsuccessful actress, she is in fact guilty of murdering Camilla Rhodes. Indeed, at the heart of the film is an anxiety concerning humiliation, desubjectification, and betrayal. It is a betrayal not only between two lovers, but also of an image constructed in order to function as a person more generally.

The death of Betty's dream leads to the film's "sad illusion" and the revealing of the illusion takes place in one of the film's central haunts, the Club Silencio. As viewers to the film, we are witness to a performance, both on the screen but also within the medium of cinema itself. The question that haunts Club Silencio concerns our own complicity in the construction of a narrative-based identity. For it is in this place where the illusion of both cinema and of identity is called into question. A magician is on stage, introducing the act: "There is no band, this is all a tape recording ... it is all recorded." In a key scene, a moving rendition of Roy Orbison's "Crying" sung in Spanish is given by Rebekah Del Rio. Suddenly she collapses, yet where there should be silence, the song goes on without her. In response, both Rita and Betty, having now recognized that what they are seeing is an illusion, tremble with anxiety. This confrontation with the illusory dimension of identity triggers a series of disasters in Betty's dream. It is now time, as one of Lynch's sinister characters says, to wake up.

In the final part of the film, "love," Lynch provides us with an extraordinary study of the conflict between anxiety and illusion. This final segment returns us to what is ostensibly the "real" version of what happened between Diane and Camilla. We are in Diane's grim apartment. Her own appearance is also disheveled and devoid of life. From nowhere, she sees Camilla: "You've come back," she whimpers. As the film draws to its end, the viewer is given the keys to unlock the broken narrative and identities of *Mulholland Drive*. Diane recounts how she received an inheritance from her aunt, and thereafter made the journey from Ontario to Hollywood. There, she will meet Camilla on the set of a film, losing out on the lead part. Over dinner, Camilla and Kesher—director and evident lover of Camilla—indicate they are on the verge of getting engaged. Humiliated, distraught, and having lost everything she cares for, Diane trembles with tears in her eyes and rage seething in her face. At the end, Diane is back in her apartment, pursued by her phantoms. Having shot herself in the mouth, blue smoke emerges from above the bed, and a constellation of images fills the cloud: the face of an abject homeless figure featured earlier on, the LA skyline, the fused smiles of Betty and Rita, and the blue interior of Club Silencio, each image dissolving into one another.

AN UNBEARABLE ANXIETY

From the outset, an unbearable anxiety haunts *Mulholland Drive*. The anxiety cannot be entirely placed in one definite spot but instead drifts from scene to scene, permeating the film's atmosphere as a whole. This placeless anxiety invites us the viewers to restore it to narrative wholeness, to find a place for it by situating the film in-between what we term "reality" and "dream." Notably, one of the film's recurring motifs is "to get rid of that God-awful feeling," anxiety. Betty's presence as one of pink hope is a response to that "God-awful feeling," and at first glance, it looks as though the film is a document on the failure to be a successful actress and instead to remain at the level of aspiring actress, forever on the verge of an unrealized dream. But in fact, the film's location of anxiety is situated neither in dream nor in reality in strict terms, but instead in the transitional state between each category. Indeed, considered as a whole, the film is the consummate expression of anxiety: a nebulous, formless presence, which manifests itself in all things, yet which transcends those things.[3]

Against this backdrop, dreaming becomes the means for a transformation of an otherwise intolerable reality. Thus, Camilla's transformation into Rita is only possible thanks to the inclusion of her amnesia. This lacuna in her memory provides Diane with a *tabula rasa* upon which a new identity can be inscribed. As we see throughout, however, an insufferable anxiety makes itself visible within the dream. The edge of the dream proves too porous, and what unfolds is the dissolution of the boundary line between dream and reality. Dreaming becomes a reality, and reality becomes a dream. Omens and totems from Diane's anxious existence uncannily enter the scene of the dream: articles of clothing, domestic objects, lamps, ashtrays, the abject figure hidden behind the café, and above all a rotting corpse on the bed, all make an eerie appearance in a world unconsciously engineered to be a fictional retort to the nightmare of life.

It is precisely in this disjunction between Diane and Betty—and thus in the transition between dreamfulness and wakefulness—that an anxiety greater than that of failing to live up to one's dream becomes a visible specter. Betty's failure to remain as Betty is more than a validation of Sartre's concept of bad faith, as some commentators on *Mulholland Drive* have thought.[4] Maintaining a role, adopting a persona, is not enough. At stake in her anxiety is not simply the dizzying freedom of deceiving herself in order to maintain the pretense of being successful. The film's unbearable anxiety is not that we fail to become the people we desire to be and thus seek refuge in another role, but that *the very concept of personhood is itself a sad illusion*, irrespective of the roles we assume.

BETWEEN SLEEP AND WAKEFULNESS

In Lynch's *Mulholland Drive*, there are several scenes that deal with this black hole of personhood. One striking scene occurs at the end of the perfect mystery. In search of clues as to Rita's missing identity, she and Betty are led to an apartment complex in the suburbs of LA. "Does it look familiar?" Betty asks. At the Sierra Bonita apartments, they find a neighbor who directs them to the apartment of Diane Selwyn. Betty makes her way in, and there discovers a terrible secret: a rotting corpse, with Diane's hair and Camilla's dress, placed on the same bed where Diane will ultimately end up shooting herself. In the scene that follows this discovery, Betty and Rita flee from the apartment, their faces now fracturing into the same fragmented space. Faced with this scene, we might be tempted to take the corpse as an indication that Diane is already dead, and that what we are witnessing through the lens of Rita and Betty's vision is a haunting of sorts. But another encounter dwells here: not only that of the indistinction between dreaming and reality, but of the very passage *between* the two states. Betty's encounter with the corpse inside of the apartment marks an encounter with a reality outside of the dream. Something belonging to Diane has made it into the dreamscape, an imminent death, be it her own or Camilla's. Why is this encounter so unbearably anxiety inducing, why does it lead to the fragmentation of selfhood? One reason is that it takes place neither in a world of dreaming nor in a world of wakefulness, but in the passageway between these worlds, as that of a hypnagogic state.

To understand the anxiety tied up with *hypnagogia*, let us consider by contrast the experience of dreaming. Consider in particular how both dreaming and wakefulness open themselves up as coherent worlds; they are worlds in which each of us is at the center of things. No matter how uncanny, both dreaming and waking life appear for us as variants of a sensible world, in which the singularity of our selfhood is confirmed. It is we who are the dreamers of our nightmare; we who are subjects of our own waking lives. When the nightmare proves unbearable, then something within us stirs us from our slumbers, returning us to the world of familiar constancy. There, we reassemble the intimate sense of being who we are, habitual and irreducibly in one's own skin.

The history of dreaming within philosophy attests to this function as providing evidence of the singularity of the self. The famous first meditation of Descartes is predicated on a consciousness that affirms its own existence even in the flight of imagination. The dream world, if existing as a fantasy, is nevertheless comprised from elements belonging to the non-dream world; at any given point, there is always a latent atmosphere of familiarity, even if it is yet to be explicitly registered. Whether or not the things of my dream are themselves real or not is contingent; what matters from a Cartesian perspective is that there exists a self that is the zero point of its own dreamscape. The dream returns me to myself, just as perceptual awareness of "reality" achieves the same end. In nightmares, we often tell ourselves—silently or otherwise—that we are merely dreaming and seek to break the nightmare in order to return to less anxious surroundings. Who is it, though, that accompanies us in our dreams when the conscious dreamer is him or herself asleep? From a Sartrean perspective, this minimal consciousness is suggestive of a reflective consciousness operating beneath that of the Cartesian ego, as he writes: "My reflective certainty of dreaming therefore comes from the fact that my primitive and unreflective consciousness must contain in itself a kind of latent and non-positional knowledge that reflection then makes explicit."[5] Dreaming appears here as a special kind of consciousness, one that captivates us with such efficacy that the very concept of reality is displaced. Of course, the question of how the world can be both one thing and another thing at the same time will form the central motif of Sartre's account of bad faith as presented in *Being and Nothingness*. That I am able to depict myself as a certain fiction is only possible through a tacit awareness of myself as being different from that fiction. Imagination, as understood in this context, has a concealing function—it obscures and veils cracks in reality. Throughout these imaginative variations, moreover, the self may come to the edge of its own constructed narrative, and this occurs as much in dreaming as it does in waking life. Sartre's vivid accounts of subjects denying their own contingency can be rephrased in terms of a nightmare that confronts us with an aspect of ourselves we would otherwise wish to discard. In each case, dreaming and waking life renews selfhood even—or especially—through its upheavals and anxieties.

For Merleau-Ponty, the alliance between dreaming and reality is phrased less in terms of the variations of consciousness and more in terms of a being that is general to existence more broadly and accessed through the primacy of the body. The world of dreaming is a meaningful world, unfolding in a manner that is peculiar to itself but never entirely divorced from waking life, such that it becomes a closed unit. Dreams intrude upon waking life and waking life enters into the dream, and there is often a reversibility between the two aspects. What survives the passage between dreaming and waking is the body, and it is through the body that the different modalities and images of the dream begin to assume a sense.[6] Dreaming for both Merleau-Ponty and Sartre certifies our worldliness. It may be a world in which our sense of self is modified and captivated by other forces, but it remains a world that opens itself up as a discernible realm that is to varying extents navigable.

Hypnagogia presents us with a less assured world. It is "leading into sleep," and as such, *hypnagogia* is to be distinguished from its counterpart, *hypnopompia*, which refers to the onset of wakefulness. The difference is not only temporal, but also thematic. *Hypnagogia* is characterized by the spontaneous production of vivid images that occur on the fringe of sleep and wakefulness. A liminal zone opens up that neither belongs to sleep nor wakefulness, much less dream and reality, but instead occupies the blurred boundaries between these realms. Depending on if we are falling into sleep or emerging from it, our capacity to reflect upon *hypnagogic* images is modified accordingly. When falling into sleep, an already established sense of self is the primary context against which hypnagogic images emerge. The advent of hypnagogic images is thus dependent on the gradual loosening of one's sense of self, such that there is the sense of falling *into* sleep. *Hypnopompia*, on the other hand, is marked by the primacy of images that belong less to a static self and more to a world of dreaming, which is carried over into waking life. Upon awakening, those same images that captivate us when falling into sleep are readily consolidated with the self that emerges from sleep, such that the residual blurring of boundaries is soon restored.

Both *hypnopompia* and *hypnagogia* are fragile states, easily broken by an excess of self-observation. On the verge of sleep and upon emerging from sleep, images of dream and reality collide and dissolve. If the image appears for the semi-dreamer, then it does so fleetingly. To fix one's attention too readily on the image means destroying it. There is here the indication of an emerging dream without that dream coming into full fruition. The outline of a dream forms in and around our awareness, at times preserving the boundary line between oneself and one's surroundings, and at other times effectively undermining any such distinction.

INTO THE GAPS

Historically, *hypnagogia* has been regarded as a source of inspiration, carrying with it a certain aesthetic pleasure.[7] Indeed, Lynch seems to suggest that he situates himself in a hypnagogic state when catching the big fish, to reference the title of his reflections on consciousness and creativity.[8] He describes it in the following way: "Inside every human being is an ocean of pure, vibrant consciousness. When you 'transcend' in Transcendental Meditation, you dive down into that ocean of pure consciousness. You splash into it. And it's bliss. You can vibrate with this bliss. Experiencing pure consciousness enlivens it, expands it. It starts to unfold and grow."[9] Lynch's account of the ecstatic leap into pure consciousness is foreshadowed by the accounts described by Proust and Poe of their own hypnagogic reveries. For each of them, "transcendence" in the Lynchian sense of the term is not a radical departure from waking life, but instead a strengthening of our already existing bonds with the world. Strikingly, Lynch will go on to align transcendence with *hypnagogia* explicitly.

> Many people have already experienced transcending, but they may not realize it. It's an experience that you can have just before you go to sleep. You're awake, but you experience a sort of fall, and you maybe see some white light and get a little jolt of bliss. And you say, "Holy jumping George!" When you go from one state of consciousness to another—for instance, from waking to sleeping—you pass through a gap. And in that gap, you can transcend. I picture it like a round white room that has yellow, red, and blue curtains covering the white wall. The curtains are three states of consciousness: waking, sleeping, and dreaming. But in the gap between each curtain, you can see the white of the Absolute—the pure bliss consciousness. You can transcend in that little piece of white. Then you come to the next state of consciousness. The white room really is all around you all the time, even though the curtains cover most of it; so it's here, there, and everywhere. And sometimes, without knowing it or knowing how, people have transcended. With Transcendental Meditation, from the waking state of consciousness you can experience that white wall anytime when you sit and meditate. That's the beautiful thing about it.[10]

Lynch's description of falling into the white light is both idyllic and illuminating. The gaps that appear in this state are not conducive to anxiety, as though a confrontation with them would tear the self asunder. Rather, they appear as sources of insight, from which missing pieces and fragments, ordinarily concealed by an overly occupied consciousness, suddenly appear. How, then, do we move from this harmonious engagement with the gaps in existence to an anxiety ridden gap, which threatens to swallow selfhood, as we see time and again in the fractured images of Rita and Betty? Despite his insistence on the blissful nature of transcendence, Lynch's films are saturated with an undertow of disquiet. At times, Lynch's rapport with the gaps between things assumes a more unnerving tone. In a series of interviews, Lynch reflects on his childhood fear of boarding a train in order to journey to Brooklyn. The fear takes form in a primordial way: "I would go to New York City and I would see things. And it scared the hell out of me. In the subway I remember a wind from the approaching train, then a smell and a sound. I had a taste of horror every time I went to New York."[11] Lynch's encounter with "another world . . . just beneath the surface" marks an early confrontation with "a wild pain and decay [that] accompanies everything."[12] Perhaps it is not too forced to suggest that this "gap" uncovered on the subway forms the unhomely counterpart of the white gaps constituting Lynch's blissful transcendence. Only here, the gaps between identities fails to converge into a singular whole. New York and Brooklyn remain irreconcilable with the "goodness in blue skies and flowers."[13]

Subjects with a more fragile sense of self than that of Lynch may encounter the gaps between things with an anxiety that is more apparent than a state of bliss. During the hypnagogic state, columns of familiarity, including that of a centralized subject, are suspended; in place, an impersonal consciousness, as it were, goes on without us. At once the site of inspiration, there are also anxiety inducing elements to be found in *hypnagogia*, given that it provides evidence of a consciousness outside of our ego, which we have limited access to but nevertheless casts a presence in our waking lives. In his *General Psychopathology*, Jaspers traces the movement involved in *hypnagogia*:

> Everything grows fleeting, vague and loses its structure; thoughts, feelings, perceptions, images merge in confusion, glide away, slip about and get derailed, whilst at the same time we may have exotic experiences, sense deep meanings or the presence of the infinite. One's own activity merges into an accepting and a yielding until, in spite of the unity of consciousness, self-awareness completely dissolves away.[14]

Jaspers describes a destabilizing experience. The ego that ordinarily frames and delimits consciousness is suddenly deprived of its sovereignty. In its place, a consciousness no longer constricted is saturated with a meaning that transcends the confines of selfhood. Thoughts and images are derailed, such that what is peculiar to one's sense of self is gradually eroded. Edges and boundaries are dissolved, and the laws that ordinarily govern perception are no longer operational. Perspective along with a sense of individuation is bracketed; things that are usually recognized as having a form cease to function in their native fashion. Gaps appear, intervals between things. Of this gap, Sartre writes that objects appear for us before they come into focus.[15] In this hinterland of perception, it is not only visual observation that undergoes a modification; the whole body, as a spatial and temporal thing, also shifts: "One feels one's body very confusedly, even more vaguely the contact with the sheets and the mattress. The spatial position of the body is very poorly defined. The orientation is prone to blatant disorders. The perception of time is uncertain."[16] This confused state breaks down the certainty of selfhood as in inflexible boundary against the world. What remains is a consciousness accompanied by a radically weakened but never fully expired sense of self. Consciousness remains intact, "captivated," in Sartre's terminology, by its own imaginings. Images are not willed to appear, but instead come of their own accord, freely. Sartre: "One will notice that a totally new way of thinking appears here: it is a thought that can be caught in any trap, that accepts all invitations, that posits objects differently from waking thought, in the sense that it is no longer absolutely distinguished from them."[17]

The line drawn here between pleasure and anxiety is almost imperceptible. The pleasurable dimension of *hypnagogia* hinges on a capacity to tolerate ambiguity; whilst the anxious experience of such a state is marked by a resistance to uncertainty, given that the experience of ambiguity is presented as a threat to a weakened sense of selfhood. What emerges in *hypnagogia* is a momentary suspension of being a fixed self. The centralized zero point that delineates where the agent begins and ends gets deferred. In its place, a *partial* consciousness with no fixed identity transpires, whilst the residue of selfhood continues to gaze on throughout this unveiling in what Sartre describes as a *spellbound* state. Sartre goes on to describe pathological instances of *hypnagogic* images, whereupon patients with a "weakening of attention to life" can lead to a state of delirium.[18]

"HE'S THE ONE WHO'S DOING IT"

The anxiety peculiar to *hypnagogia* does not concern simply the unmasking of one's sense of being a particular kind of self, be it an actor, a waitress, or an academic. Rather, it points to the very instability of selfhood more specifically. The space between waking and sleeping, between dream and reality is a tenebrous space, charged with an instability that is framed by the refusal to settle in one particular area. "This is why," Sartre writes, "the transitory, unstable hypnagogic state is, in a sense, an artificial state. It is "the dream that cannot form itself."[19] This unformed dream carries with it a "certain nervousness," which prevents us from being at ease in the process of falling asleep. To sleep, to enter that other realm which runs concurrent to waking life, we need to take leave of our senses and place our trust in the passageway between states.

Lynch's *Mulholland Drive* presents us with the uncanny sense of this nervous state extended over the duration of an entire film. Diane Selwyn is herself a liminal character, existing on the fringe of divergent states of consciousness. At no point does she completely transform into Betty, nor is her "reality" completed effaced by illusion. Rather, as Diane she occupies a liminal space between each of these poles, becoming the medium for a set of opposites, each of which resides in the same paradoxical space. The discovery of the corpse is one expression of this suspended state between dreaming and waking, a moment of self-recognition that reappears in another scene with a neighbor of Betty's, a psychic no less. After introducing herself as Betty, the neighbor responds with a forlorn expression, "No, it's not." These vestiges of Diane appearing in the world of Betty are neither accidental nor devoid of effect. Rather, they signal the exact point whereby the subject of the nightmare is called into question, and are registered as threats. Whereas Lynch sees the "white of the Absolute—the pure bliss consciousness" in the gaps demarcating one area of consciousness from another, Diane Selwyn is engulfed by anxiety. The gaps that appear for her do so as instances of "wild pain and decay" that ravished Lynch's voyage into New York. With each gap that appears, the ground upon which Betty's dream is situated becomes increasingly more fragile, until in the final gasp all that remains is the obscure boundary that can no longer be relied on to preserve the integrity of selfhood.

One scene in particular articulates the manifold anxieties that operate within *Mulholland Drive*. We are in Winkie's diner on Sunset Boulevard and two men are talking. One of the men is nervous and sweating. He appears agitated and unsteady, and introduces the topic of discussion by way of a disclaimer, stating that "it's kind of embarrassing . . . I had a dream about this place." He then goes on to describe the content of the dream.

> It's not day or night. It . . . it's kind of half-night, you know? But, it looks just like this—except for the light. And I'm scared like I can't tell you. Of all people, you're standing right over there, by that counter. You're in both dreams and you're scared. I get even more frightened when I see how afraid you are, and then I realize what it is. There's a man . . . in back of this place. He's the one who's doing it. I can see him through the wall. I can see his face. . . . I hope that I never see that face, ever, outside of a dream. . . . That's it.

The dialogue is phrased in the manner of a confession. The dreamer wants to expel "the God awful feeling" that has been haunting him, and its power is so forceful that he can even see the man in the back of this place through walls. As viewers, we are then led through the exit of Winkie's to the back of the place and down a series of steps. As we embark on this journey, the droning soundtrack accompanying this scene intensifies with a brooding aura. The perspiring dreamer is underneath the bright Los Angeles light, his forehead glistening with anxiety and incipient panic. He pauses at the entrance sign before solemnly continuing the trek, walking now with the fatalistic dread of being carried to his own death. He approaches the wall behind Winkie's diner, slows down at the edge, and then—suddenly—a figure of abjection comes into view. Two dark eyes peer out from a morass of even darker materials. It is a human figure of sorts, but deranged into a demonic, otherworldly appearance. Upon seeing "the one who's doing it," the anxious dreamer recoils with shock and dies.

The Winkie's diner scene is both brilliant and terrifying, arguably one of Lynch's most powerful scenes as a filmmaker. Its power is framed by its capacity to invoke an eerie sense of anxiety in the midst of what is ostensibly a safe space, as Lynch himself declares: "There's a safety in thinking in a diner. You can have your coffee or your milk shake, and you can go off into strange dark areas, and always come back to the safety of the diner."[20] In Winkie's, the safety of the diner is put into question; there is no small danger that an innocuous cup of coffee might lead to some dreadful fate. Neither day nor night, the scene collapses a series of boundaries, which prevent us from categorizing it as a nightmare alone. Part of this eeriness is centered on the uncertainty central to the scene's atmosphere. Something is not quite right; it is evident on the man's face and apparent in his speech. As the dreamer's interlocutor become infected by anxiety, so the scene intensifies in its menacing dread. Now, both of their faces are beginning to sense a danger that we as the viewers do not yet have access to. When the dreamer's hitherto calm interlocutor gets up to pay the bill, we then realize that the dream is morphing into a reality and vice versa. "Of all people, you're standing right over there, by that counter." There he is, by the counter; anxiety is appearing in the gaps between conflicting states, each of which proceeds to disorient and disarm us. That the homeless figure of darkness appears in broad daylight, in searing sunlight no less, is instructive of the transitional zone in which *Mulholland Drive* takes place. The everyday world is not erased by the onset of a nightmare; rather, it is preserved precisely in its singular everydayness. As preserved, the onset of anxiety does not mark a radical departure from what is already familiar to us, but instead confirms and underscores an instability that was there all along.

It is this unfamiliar familiarity that frames the scene's many anxieties. In fact, at least three anxieties can be elicited from this scene alone. In the first case, there is the surrounding impression of a generalized anxiety, taken up in the motion of the camera, hovering above and below the heads of the actors without ever settling in one fixed point. Even—especially—in this ostensibly prosaic setting, there is the overriding sense that something is not quite right. This disquiet is confirmed in the second expression of anxiety, that of encountering the object of a nightmare: the destitute and abject figure lurking behind the diner. Here, we have a variant of exposure therapy—an attempt at expunging anxiety through confronting it directly. Only, the encounter backfires, proving deadly for the dreamer. Throughout both this generalized and object-related anxiety, there is, however, another anxiety, which is less easily placed. It concerns neither atmosphere nor specific thing, but instead the very subjective framework upon which the contents of the world appear for us. Lynch's orientation toward hypnagogic states means that he undercuts the centrality of a fixed subject, revealing a pre-conceptual advent of consciousness, oneiric and disquieting. In *Mulholland Drive*, this oneirism is manifest as an irreducible anxiety, for it is an anxiety that concerns the very placelessness of the dreamer, asking us to question whether we are essentially the subjects of our own nightmares.

"I hope that I never see that face, ever, outside of a dream." The anxiety at work in *Mulholland Drive* is not the angst that belongs to Heidegger or Sartre; there are no redeeming features that we can salvage from anxiety in order to piece back together a more authentic subject. Lynch's anxiety provides no such resolution. In the end, the desire to never see anxiety outside of a dream proves ineffectual. Neither dream nor reality is insulated from each other; they are both exposed to the same porousness. The same is true of identity: it is neither totally destroyed nor entirely preserved in Lynch's film. Rather, identity forms and deforms, folds back upon familiar states of existence, before untangling the knots that enable a person to persist in and through time. The lies we tell ourselves are not simply designed to ensure our social standing in the world as agents of a civilized culture; they are covertly deployed to preserve our integrity as subjects at a more elemental level. Anxiety pierces through the lie, and in doing so reveals itself as a transcendent anxiety, unable to be confined to the objects of fear we locate in the world, much less able to be domesticated to the realm of illusion and narrative, marking itself instead as an unbearable hole not only surrounding the question of "who am I," but more fundamentally "what am I."

NOTES

1. David Lynch, *Lynch on Lynch*, ed. Chris Rodley (New York: Faber and Faber, 2005), 266.
2. David Lynch (Producer), and David Lynch (Director). *Mulholland Drive*, United States: Universal Studios Home Entertainment, 2001.
3. Dylan Trigg, *Topophobia: A Phenomenology of Anxiety* (London: Bloomsbury, 2016).

4. Jennifer McMahon, "City of Dreams: Bad Faith in *Mulholland Drive*," in *The Philosophy of David Lynch*, eds. William Devlin and Shai Biderman, 113-126 (Lexington: University Press of Kentucky, 2001).
5. Jean-Paul Sartre, *The Imaginary* (London: Routledge, 2004), 161.
6. Maurice Merleau-Ponty, *Phenomenology of Perception* (London: Routledge, 2012).
7. Andreas Mavromatis, *Hypnagogia: The Unique State of Consciousness Between Wakefulness and Sleep* (London: Routledge, 1991).
8. David Lynch, *Catching the Big Fish: Mediation, Consciousness, and Creativity* (New York: TarcherPerigee, 2007).
9. Lynch, *Lynch on Lynch*, 27.
10. Lynch, *Lynch on Lynch*, 49.
11. McMahon, "City of Dreams," 8.
12. McMahon, "City of Dreams," 8.
13. McMahon, "City of Dreams," 8.
14. Karl Jaspers, *General Psychopathology*, Vol. 2. (Baltimore: Johns Hopkins University Press, 1997), 146.
15. Jean-Paul Sartre. *The Imaginary* (London: Routledge, 2004), 39.
16. Sartre, *The Imaginary*, 40.
17. Sartre, *The Imaginary*, 41.
18. Sartre, *The Imaginary*, 44.
19. Sartre, *The Imaginary*, 44.
20. Lynch, *Lynch on Lynch*, 39.

BIBLIOGRAPHY

Jaspers, Karl. *General Psychopathology*, Vol. 2. Baltimore: Johns Hopkins University Press, 1997.
Lynch, David. *Catching the Big Fish: Mediation, Consciousness, and Creativity*. New York: TarcherPerigee, 2007.
Lynch, David. *Lynch on Lynch*. Edited by Chris Rodley. New York: Faber and Faber, 2005.
Lynch, David (Producer). Lynch, David (Director). *Mulholland Drive*. United States: Universal Studios Home Entertainment, 2001.
Mavromatis, Andreas. *Hypnagogia: The Unique State of Consciousness Between Wakefulness and Sleep*. London: Routledge, 1991.
McMahon, Jennifer. "City of Dreams: Bad Faith in *Mulholland Drive*." In *The Philosophy of David Lynch*, edited by William Devlin and Shai Biderman, 113-126. Lexington: University Press of Kentucky, 2001.
Merleau-Ponty, Maurice. *Phenomenology of Perception*. London: Routledge, 2012.
Sartre, Jean-Paul. *The Imaginary*. London: Routledge, 2004.
Trigg, Dylan. *Topophobia: A Phenomenology of Anxiety*. London: Bloomsbury, 2016.

TWO

Transcendence and Tragedy in *My Son, My Son, What Have Ye Done*

Herbert Golder

I feel far more qualified to speak about the second of the two themes announced by my title, tragedy, than I do about transcendence. About tragedy I know, well, something. I have always been powerfully and mysteriously drawn to tragedy. I actually went so far as to make it my profession: I mainly teach, write about, and translate Greek tragedy. Admittedly a very strange business: Tragedy for a living.

In thinking about what then to write, I was reminded of a brief exchange between T. E. Lawrence and his publisher, which was reprinted in the front matter of the 1935 edition of the *Seven Pillars of Wisdom*: Publisher's query on Slip 53 of Lawrence's manuscript: "'Meleager, the immoral poet.' I have put 'immortal' poet, but the author may mean immoral after all." Lawrence's response to his publisher: "Immorality I know. Immortality I cannot judge. As you please: Meleager will not sue us for libel."[1]

I face something of the same dilemma. Tragedy I know. Transcendence I cannot judge. But I am also pretty confident no one will sue me if I conflate the two. And yet . . . I do have a suspicion that the former may be the precondition of the latter—a suspicion deeply reinforced by Karl Jaspers' lifelong meditation on this profoundly paradoxical idea, of the bounded revealing the horizon of, even a gateway to, the unbounded.

In his mature work, *Von der Wahrheit*, 1947, in a section later to be translated as *Tragedy Is Not Enough*, Jaspers writes: "*There is no tragedy without transcendence*. Even defiance unto death in a hopeless battle against gods and fate is an act of transcending: it is a movement toward man's proper essence, which he comes to know as his own in the presence of his doom."[2]

And elsewhere in the same work:

> Genuine awareness of the tragic... is more than mere contemplation of suffering and death, flux and extinction. If these things are to become tragic, man must act. It is only then, through his own actions, that man enters into the tragic involvement that inevitably must destroy him. What will be ruined here is not merely man's life as concrete existence, but every concrete embodiment of whatever perfection he sought. Man's mind fails and breaks down in the very wealth of his potentialities. Every one of these potentialities, as it becomes fulfilled, provokes and reaps disaster. A yearning for deliverance has always gone hand in hand with the knowledge of the tragic. When man encounters the hard fact of tragedy, he faces an inexorable limit. At this limit, he finds no guarantee of general salvation. Rather, it is in acting out his own personality, in realizing his selfhood even unto death, that he finds redemption and deliverance. He may find his deliverance through his sheer strength to bear the unknown without question, and to endure it with unshakable defiance. This, however, is the mere seed of deliverance, its barest possible form. Or he may find deliverance by opening his eyes to the nature of the tragic process which, brought to light, can purify the mind.[3]

Still Jaspers:

> Tragedy views in tremendous perspectives all that actually exists and occurs; and in its climax of silence, tragedy suggests and brings to realization the highest possibility of man.
>
> These tragic visions and perspectives contain a hidden philosophy, for they lend meaning to an otherwise meaningless doom. Although we cannot translate this hidden philosophy into intellectual terms, we can by philosophic interpretation throw it into bolder relief. We acquire this hidden philosophy by re-experiencing its original visions. There can be no substitute for this world of visions.[4]

In the final section of this work, Jaspers returns to where he began, the limits of philosophy—in its speculative, deductive systemizations—when it comes to its understanding and experience of the tragic and, by extension, the transcendent. He writes:

> Myths, images, and stories of tragic inspiration are quite capable of containing truth without losing their uncommitted, hovering character. If perceived in its purity, the original vision of the tragic already contains the essence of philosophy: movement, question, open-mindedness, emotion, wonder, truthfulness, lack of illusion.[5]

Jaspers acknowledges the limits of interpretation and the power, primacy and irreducibility of myths, symbols, and images themselves.[6] They are, to use his term, the "ciphers" that point beyond their vivid particularity and concreteness, even as they intimate and incarnate—in a way that philosophy can only approximate and describe—Being, the All-Encompassing, itself.

There is a wonderful story about Plato, no doubt apocryphal, but revealing nonetheless about the tragic and the transcendent. It was said that, as a young man, he had wanted to be a poet. Until, that is, he hit upon a certain passage in Homer, a simile in Book 12 of the *Iliad*. Book 12 begins with a glimpse into the inevitable future. After many Greeks have perished and the city of Troy itself has finally fallen, the gods will wipe away the protective rampart the Greeks had built and around which so many men had fought and died—wipe it clean off the face of the earth, buried in the sands, as if it had never even existed, "leveling all by the blue running sea." So it will come to pass, in the fullness of time. But in the present tense of the story, the bloodiest battle in the poem now rages around this bulwark, which the Trojans will eventually breach. As the fighting intensifies and its din grows deafening, Homer suddenly veers off into a description of another world, a winter landscape where falling snow has muffled the whole world white, describing what George Eliot once called, in another context, that "roar which lies on the other side of silence," which we would die of, were we to hear it.[7] Plato, the story goes, read this simile and, in awe, decided to give up trying to be a poet and instead try his hand at philosophy. Homer writes,

> Imagine,
> flakes of snow that come down thick and fast
> on a winter day when Zeus who views the wide world
> brings on a fall of snow, showing mankind
> his means of making war. He lulls the winds
> and sifts white flakes in stillness hour by hour
> until hilltop and foreland are all hid
> as are farmers' meadowlands and fields,
> while snow comes down over the hoary sea,
> on harbors and on shores. Though running surf
> repel it, all things else are muffled white,
> weighed down by snow from heaven, a storm of Zeus.
> So thick the stones flew. Here they fell
> on Trojans, there from Trojans on Akhaians,
> by all hands thrown and thudding along the wall.[8]

Simone Weil has described the similes in Homer as moments when men take possession of their souls.[9] Less than 200 lines later, as the battle reaches its peak intensity, and just before Hektor finally smashes through the Greek wall, Homer pulls us away from the battle and describes "an honest cottage spinner / balancing weight in one pan of the scales / and wool yarn on the other, trying to earn / a pittance for her children: evenly poised / as that were these great powers making war . . ."[10]

In both instances, as throughout the *Iliad*, Homer parts the foreground curtain of blood and reveals that larger tapestry of life: the all-muffling snow amplifying even as it mutes the sounds of human anguish. In his tragic finitude, man stands apart from that never-ending, Zeus-sent snow. And yet, Homer seems to suggest, by assimilating man to it, even as he is dying, he is also, in some mysterious way, a part of it. And in that homely image of the poor, honest woman weighing her wool, but above all through that very ordinary, but in the context, utterly extraordinary phrase, "for her children," the thousand shapes of death disperse, for a moment, and life reasserts its eternally recrudescent power and purpose.

My topic here confronts me with several challenges. Professor Nichols specifically requested a chapter about transcendence and tragedy in the film *My Son, My Son, What Have Ye Done* (2009).[11] This is difficult for me to do for a few reasons. Firstly, I suspect that many readers have not seen the film. Secondly, I cowrote the film with Werner Herzog, and so, it is close to me in a way that does not easily allow for an academic discussion. Then, there is Herzog's own, inveterate disavowal of any and all efforts at intellectualizing his films and his openly hostile dismissal of most academic analyses of them.[12] Granted, I am an academic, but I am also Herzog's creative collaborator. It's a bit of a bind. On top of all this, the editor of Herzog's recent book, *A Guide to the Perplexed*, hailed me in his introduction, for the chapter I contributed to the volume at Herzog's invitation, as "a bulwark against theoretical utterances about the films."[13]

What then can I contribute on my invited topic to this learned collection? Jaspers himself, in Paul Ricoeur's words, "refuses to absolutize the tragic into a philosophical pantragicism."[14] Jaspers argues that, "tragedy resides only in the phenomena of this world. For through the tragic, something different speaks to us, something that is no longer tragic."[15] Ricoeur, quoting Jaspers, and modifying a little, says, "In the face of the tragic, Being is revealed in foundering."[16] Again, Jaspers himself:

> Every one of the great poems has a meaning which cannot be exhausted by interpretation. They offer no more than directions for interpretation to pursue. Where complete rational interpretation is possible, poetry becomes superfluous. . . . Where interpretation heightens their accessibility precisely by virtue of a profound vision that is uncharted, that is not exhaustible by any analysis or interpretation . . .[17]

Later in the same work,

> Instead of systematizing tragic knowledge through speculative deduction, instead of stripping it of its polarity and turning it into a philosophic absolute, we must instead so understand tragic knowledge as to preserve it as an original experience. The original tragic vision consists in thoughts and questions experienced in concrete images . . .[18]

Let me start there, with concrete images. The vision that became the film *My Son, My Son, What Have Ye Done* began with very concrete images.

Jaspers has defined the mythical interpretation of the tragic as "thinking in terms of pictures—of pictures taken for realities."[19] "Myths, images, and stories of tragic inspiration are quite capable of containing truth without losing their uncommitted, hovering character."[20] Through their truth, according to Jaspers, if truly, radically tragic, that something beyond the tragic—the transcendent—speaks to us.

I must take a few steps back and explain the genesis and the story of this film. Of course, anyone who knows the films of Werner Herzog must know that it would be easy to make a general case for the presence of tragedy and transcendence in his films. They are so full of indelible images of human beings *in extremis*, envisioned in stories that unfold at the extreme limits of our condition, both its upper reaches and lower depths, where, like an element in nature subjected to extreme pressure or extreme heat, human beings reveal their true and elementally essential make-up. The fierceness and determination with which they confront and challenge those limits that the universe imposes upon us—what the Greeks called *Anangke*—are directly proportionate to the ecstatic truth and intimation of—what Shakespeare called—"a world elsewhere" that they awaken inside us. No matter how savage, formidable, or inhospitable the landscapes of his films, his characters wrestle a human meaning out of them—and sometimes soar beyond their bounds.[21]

But this is taking yet few more steps backward to situate Herzog's films generally in a conversation about tragedy and transcendence. Our project here, with this film, did not begin with any preconceived idea, or pattern of meaning, philosophical reflection, or generic mold. It began with my serendipitous discovery of a story, an obscure homicide that struck me as being about something more than the tragedy of those directly involved. A talented young actor in San Diego, named Mark Yavorsky, had been rehearsing the role of Orestes for a stage production of the *Oresteia*. He ended up, however, committing in reality the crime he was to enact in the play: he murdered his mother.[22] I was immediately fascinated that any distinction between myth and reality had disappeared altogether here. Of course, the man must have been clinically insane; and in fact, he had been judged not guilty by reason of insanity and had spent nearly ten years in a maximum-security facility for the criminally insane. That could have been the end of the story right there. As Jaspers has written,

> Poetry depicting only horror as such, only brutality, murder, intrigue—in short, everything terrible—is not, by that token, tragic. For in tragedy the hero should have the knowledge of the tragic and the spectator should be led to share it. This is the origin of the quest for deliverance from the tragic, the quest for fundamental reality.[23]

As I said, I sensed there was more than what met the eye here. I read the case files carefully and became convinced—from hints between the lines—that although Mark had admittedly been grossly psychotic at the time of the murder, a great deal more had also been going on. There were many clues in the court and police files, but I will mention just a few. At first they may seem inconsequential, but collectively they started to add up to something for me. Among his effects, thought important enough to be confiscated by the police after the murder, was a notice for one and only one overdue library book. The book was H.D.F. Kitto's *The Greeks*, a book that put the Greeks' uniquely tragic vision at the heart of the greatness and profundity of the culture they produced.[24] Mark, I realized, had been *studying* all this. Then, there were things like the comments he had made in the police van after his arrest: admittedly the ravings of a madman, but these were interspersed with what I can only call *moments of fatal lucidity* about the fate of Orestes, the Furies, even the symbolic meaning of his crime. His talk of having made the ultimate sacrifice—by killing his own mother—made no normative sense, but his larger claims for doing so—waking up the world, whose man-made destruction he believed imminent—to save it from itself—made sense symbolically, or even as forebodings that could prove to be prophetic. In the *Oresteia* of Aeschylus, Orestes *has to* kill Klytemnestra; otherwise, the human world simply does not move forward, and a more enlightened world, based on the ideals of deliberative justice, remains forever shrouded in the blood claims of archaic night. Later, Mark would write, "If only I had been a good god-fearing pagan, I wouldn't have had to turn myself into a metaphor."

Many other things caught my eye that had never been noted by any of the clinical professionals. One was a story in the police files of his escape from custody. After close to a decade in a maximum-security facility for the criminally insane, and now remanded to the custody of a conditional release program, Mark was told he would never be cured and that he would always be heavily medicated with anti-psychotics. Convinced, however, that he was actually quite sane, he escaped. He was on the lam for a year and a half. The police finally arrested him 2500 miles away on the night he was about to start a new job: *opening act in a stand-up comedy club*. His car had a bumper sticker on it that read: "God couldn't be everywhere, that's why he created mothers." Even the *Oresteia* ends, perforce, with the transformation of the Furies into the Eumenides, the Kindly Ones. I knew that Mark indeed had some sort of perspective on all this and on what he had done. I sensed beyond his personal tragedy, a generic tragedy—and one that therefore connected to something deeper. The Greek play, he would later tell me, crystalized myriad mythic elements in his psyche.

I wrote Mark a letter saying that, as a student of Greek tragedy, I was interested in the poetry of his madness. He invited me to visit. A highly intelligent, widely read man with a graduate degree in English Literature, a published poet, a once promising, award-winning actor who had moreover attended college on a basketball scholarship, Mark then let me into the labyrinth of his mind. Through my conversations with him, through reading his letters, poetry, and diaries, written before and after the fact, I could see that he had thought long and hard about what he had done, that it had all been *premeditated* but in a sense radically different from that normally meant when referring to a crime. Mark had quite consciously chosen a *mythical destiny*, and the inextricability of that choice from his psychopathy is what especially intrigued me. Among the numerous quotes, iconic images, memorabilia, and photos that covered his walls like a collage, one phrase in particular caught my eye. It was from Sartre's *The Flies*:

> Zeus: Who then made you?
> Orestes: You. But, you blundered; you should have not have made me free...[25]

Mark would tell me that he had not suffered from a functional psychosis, like schizophrenia, nor an organic psychosis, like brain damage, but rather from what he chose to categorize as an active-poetic mystical psychosis: a modern parallel to what used to be described as a metaphysical "dark night of the soul," in reference to the spiritual crises of saints and sages, although, by his own admission, he could claim neither sanctity nor wisdom.

The more I spoke with him and the more I read of what he had written—especially his reflections on the numbing soullessness of modern life—I came to see Mark's story as being much more than a domestic tragedy. Instead, something like the following is how I came to see it: I saw Mark's strange story as being that of an exceedingly gifted and once very promising young man who had come to feel—because he sensed acutely what most are numb to or take for granted—increasingly oppressed by the artificiality, insincerity and spiritual deadness of the world around him, but who came to discover, first in religion and then art but ultimately through Greek tragic myth, a much more intense and vibrant world of myth and vision. However, instead of being apotheosized through the latter world, he had fallen tragically between the cracks of both.

This all set me to thinking, and led to the disturbing question: What, I wondered, absent the modalities of ancient experience, could a mythic fate lead to today, given the limits and diminished horizons of modern experience—what could it lead to, other than madness, or like Mark, to a case of terminal Greek tragedy?[26]

That is where the idea for this film began. And it unfolded as a series of images, sometimes conjured by words, sometimes as what Jaspers called, apropos the mythic understanding of tragedy, which is prior to any philosophical interpretation of it: "thinking in terms of pictures—of pictures taken for realities."[27]

But before I continue, I would like to interject a further reflection on Jaspers. I am fascinated by the fact that it was his studies in psychopathy, even criminal insanity, that led him to philosophy.[28] There is surely some connection between thinking beyond the normative categories—especially given Jaspers' own powerfully articulated views on the diminished capacities of post-Enlightenment thought generally, and on the ever-narrowing and blinkered worldview wrought by the modern materialism of science and technology, and the social and political systems they engender—some connection between non-normative thinking and the possibility of glimpsing, or having an intimation of, ultimate reality, the absolute Being to which, through tragedy, the ciphers point at the moment of shipwreck.

Between the second and third editions of his *General Psychopathology*, Jaspers published a psychopathological analysis of *Strindberg and van Gogh*. In the study, he speculates that the highest forms of artistic expression in any particular cultural epoch may be especially suited to a particular form of disease. In the concluding two chapters, "On the relation between schizophrenia and schizophrenic creations" and "schizophrenia and modern culture," he pursued the question of what was "unique" in the works of schizophrenic personalities, something which "has a specific character with a defined place in the cosmos of spirituality, but which materializes in reality only if and when the conditions are created by the process of the disease."[29] He speaks of the emergence of "new forces . . . which in their turn objectify themselves, forces which are spiritual, i.e., neither sick nor healthy, but which thrive in the soil of the disease."[30] Noting different psychopathologies in artists of other eras, but a striking absence of schizophrenia per se, he asks in his conclusion, "May schizophrenia be the condition of authenticity in such periods, which in previous times could be experienced and portrayed without schizophrenia?"[31]

I saw Mark's psychosis as, on one level, symptomatic, and an expression of, but at the same time a reaction against, a larger spiritual and societal malaise, acutely felt in our time, which T. S. Eliot once called the "dissociation of sensibility," a separation of thought and feeling, and everything that such a rupture implies, which he thought had afflicted modern man, *mutatis mutandis*, since about the mid-seventeenth century.[32] Scrupulously examining the history of thought in its broadest perspective, Jaspers too has argued that certain areas of experience, notably that of true tragedy and the transcendent experience it enables, have been saliently lost to modern man ever since the Enlightenment.[33] That Mark's schizophrenia skewed his perceptions, an apposite reaction to a world out of kilter, in no way invalidates the perceptions themselves; in fact, schizophrenia may very well be, to use Jaspers' term, "the condition of authenticity" required to see beyond the beguiling surface of a manifestly unhealthy world. Mark's psychosis manifested itself as an effort to interpret his existence transcendentally, or to experience—what I call—a mythic fate. He related his being in the world to the All-Encompassing, and it is the inconcinnity between that aspiration, and concomitant intimation, and the world as it now is that turns his tragedy into his travesty, into what I called a case of terminal Greek tragedy.

I was especially struck by Jaspers' highly perceptive account of Hamlet's madness in *Von der Wahrheit*—what he referred to as "the mask of madness"—which takes into account the full complexity and inevitability of that madness, even its being a matter of existential choice, if one forced on Hamlet, under the circumstances. I thought Jaspers' notion characterized to some degree what I had originally sensed in, and tried then to express in fictionalizing, Mark's story:

> Hamlet's knowledge and his desire for knowledge set him apart from the world. In it, he cannot be of it. He acts the part of a madman. In this counterfeit world, madness is the mask that allows him not to lie about his real feelings, not to feign respect where he feels none. He can speak the truth through irony. Whatever he says, true or untrue—equivocal for all—he can cover with the mask of madness. He chooses madness as his proper role because truth admits of no other.[34]

As Jaspers did in his own studies of psychopathy, I used a good deal of Mark's own "concrete psychopathological material" to explore the meaning, substance, and experience of his story, and the larger story to which it led me.[35] Quoting Hamlet's famous "There's a divinity that shapes our ends, / Rough-hew them how we will," Jaspers says Hamlet's words point not to nothingness but to transcendence.[36] I said earlier that the film's genesis lay in concrete images, "thinking in pictures" (some Mark's, some our own). I can rattle off a few of them, and although they conjure visions in my mind's eye, they might not seem to make much sense out of context: Acting "Sane," Real People, Raging River, Paradise, Mirage, Freeze Frames, Stray Dialogue, Lost Place, Quaker Oats and God, Fate and Necessity (Greek tragedy), Preaching the Gospel, Mexican Ballad, Giant Chicken, the Monstrosity of Nature, The Curse, Revenge. There we have it: a recipe for tragedy and, at least, thrown into the mix, an intimation of transcendence.

Our story: The film begins at the crime scene, the murder having already taken place in a neighbor's house across the street. The murderer, named Brad in the film and played by Michael Shannon, has holed up in his own home on the opposite side of the street. Two people whom he had telephoned just before killing his mother, his fiancée, played by Chloë Sevigny, and the director of the *Oresteia* production, played by Udo Kier, arrive on the scene and are interrogated by a detective, played by Willem Dafoe, who is attempting, as detectives do, to understand who the perpetrator is and what might have precipitated this killing. So the story of Brad unfolds as a series of flashbacks, as each of the interlocutors proceeds to describe how, after a trip to Peru, a white-river kayaking trip that ended in tragedy, Brad changed, and then to describe various things that he did that struck those who knew him as stranger and stranger. And although some of what follows will take us to some unusual and even rather faraway places, the Urubamba Valley and the Andes Mountains in Peru, Kashkar in Western China, Calaveras Big Tree Forest in Northern California, Plaza Santa Cecilia in Tijuana, and what was, at the time we filmed, the largest ostrich ranch in America, in the desert outside Victorville, we keep coming back to the standoff, since Brad has taken, so he claims, several hostages. And threaded through these flashbacks are the rehearsals, and then the production, of the Greek play, the story of Orestes killing Klytemnestra, which concentrates and binds together all the disparate strands of this story and brings everything to a climax.

But what of these exotic places and the visions of intense experience they embody? What possible connection can exist between the production of an ancient Greek tragedy, say, and a pride of ostriches galloping across the desert—"dinosaurs in drag" as we call them—or the deafening fury of the Urubamba's raging rapids in full spate at the height of the rainy season, or the dignified and weathered faces of Uyghur tribesmen in the thousand-year-old market of Kashkar?

These images, and others both like and unlike them in the film, suggest, each in its own way, the persistence of something very ancient into the present. But it is only Brad who sees them, or, even if and when visible to others, only Brad who sees so as to be affected by them, by what I can only call "the ancient experience" they variously embody. These "ancient experiences," and other moments of what I will call "authentic encounters" in the film, stand in stark contrast to, and almost serve as an indictment of, the contemporary world of suburban Southern California where the immediate story, the "crime drama," of the film is set. In this so-called real world, nothing any longer seems, at least to Brad, very real. Nor does it to us, if we are paying attention. There is a scene in the Bonaventure Hotel in Los Angeles where Brad walks through the lobby and the viewer cannot really tell, as indeed Brad himself cannot, whether the waterfall in the atrium is actually cascading water or a screen of glass beads; or if the elaborate tropical gardens are actually living plants or painted plastic. The confusion is intentional. Brad is surrounded by, and painfully aware of, the simulations and counterfeits that most are content to accept as realities, or simply to take for granted. Through highly stylized dialogue and mise-en-scène, we are given the impression that simulation and dissimulation have become a way of life, a *modus vivendi* so pervasive that attempts at human communication seem severely circumscribed, reduced almost to rote formulae; and even efforts at human intimacy, in being a cry from a place not really belonging to this, but another, world, ring hollow and untrue. Brad's tragedy then is to suffer this, to suffer this unto shipwreck.[37]

In his "breaks" with this world, Brad envisages another. There are several occasions in the film when everything suddenly, seemingly freezes, but Brad, and we the viewers, are the only ones who actually see it. It happens in a park filled with people. For an instant, everyone and everything appears to move as if in slow motion. It happens at the dinner table: Brad, his fiancée, and his mother unexpectedly freeze before the camera and hold their positions. These scenes and others in the film like them are, for me, not unrelated to those other glimpses into a "world elsewhere" in the film, like the glowering clouds just beyond the peaks of the Andes, the tumultuous river in the jungle valley, the stump of a giant sequoia in the snow, or the accusing stare of an ancient Turkman. In one scene of the film, as Brad is rehearsing the scene from the stage play of the *Oresteia* in which he confronts his mother Klytemnestra, played here by his fiancée, and in the middle of which Brad skips a hundred lines, because, as he says, "it makes more sense this way," he suddenly stops the rehearsal altogether to speak with the director about basketball. He describes being in midcourt, a second before the buzzer is about to ring, going up into the air, and then, suspended in midair, releasing his fifty-footer. Neither the director nor the others have any idea what he is talking about. Visibly in pain, Brad tries to explain: he tells the bewildered director that he thinks he has found "it . . . the still point, the unwobbling pivot of the world."

The world freezes or slows down around Brad; the mythic world, like the Greek play, becomes tragic reality for him; a sense of the awesome, even numinous, power of nature fills the screen when we see the landscape through his eyes. To him, even birds molt into the stuff of sacred legend (we have him recite a short passage on ostriches from the *Book of Job* after a visit to his uncle's ostrich farm) as well as pre-history (ostriches, "dinosaurs in drag," are after all more than one-hundred million years old). Just prior to the *Oresteia* production from which he has been removed but now attends as a spectator with his mother, a glass, tunnel-like structure of concentric circles that forms part of the roof above an escalator becomes, in his eyes, "the tunnel of time—the perfect place to stage a cosmic melodrama." The mysterious refraction of light created by his arrangement of prescription glasses in a circle in a hotel room in Tijuana becomes one of his ways of "bringing heaven to earth." Brad even sees, in the stout pilgrim featured on a box of Quaker Oats, God hiding in the cupboard.[38]

Where others do not see beyond a very superficial surface, such as his mother, for instance, who giddily greets his preoccupation with Quaker Oats as a preference for health food over eggs and bacon, Brad sees more deeply into things, glimpsing something like an ultimate reality—or at least the ciphers that point unmistakably to its existence, to that which transcends *Existenz*, to Being. If his metaphors seem hyperbolic, that is because poetic truth resonates only in that higher register.[39]

But, as I said above, Brad's tragedy turns travesty. Absent the modalities of ancient experience, and given the diminished horizons of modern life, his mythic destiny perforce devolves into, and is expressed only through, "the mask of madness." Brad suffers in his person acutely, in fact, killingly, the inanities and mundanities of social intercourse—the "hell" that Sartre said was other people—as well as the monstrousness of nature in its awful indifference to man, to which Brad alone in the story seems keenly attuned. Jaspers spoke of "a movement toward man's proper essence, which he comes to know as his own in the presence of his doom."[40] As the world spins and whirls increasingly out of control around him, Brad finds the "still point, the unwobbling pivot of the world," the ground of Being itself. As I suggested above, in this modern story, Brad is not apotheosized through his discovery of this more vibrant and visionary world, so much as he falls tragically into the chasm that separates it from the sublunary world he has moved beyond, descending into a vortex of madness.

Brad's pain and isolation are palpable, but these are not I think the feelings with which the film leaves you. The visions haunt. One in particular, which advances the narrative no more than does a simile in Homer, but sums up what I feel may be the essence of the film, occurs about two-thirds of the way through it. Following the interrupted theatrical rehearsal mentioned above, in which Brad has revealed his discovery of the world's still point, we cut to a long, slow tracking shot of the exterior of the house where he is holed up—a pastel pink facade, fronted by a lawn of cacti of different shapes and sizes. Meanwhile, we hear, on the soundtrack, the words of the Aeschylean chorus played back from the earlier scene we have just left. They recite the numberless terrors of nature, from flaming comets that stab down through the sky to monsters that dwell in the deep, and, not least among earth's pain-begetting horrors, the audacity and daring of man. As they chant, the camera slowly zooms in on the front of the house. Brad appears for a moment at the door, shotgun in hand, hollering something about a rooster and the rider of the apocalypse. Then, by means of what is called a swish pan, we find ourselves in a snowy landscape, witnessing a conversation between Brad and his eccentric Uncle Ted (played by Brad Dourif), in which his bizarre uncle at first corrects Brad, who has repeated his line from the immediately preceding scene—"The rider of the apocalypse"—admonishing him, "no, not the rider, it was the horse owner, the goddam horse owner who wouldn't let me have the horse." Uncle Ted then shows Brad a photograph of a miniature horse, next to a normal one, and, as the camera cuts to what we saw previously in the background, but now in the closer shot realize is a midget in a tuxedo pacing atop a gigantic tree stump, Uncle Ted asks Brad to imagine his giant rooster Wilbur chasing the smallest horse in the world, ridden by the midget, around the biggest tree on this planet. As Uncle Ted speaks off camera, our eyes are on the little man as he walks cautiously across the massive stump. As we watch him, the heartrendingly beautiful Mexican ballad *Cucurrucucu Paloma* sung by Caetano Veloso begins to play. Then, cutting back to Uncle Ted, he tells Brad that his "rooster would stand taller than the rider and horse together," and that "it was going to be a commercial" and "it was going to make a bunch of money." But, when Brad asks what the commercial was going to be for, Uncle Ted looks puzzled and says, "How should I know, but it was going to be great!"

The film then cuts to a wider shot of Uncle Ted and Brad standing, now posed, in front of the midget on the gargantuan stump of the giant sequoia. All three face the camera as the plaintively beautiful Mexican ballad (of a broken-hearted man's soul turned into a dove) continues to play. The camera slowly zooms in on the three as they look back at us. This tableau of the three men staring directly into the camera, with only Brad looking thoughtfully down and away for but a second, lasts an entire minute. This may not sound like much, but if you consider that the average shot length in most films is a mere few seconds—it's an eternity.

I am not sure I could even begin to unpack everything that is going on here. But I want to make two points. Firstly, I cannot tell you how dignified that little man looks to me in his tuxedo as he stands there, proud and straight-backed, almost like a statue, on top of that monstrously disproportionate prodigy of nature that, even felled, dwarfs him and any and all human scale, intimating an order of magnitude and being beyond our sphere. Secondly, and this is my final point, I want to return to Brad's question, to which Uncle Ted had no answer: A commercial for what?

This is the conundrum that the visionary moments in this story, and I think in Herzog's films generally, pose. The metaphor is vividly present, but it is sometimes difficult to say just what it is a metaphor of. Not only is it difficult to say what it means—which is the case I think with any true metaphor—but it is difficult to say just what the image is being compared to. In the earlier example from Homer, the barrage of missiles and deafening tumult of men in mortal combat is being compared to a snowstorm sent by Zeus. But here, *just what is it* that is being compared to a midget on a giant tree stump? We have the image, the metaphor, but no clear indication of just what is like a midget on a giant stump. We have what is referred to as the "figure," but not what is called the "ground." I would like to suggest this may have something to do with the fact that our modern and "untragic" world, in Jaspers' sense, is no longer authentically grounded in the way Homer's archaic and tragic world once was, where something like elemental vision presupposed an integrity of man and Being. It was once possible to see similarity in dissimilarity—which T. S. Eliot called the supreme power of the poet—to see, in and through the tragedy of man, the power of transcendence.[41]

We, on the other hand, lack sufficiently dignified images of our humanity. Herzog has often spoken about the grave danger inadequate imagery poses for our civilization. The "ground" is lacking. So the tragic story of *My Son, My Son* unfolds through a series of transcendent visions that we struggle to keep up with because we do not have anything we can compare them to; we do not have, in our modern experience or self-image, the gravity to weather Homer's heaven-sent storm. So the "figures" conjured by Brad, ungrounded in the foreground world of the film, stand as challenges, to imagine a humanity large enough to be assimilated to them.

Brad's hostages, by the way, turn out to be his pet flamingos. But before we can figure out what it is like taking a flamingo hostage, Brad tells the detective, as he is being arrested, to "forget about flamingos," that he sees "ostriches, ostriches running"—and, as he says this, a music begins and an image of these primordial creatures in full gallop stirring a cloud of dust appears. Then, as we cut away from the ostriches, and back to Brad about to enter the police car, he asks the detective, "whatever happened to my basketball," which the film cuts to, as the Mexican ballad of a legendary desperado, a man who "lived beyond reason," begins to play. The ball is just where Brad last left it, in the crook of a tree in the park, silhouetted against the skyline of the city, downtown San Diego, "a city on a hill," that looks phantasmal in the distance, like a mirage. The final image, the ball in the tree, recalls Brad's discovery of that still-point, that unwobbling pivot of the world—the transcendence to which Jaspers believed only true tragedy can lead.[42]

One final grace note, in defense of ostriches: Evoking the miracles of his Creation in response to Job, God admires the speed of his ostrich which, though earthbound, seems nevertheless to fly: "When the time cometh, she raiseth her wings on high, and scorneth the horse and his rider."[43] And, if herds of galloping creatures do not strike you as an apt image of the sublime, consider this: In his treatise *On the Sublime*, searching for those words and images with the power to conjure a transcendent experience, the ancient critic Longinus likened the inimitably powerful image of God's singular creation of light and the world, notably from the void, out of nothingness, in *Genesis*, to descriptions in Homer of the vaulting strides of the gods' horses—"between earth and starry heaven, a single leap taking them as far as a man can see with his eyes from a mountain top, staring out over the wine-dark sea into the vanishing sky."[44]

NOTES

1. The correspondence between T. E. Lawrence and his publisher concerned the printing of *Revolt in the Desert*, an abridged version of an earlier edition of the former. T. E. Lawrence, *Seven Pillars of Wisdom* (Garden City, NY: Doubleday, Doran & Company, Inc., 1935), 25.

2. Karl Jaspers, *Tragedy Is Not Enough*, trans. Harold A. T Reiche, Harry T. Moore, and Karl W. Deutsche (Boston: The Beacon Press, 1952), 41. Karl Jaspers, *Von der Wahrheit* (Münich: R. Piper, 1947).

3. Jaspers, *Tragedy Not Enough*, 43.

4. Jaspers, *Tragedy Not Enough*, 27.

5. Jaspers, *Tragedy Not Enough*, 103.

6. "The symbol is *infinite*. In pursuing the symbol, and with it the experience of essential reality, thought stands still. No thought is adequate to the symbol. The symbol opens us up for Being and shows us all Being." Karl Jaspers, *Truth and Symbol*, trans. Jean T. Wilde, William Kluback, and William Kimmel. (New York: Twayne Publishers, 1959), 40.

7. George Eliot. *Middlemarch* (London: Penguin Books, 2008), 226.

8. Homer, *The Iliad*, trans. Robert Fitzgerald (New York: Farrar, Straus & Giroux, 2004), 283-4. Homer, *The Iliad*, in *Oxford Classical Texts, Homeri Opera*, Vol. 1., eds. David B. Munro and Thomas W. Allen (Oxford: Clarendon Press, 1963), XII. 278-89.

9. Simone Weil writes of moments of "grace" in the poem. I include the poem's similes, integral to its texture and part of its essential make-up, among these. Simone Weil, *The Iliad or The Poem of Force*, trans. Mary McCarthy (Wallingford, PA: Pendle Hill, 1978), 27.

10. Homer, *The Iliad*, Fitzgerald, 288. Homer, *The Iliad*, Oxford Classical, XII. 433-6.

11. Bassett, E. (Producer), & Herzog, W. (Director). *My Son, My Son, What Have Ye Done*? United States: Industrial Entertainment, 2009.

12. Werner Herzog. *Werner Herzog, A Guide for the Perplexed, Conversations with Paul Cronin*, ed. Paul Cronin (London, UK: Faber and Faber, 2014), 77f, 177f.

13. Paul Cronin, "Visionary Vehemence," in *Werner Herzog, A Guide for the Perplexed, Conversations with Paul Cronin*, ed. Paul Cronin (London, UK: Faber and Faber, 2014) Herzog, *Werner Herzog*, xl. and passim.

14. Paul Ricoeur, "The Relation of Jaspers' Philosophy to Religion," in *The Philosophy of Karl Jaspers*, ed. Paul Arthur Schilpp (La Salle, IL: Open Court Publishing Co., 1957), 618.

15. Jaspers, *Tragedy Not Enough*, 94.

16. Ricoeur, "Jaspers' Philosophy to Religion," 614. Ricoeur also quotes Karl Jaspers here. Compare with Jaspers, *Tragedy Not Enough*, 80.

17. Jaspers, *Tragedy Not Enough*, 43.

18. Jaspers, *Tragedy Not Enough*, 102.

19. Jaspers, *Tragedy Not Enough*, 90.

20. Jaspers, *Tragedy Not Enough*, 103.

21. See Herbert Golder, "Shooting on the Lam," in *Werner Herzog, A Guide for the Perplexed, Conversations with Paul Cronin*, ed. by Paul Cronin (London, UK: Faber and Faber, 2014), 478-88. Also, see my forthcoming film, *Ballad of a Righteous Merchant* (world premiere, Montreal World Film Festival 2017), from which I quote and paraphrase in this paragraph.

22. This was a 1979 production mounted by the Theater Department at the University of California at San Diego, where Mark, already having received awards for his work in regional theater, was enrolled as an MFA candidate in acting. Because he was a few years older than the other students, Mark had originally been cast as Agamemnon, which had not sat well with him. He wanted to play Orestes; memorized all the latter's lines; and was quite demonstrative about his dissatisfaction during rehearsals.

23. Jaspers, *Tragedy Not Enough*, 74.

24. H. D. F. Kitto, *The Greeks* (New York: Penguin Books Ltd, 1951).

25. Jean Paul Sartre. *No Exit and Three Other Plays* (New York: Vintage Books, 1946), 120.

26. In a brilliant and insightful response to this chapter, Amanda Parris (2016) cautioned me about my blanket indictment of the "modern" and my use of the term as a "kind of floating signifier." But I think the distinction I am trying to make between the "ancient" and the "modern" and what is meant implicitly by each word, at least

rhetorically, and in terms of the argument I am presenting here, is tolerably clear. Jaspers himself was certainly preoccupied in his writings by the circumstances peculiar to modern life and to the distinctive characteristics of its decline. Amanda Parris. *Herbert Golder's My Son, My Son What Have Ye Done?* Response presented at American Philosophical Association, Pacific Division. March 31, 2016. Karl Jaspers, *Man in the Modern Age*, trans. Eden and Cedar Paul (London: Routledge & Kegan Paul, Ltd., 1951), especially 9-27, 116-24, and passim.

27. Jaspers, *Tragedy Not Enough*, 90.
28. In fact, his doctoral dissertation in medical school was entitled *Nostalgia and Crime*. Karl Jaspers, *Heimweh und Verbrechen*, Habilitation. Heidelberg University, 1909.
29. Karl Jaspers, *Strindberg und van Gogh* (München: Piper & Co., 1951), 177. Cited in Kurt Kolle, "Karl Jaspers as Psychopathologist," in *The Philosophy of Karl Jaspers*, ed. Paul Arthur Schilpp (La Salle, IL: Open Court Publishing Co., 1957), 446-7.
30. Jaspers, *Strindberg und van Gogh*, 177. Cited Kolle, "Jaspers as Psychopathologist," 447.
31. Jaspers, *Strindberg und van Gogh*, 182. Cited Kolle, "Jaspers as Psychopathologist," 447.
32. T. S. Eliot, "The Metaphysical Poets," in *Selected Essays 1917-1932* (New York: Harcourt, Brace and Company, 1932), 241-250, esp. 247.
33. "Where there is no sense of the infinite vastness of what is beyond our grasp, all we finally succeed in conveying is misery—not tragedy. This is the peculiar predicament of modern tragedy since the Enlightenment." Jaspers, *Tragedy Not Enough*, 48. See also his general history of this development, Jaspers, "Tragedy Not Enough," 28-40.
34. Jaspers, *Tragedy Not Enough*, 62.
35. Kolle, "Jaspers as Psychopathologist," 437.
36. Jaspers, *Tragedy Not Enough*, 69.
37. In her astute critique of this chapter, and the film, Amanda Parris (2016) very aptly described *My Son, My Son, What Have Ye Done?* as "an action film without action, a crime drama in which we do not see the crime and there is no dramatic development . . . [and for the scene where the police take measurements around the deceased . . .] There is a critique of the ubiquitous crime drama here, of the rational reduction of what is to what is quantifiable captured in the very notion of the procedural." Parris, Response, 2016. This is exactly what, I believe, we were trying to convey, and it is to this, and of all that it is emblematic, that Brad reacts. My respondent was also, I think, correct in characterizing the technique employed, in the writing as well as the acting, as creating a kind of Brechtian *Verfremdungseffekt*. She described the way both the stylized dialogue and the "affectless" acting "defamiliarizes the familiar" and quoted Brecht—"By this craft everyday things are removed from the realm of the self-evident"—and Walter Benjamin—"instead of identifying with the protagonist, the audience should learn to feel astonished at the circumstances under which he functions." While I appreciate her characterization of this aspect of the film—and am delighted someone responded to and could articulate so well what we were after—the classicist in me had to resist being therefore labeled "modernist" and the notion imputed of our therefore employing an "historically situated [read "modern" or "modernist"] technique." What ones admires in Brecht (and calls Brechtian) is in actuality what he admired in, and learned from, Euripides. That said, like anyone alive to the time in which he lives but likewise haunted by *le temps perdu*, "fragments I have shored against my ruins" is maybe the best that one can do. (So, a modernist after all.) On the important distinction, which came up in discussion, between the falsified and simulated realities we endeavored to present in the film, and by which Brad feels oppressed, and the kind of poetic truth and invention, even falsification, of which Herzog so often speaks, I refer the reader, as I did my respondent, to a scene in Zak Penn's *Incident at Loch Ness* (2004), a "mockumentary," in which Herzog plays himself on a mission to "find" the Loch Ness monster. Fed up with the cheap stunts orchestrated throughout the film by Penn, which include, Herzog has discovered, a tacky,

remote-controlled, Loch Ness monster mock-up, Herzog tells Penn that he has had enough, and, when Penn tries to defend his shenanigans by saying that Herzog has said that cinema is lies, Herzog insists emphatically that "there is a distinction"—that is, a distinction between his stylizations of reality and poetic inventions, his cinematic credo of ecstatic truth, of which he has often spoken and in fact speaks at the beginning of this film, and Penn's cinematic tricks, outright tawdry lies and deceit—and that being a filmmaker depends on knowing and being able to make that distinction.

38. Jaspers sees a correlation between the grandiosity of the idea the hero is living with and the fundamental reality his tragedy has the power to reveal. Jaspers, "Tragedy Not Enough," 78.

39. Herzog has described what he himself does as a filmmaker in the following way: "I can see, on the horizon, unpronounced and unproclaimed images. I can sense the hypnotic qualities of things that to everyone else look unobtrusive, then excavate and articulate these collective dreams with some clarity." Herzog, *Werner Herzog*, 74. Compare with Jaspers: "We experience nature and man only as they are reduced to their essence in sculpture, drawing, and painting. In a sense, it is when this is done, and only when this is done, that things assume their characteristic form and reveal their visible quality and soul which had previously seemed hidden." Jaspers, *Tragedy Not Enough*, 25-26.

40. Jaspers, *Tragedy Not Enough*, 41.

41. See, for example, T. S. Eliot, "Dante," in *Selected Essays, 1917-1932*, 199-237 (New York: Harcourt, Brace and Company, 1932), 199-237, especially 227-29. Aristotle called the perception of identity in difference the sign of genius. Aristotle, *Poetics*, in *Oxford Classical Texts, De Arte Poetica Liber*, ed. Rudolph Kassel. (New York: Oxford University Press, 1965), 1459a3-8.

42. The image and the idea, of being in a state of suspension in midair, came from Mark Yavorsky, who had been a basketball star, and described having this experience. It was something Herzog and I intuitively understood and responded to. Although I was not consciously thinking about either work at the time, I'm sure the phrase "unwobbling pivot" had stuck with me from the title of Ezra Pound's translation of Confucius and that "still point" must have leapt out at me, half-remembered, from those haunting lines of T. S. Eliot's "Four Quartets": "At the still point of the turning world. Neither flesh nor fleshless; / Neither from nor towards; at the still point, there the dance is, / But neither arrest nor movement. And do not call it fixity, / Where past and future are gathered. Neither movement from nor towards, / Neither ascent nor decline. Except for the point, the still point, / There would be no dance, and there is only the dance." T. S. Eliot, "Four Quartets," in *Collected Poems, 1909-1962* (New York: Harcourt, Brace & World, 1963), 177. Ezra Pound, *Confucius: The Unwobbling Pivot/The Great Digest/The Analects* (New York: New Directions Publishing Company, 1969). I also had never seen and was at the time we wrote this film completely unaware of Jeff Koon's *One Ball Total Equilibrium Tank* (1985), in which a lone basketball hovers, suspended, in the absolute center of a tank filled with water, epitomizing, as an arresting image of quite surprising power—perhaps because of its very concreteness—that still, suspended, inner state Brad describes. If I had even once ever seen a photo of it, I had completely forgotten it, and in fact only came upon one entirely by accident after having written this chapter.

43. See Job 39:18 in *The Holy Scriptures* (Philadelphia: The Jewish Publication Society, 1941).

44. Longinus compares the sense of Genesis 1:3, 9 with a conflation of several Homeric passages describing the earth trembling and seas parting as Poseidon drives his immortal team. In keeping with Longinus' spirit of creative conflations, the Homeric passage quoted here by me comes from an immediately preceding passage (IX.5) where Longinus begins his brief discussion of evoking the majesty of the divine with these lines from the *Iliad*, a description of Hera's horses vaulting from Olympus. Longinus, *On the Sublime*, ed. D. A. Russell (Oxford: Clarendon Press, 1964), IX.9. The translation of Homer is my own. Homer, *The Iliad*, Oxford Classical, V. 768f.

BIBLIOGRAPHY

Aristotle. *Poetics*. In *Oxford Classical Texts, De Arte Poetica Liber*. Edited by Rudolph Kassel. New York: Oxford University Press, 1965.
Bassett, Eric. (Producer). Werner Herzog (Director). *My Son, My Son, What Have Ye Done?* United States: Industrial Entertainment, 2009.
Eliot, George. *Middlemarch*. London: Penguin Books, 2008.
Eliot, T. S. "Four Quartets." In *Collected Poems, 1909-1962*, 173-209. New York: Harcourt, Brace & World, 1963.
_____. "The Metaphysical Poets." In *Selected Essays, 1917-1932*, 241-250. New York: Harcourt, Brace and Company, 1932.
_____. "Dante." In *Selected Essays, 1917-1932*, 199-237. New York: Harcourt, Brace and Company, 1932.
Golder, Herbert. "Shooting on the Lam." In *Werner Herzog, A Guide for the Perplexed, Conversations with Paul Cronin*, edited by Paul Cronin, 478-88. London, UK: Faber and Faber, 2014.
Herzog, Werner. *Werner Herzog, A Guide for the Perplexed, Conversations with Paul Cronin*. Edited by Paul Cronin. London, UK: Faber and Faber, 2014.
The Holy Scriptures. Philadelphia: The Jewish Publication Society, 1941.
Homer. *The Iliad*. In *Oxford Classical Texts, Homeri Opera*, Vol. 1. Edited by David B. Munro and Thomas W. Allen. Oxford: Clarendon Press, 1963.
_____. *The Iliad*. Translated by Robert Fitzgerald. New York: Farrar, Straus and & Giroux, 2004.
Jaspers, Karl. *Heimweh und Verbrechen*. Habilitation. Heidelberg University, 1909.
_____. *Man in the Modern Age*. Translated by Eden and Cedar Paul. London: Routledge & Kegan Paul, Ltd., 1951.
_____. *Strindberg und van Gogh*. München: Piper & Co., 1951.
_____. *Tragedy Is Not Enough*. Translated by Harold A. T Reiche, Harry T. Moore, and Karl W. Deutsche. Boston: The Beacon Press, 1952.
_____. *Truth and Symbol*. Translated by Jean T. Wilde, William Kluback, and William Kimmel. New York: Twayne Publishers, 1959.
_____. *Von der Wahrheit*. München: R. Piper, 1947.
Kitto, H. D. F., *The Greeks*, New York: Penguin Books Ltd, 1951.
Kolle, Kurt. Karl Jaspers as Psychopathologist. In *The Philosophy of Karl Jaspers*, edited by Paul Arthur Schilpp, 437-68. La Salle, IL: Open Court Publishing Co., 1957.
Lawrence, T. E. *Seven Pillars of Wisdom*. Garden City, NY: Doubleday, Doran & Company, Inc., 1935.
Longinus. *On the Sublime*. Edited by D. A. Russell. Oxford: Clarendon Press, 1964.
Parris, Amanda. *Herbert Golder's My Son, My Son What Have Ye Done?* Response presented at American Philosophical Association, Pacific Division. March 31, 2016.
Pound, Ezra. *Confucius: The Unwobbling Pivot/The Great Digest/The Analects*. New York: New Directions Publishing Company, 1969.
Ricoeur, Paul. "The Relation of Jaspers' Philosophy to Religion." In *The Philosophy of Karl Jaspers*, edited by Paul Arthur Schilpp, 611-42. La Salle, IL: Open Court Publishing Co., 1957.
Sartre, Jean Paul. *No Exit and Three Other Plays*. New York: Vintage Books, 1946.
Weil, Simone. *The Iliad or The Poem of Force*. Translated by Mary McCarthy. Wallingford, PA: Pendle Hill, 1978.

THREE

eXistenZ or *Existenz*: Transcendence in the Early Twenty-First Century

K. Malcolm Richards

The work of David Cronenberg makes use of an array of different genres within cinema, especially the realms of horror, science fiction, and fantasy. From his early explorations of parasitical horror, such as *Shivers* (1974) and *Rabid* (1976) to later works, such as the crime narratives of *A History of Violence* (2005) and *Eastern Promises* (2007), Cronenberg's films show a willingness to explore different genres within the world of cinematic entertainment. Yet, while working within genre cinema, he often subverts the expectations and formulas of these genres of entertainment to probe, sometimes literally, questions around the body, identity, technology, and spirituality that make use of cinema as a form of speculative philosophy. Even when he remakes a film, such as *The Fly* or adapts another writer's work, as in *Crash* (1996), *Naked Lunch* (1991), or *Cosmopolis* (2012), the results are never a re-make or adaptation of a novel. They are transformed into a Cronenberg film, works often marked by their lurking philosophical questions.

> My films are *sui generis*. It would be nice if they could form their own genre, or subgenre. It's the need to sell films that causes this kind of categorization. And, of course, there's always a critical impulse to categorize and label. But people seem to think that it's necessary to categorize before they can understand. My films really do exist on their own. There is no need to do that to experience them properly.[1]

In this chapter, the speculative philosophical questioning that potentially happens in cinema will be traced through Cronenberg's 1999 film *eXistenZ*.[2] Not only does the movie in its title invoke the concept of *Existenz*, so central to Karl Jaspers' work, but it also touches on a number of questions pertinent to the field of philosophy, especially existentialism and its inheritors, as we try to think through a world being rapidly transformed by technology in fashions almost unimaginable fifty years ago. I say "almost," as fiction, literary, cinematic, artistic, or otherwise, allows a space for thinking this unimaginable, imagining the yet to be imagined.

In particular, I will examine the film's narrative structure, its use of recurring themes, and formal devices, while looking to how the film frames questions around the body, sexuality, identity, technology, and reality, paying particular attention to moments that may be approached through questions opened up by Jaspers and existence philosophy. At the same time, I will not be trying to suggest that Cronenberg's work may simply be read through any particular philosophical lens, one formed or informed by Jaspers, Heidegger, Derrida, or whomever. Rather, Cronenberg's work transforms the questions of philosophy through cinema, while reframing these questions, on one level, for a world entering the early twenty-first century, thinking through how questions around being and *Existenz* become contoured by our evolving relation to technology, while remaining, on another level, fundamentally the same. Technology always has mediated our relation to nature, from the bow and arrow to thermonuclear weapons, which necessitates thinking through not only what this mediated relationship to nature reveals, but also thinking through our relation with technology and technology's relation to nature. To explore *eXistenZ*, I want to consider its opening scenes, looking at the "reality" constructed by Cronenberg's film. That is to say, the framework of fiction at work in *eXistenZ* both sets up and plays on expectations, making use of the freedom of fiction to initiate a questioning of everyday reality. I also want to look to the way that *eXistenZ* poses questions around the body, technology, and immersive virtual realities, questions that brush up on the territory of existence philosophy, but extend these considerations to two phenomena outside or on the fringes of philosophic consideration, video games (through the game *eXistenZ*) and cinema (through the movie *eXistenZ*). Lastly, I want to consider how the final scenes of *eXistenZ* unsettle the framing of the film as a whole and the questions that it poses, while productively refusing to answer them.

OPENINGS I

> In a sense that's the theme of many of my movies. There is no absolute reality, therefore virtual reality becomes a meaningless term. I understand it, of course, when people are talking about computer simulations and so on. But in the greater philosophical sense, and in the artistic sense, every filmmaker is creating a virtual reality. That is what you do in a film. It's not a reality . . . even if it pretends to be a very naturalistic, realistic world. It isn't. It's complete artifice.

—David Cronenberg[3]

After the title credits, the movie begins inside a church structure filled with a packed audience being screened at the entrance. The attendees sit in wooden chairs, dressed in modest, rural attire, awaiting the reveal of a new game and gaming platform. The game, *eXistenZ*, is being introduced and the attendees will get to be the first to play the game. In addition, the audience is presented the added surprise that they will get to play the game with the game's designer, Allegra Geller (Jennifer Jason Leigh). She is introduced, visually, picking through the offerings of coffee and orderly arranged snack fair on a table. She is dressed differently from everyone, metallic blue blouse with clean, gray slacks and she uses a dark, metallic blue ski-boot as a carrying case for her "game-pod" that will host the "slave-pods" being provided to the volunteers for the test run of the new game. Twelve volunteers from the reverential audience join Geller who sits in the central chair with six participants to either side of her.

From the beginning, everything in *eXistenZ* is slightly off within the world being presented. It is tempting to say that things are *unheimlich*, but, rather, the fictive world the film presents is wholly different than our world, even in its proximity. The setting is not urban and high-tech. It is modest and rural. The look is not futuristic in architecture or dress, but, rather, simple, generic, basic, more an idea of a fictional place than a tangible place. We are not given a specific location or time to anchor this world. Moreover, the colors are muted and the lighting slightly dark, making the simplicity of the imagery murky, something that echoes the murky minimalism of Howard Shore's droning soundtrack. All of these departures from the expectations of our world are part of what cinematic fiction permits, but they also point to some of the ways that Cronenberg's film constructs a fictive framework for the narrative of *eXistenZ*, presenting a world that is simultaneously unspectacular, yet spectacularly different than ours. The structures minimally indicate place. The church is established through a central stain glass window, the flanking windows on either side bearing advertising banners for the game *eXistenZ*. Without any anchoring specificity, the movie just starts and the viewer has to negotiate the narrative making use of what is familiar from the genres of science fiction, noir, horror, and action, relying on what is most familiar, even when what is being introduced is unimaginable except in genre fiction. In using the framework of fiction to present a narrative not tied to a determinate reality, *eXistenZ* constructs a world with great freedom to play with possibilities.

In addition, the opening portion of the film, up to when Pikul (Jude Law) first enters the game *eXistenZ*, establishes a number of themes that populate not only *eXistenZ*, but also appear in *Videodrome* and other films in Cronenberg's *oeuvre*. First, *eXistenZ* presents a fictive world where nothing is what it is, or, rather, everything is not what it presents itself to be. A church is the location for the worship of a video game and the game designer. A gas station is not simply a gas station, but a place performing illegal bio-port installations at night. A ski lodge is not a ski lodge, but a medical research laboratory exploring the use of synthetic DNA with the organs of mutated reptilian-amphibian-hybrid creatures. Dissimulation permeates the cinematic reality of the world of *eXistenZ*. When Geller and Pikul arrive at a ski chalet to meet one of Geller's friends, Kiri Vinokur (Ian Holm), she responds to Pikul's query of what they do if anyone comes to the ski lodge wanting to ski by saying, "Come on Pikul. Nobody actually physically skis anymore. You know that."

Second, the names of locations and people point to the fictive nature of this reality, even as it establishes the film's narrative. Geller refers to the locals as country people, even though she notes that a number of game people are in the country due to the development of the industry. When they are thinking of where to get a bio-port installed around the middle of the night, Pikul jokingly suggests that they look for a country gas station. In the next scene, they arrive at a station named Country Gas Station. Moreover, the mechanic who runs the station is named Gas (Willem Dafoe). The look of the film accentuates this quasi-generic feel to the world being depicted, even as the imagery builds visually on elements not simply from science fiction, but also film noir. All of this supplements the sense that nothing is what it is, that while everything is seemingly familiar, we are in a world very different than our own.

Third, there is a complex element to the melding of the organic with the technological in *eXistenZ* that also brushes up on themes within Cronenberg's 1983 film *Videodrome*.[4] The hybridization of the organic and the technological comes to the fore most visibly in the game-pods that wiggle and writhe, making squealing noises as they are touched. Living creatures, the game-pods are plugged into the user's body and run off their energy and bio-feedback. Through this symbiosis, the game-pods allow the gamer's own consciousness to have an impact on the themes of the game. The game not only needs the gamer, the gamer needs other gamers to fully engage the immersive environment. Geller, in explaining her game and the need to have someone else enter *eXistenZ* with her, says to Pikul, "Of course without another player you're only a tourist. It's frustrating." While the game environment is shaped in part by the participants, it is also a world coordinated by scripted characters. Not only does Geller critique some of the characters in her game, when she and Pikul first enter the game, she also tries to explain to Pikul, who is experiencing a game for the first time, where some of the motivations that he is feeling are coming from, noting how part of the game is learning about your character and what your character is like, something that can only be done by playing the character. After initially adjusting to the seamless entry into a convincing simulated reality, Pikul asks what the goal of the game is, to which Geller responds "You have to play the game to find out why you're playing the game." When Pikul first experiences saying something that he did not expect to say, Geller enthusiastically explains, "It's your character that said it. It's a kind of schizophrenic feeling, isn't it? You'll get used to it. There are things that have to be said to advance the plot and establish the character. And those things get said whether you want to say them or not." Later, Pikul questions the role of free will within the supposed open-ended universe provided by Geller's game *eXistenZ*. To Pikul's observation that that free world does not seem to be a big part of this virtual world, Geller replies, "It's like real life. There's just enough to make it interesting."

When the game participants are linked up through their game-pods, the users are presented, if viewed from outside the game world, as users. That is to say, they appear, on one level, as addicts, their heads and torsos moving rhythmically in isolation together without any consciousness of "reality," an activity that almost mimics the nodding of heroin addicts as represented cinematically, pointing to an element of addiction and technology, or, as I will term it, techno-narcosis that not only populates *eXistenZ*, but also permeates *Videodrome*. Geller, in her urge to play the game, even while being hunted down for assassination, embodies addictive behavior. After Pikul pauses the game, she is impatient to re-enter it. In addition, the fervent enthusiasm of the crowd at the church in the opening scene presents a group of eager addicts, awaiting the newest hit game. One of the audience members steps forward and yells "Allegra! Allegra!" The narcotized movements of the first enclave of gamers also accentuate the associations visually set up by the initial meeting place of the church. Geller's visual introduction, at the coffee table, creates associations with an AA group meeting. She stands reserved and introverted, waiting to join the group meeting. Yet, instead of battling addiction, these individuals are eagerly giving into it, suggesting a world where an addiction to technology is the norm, leading potentially to a numbing of reality through synthetic overstimulation, a techno-narcosis.

In addition to the techno-narcotic dimension of the melding of the organic and the technological, there is also a related combination of technology and the erotic or, rather, a techno-erotic element to *eXistenZ*. The techno-erotic manifests most notably in the shape, movements and sounds made by the game-pod. Fleshy and alive, it responds to the flicking and rubbing of the over-determined nipple/clitoral/labial forms that comprise the interface. The techno-erotic is also something at play in the presentation of Pikul and Geller, as their bodies lay listlessly on the bed when they are within *eXistenZ*. The writhing of their bodies is not just narcotic-like, but also erotic, even if their bodies are only connected through the umbilical cords or, as they are termed, *UmbyCords* of the game pods. Geller, in particular, constantly wraps the *UmbyCord* around her body and head, at times putting it in her mouth, in ways that heighten the sensuality of this corporeal link between eroticism and technology.

The bio-ports themselves become eroticized locations, excited, licked, and penetrated, something that opens up to other dimensions of the techno-erotic within Cronenberg's work. The techno-erotic becomes a means to thinking through aspects of the body after virtual technologies.

Lastly, there is a collision of religion and the realm of technology, something that could suggest points to a techno-theology. Beyond any number of superficial allusions to religion, from the church setting to the worship of Geller, "the game pod goddess herself," and the presentation of her seated with six apostles to either side, this techno-theological element, something present also in *Videodrome*, manifests itself in other forms throughout the film. For instance, Gas, the mechanic, when he recognizes Geller, drops to her feet, in a reverential manner. The newspaper clipping that he pulls out of his wallet, a curiously old media image, seems to be a shroud in the virtual world of *eXistenz*. He notes how her work has changed his life, showing a form of worship reserved for a divine figure, echoing the reverence that greets her introduction in the film. This techno-theological element also arises in the themes of Geller's games. In talking with Pikul, Gas, wearing mechanic overalls that bear his name on the ubiquitous oval patch, says of one of Geller's earlier games, *ArtGod*, "Did you ever play her game *ArtGod*? One word capital 'A,' capital 'G.' Thou, the player of the game, art God. Very spiritual. Funny too. God the artist, the mechanic . . . funny." The techno-theological dimension, a worship of technology and worship through technology, also manifests itself in the way Geller presents her games. When she introduces *eXistenZ*, she says to the audience, "The world of games is in a kind of a trance. People are programmed to accept so little. But the possibilities are so great. *eXistenZ* is not just a game. It's an entirely new game system and it involves a whole lot of new toys which you're going to be the first to try out." She sees possibilities in a world of narcosis. She seems to even offer transcendence through technology, though the authenticity of this transcendence, something that will be discussed later, is always suspect, always a premise, not a promise. It is something that toys with us.

OPENINGS II

The phrase "biological horror"—often attached to my work—really refers to the fact that my films are very body-conscious. They're very conscious of physical existence as a living organism, rather than other horror films or science-fiction films which are very technologically oriented, or concerned with the supernatural, and in that sense are very disembodied.
—David Cronenberg[5]

eXistenZ also shows an interest in physical openings, passages between inside and outside, and this provides an opportunity for the film to explore themes around the body in a way that de-familiarizes them from normative cinematic treatments, providing ways of presenting questions around the body, gender, and sexuality made possible by fiction. Given the subject of video games, Cronenberg's work, in its own manner, anticipates phenomena such as MUD, MMOG, MMOFPS, MMORPG and other multi-user online gaming platforms, even if it does so in a fashion that is wholly different from anything that exists in our culture.[6] By doing this, *eXistenZ* avoids one of the pitfalls of many cybernetic, virtual reality films. Many films within this genre force a futuristic look or try to embody something of the digital formally, such as the use of pixilation or other digital traces to emphasize the difference between the virtual and reality itself.[7] They often use the most advanced technical effects to no long-term effect, as they create a look that quickly becomes dated given the rapid advancement of technology and design. They think the technical only through the surface or appearance, not thinking about how the technical may change our relation to reality and being. Instead, *eXistenZ* creates a world where the difference between the appearance of reality and virtual reality is minimal. There are proximate differences between the realities, but to differentiate the video game realm from the realm of reality may be a faulty assumption as will be explored later.

Bodily openings factor into all the participants in the game *eXistenZ*, notably through the bio-port into which the game pod's *UmbyCord* is plugged. This physical opening, allowing for the merger of technology and the body, gets a lot of play in Cronenberg's filmic hands. Not only does it evoke other displaced orifices on bodies within his cinematic work, such as the opening in the armpit of Rose in *Rabid* that houses an over-determined fecal-phallic parasite that pricks its victims, turning the female protagonist into a predator of men and her victims into ravenous flesh-eaters, it also allows Cronenberg's film to reframe gender difference through a number of scenes where the bio-port receives attention. For instance, when the viewer first discovers that Pikul does not have a bio-port, he states his anxiety over being penetrated.

> Pikul: I've been dying to play your games, but I have this phobia about having my body penetrated . . . surgically . . . you know what I mean.
>
> Geller: No, I'm not sure that I do.
>
> Pikul: Getting a bio-port fitted.

While this introduces a larger theme around Pikul's anxieties over his physical self, in this particular situation, directing his fear about being penetrated to a female character, accentuates the different experiences of the body at stake, Geller's response, in its delivery, marking Pikul's lack of thinking beyond his own heterosexual, male response of phobic fear around being penetrated. Pikul feels vulnerable and, later, shortly after he gets a bio-port, he does not like the experience as Geller prepares to plug him into *eXistenZ*. The entire scene plays on a techno-erotic/techno-narcotic quality. She is preparing to physically penetrate the gaming virgin, Pikul, licking the bio-organic *UmbyCord*, replete with veins/wires and ending in a pointed tip, while she fingers his bio-port hole to which she applies lubricant. He responds anxiously,

Pikul: What's that for. It feels cold.

Geller: New ports are sometimes a bit tight. Wouldn't want to hurt you.

(Plugs UmbyCord into Pikul)

Pikul: How come bio-ports don't get infected, I mean they open right into your body.

Geller: Listen to what you're saying, Pikul. Don't be ludicrous. (Opens mouth)

Pikul: Don't you think you could call me Ted.

Geller: Maybe afterwards.

Later, at Vinokur's ski lodge, Pikul receives a new bio-port to replace the sabotaging port installed by Gas. This leads to Pikul's second confrontation with his anxieties over losing his gaming virginity, as well as Geller's aggressive desire to penetrate his bio-port hole.

Pikul: It hurts. I think it's infected.

Geller: No it's not infected. It's just excited. It wants action.

Pikul: I really don't think that I want action. I mean me the bearer of the excited bio-port.

A techno-erotic dimension also occurs inside the game, not only through the mimicking of the bio-pod technology in *eXistenZ*'s game world, where the game pods enter the body completely without any connecting *UmbyCord*, but also in the characters' interactions together. Pikul unexpectedly licks Geller's bio-port, noting that that was not his intention. Geller says that this is okay, that Pikul is feeling a game-urge, one programmed into the character to spur on their movement through the game's narrative. The players lose their identity as they succumb to the urges programmed into the character. As they continue foreplay, Geller says of their sexual interaction, "Our characters are obviously supposed to jump on each other. It's most probably a pathetically mechanical attempt to heighten the emotional tension of the next game sequence. No use fighting it." In the midst of their foreplay, Pikul pauses, now expressing a newfound anxiety around his body.

> Pikul: I'm very worried about my body.
>
> Geller: Your what?
>
> Pikul: Where are our real bodies? Are they all right, what if they're hungry, what if there's danger?
>
> Geller: They're just where we left them. They're sitting quietly, eyes closed. It's just like meditating.
>
> Pikul: I feel really vulnerable. Disembodied.

Besides again expressing anxieties around his body being vulnerable, we also see another manifestation of the techno-theological in the evocation of the meditative terms that Geller uses to describe the plugged-in gamer's body. As is visually evident, the peace of these bodies is proximate to the erotic and the narcotic, something that Geller's own view as enthusiastic user presents as peaceful and spiritual to assure the new gamer's bodily anxieties.

Later, as Pikul and Geller proceed further into the game, he expresses anxiety over what his real body is doing. He expresses his discomfort, one that points to not just an anxiety over the potential loss of his real body, but also a loss of any concept of the "real." He says,

> Pikul: I'm feeling a little disconnected from my real life. I'm kind of losing touch with the texture of it. You know what I mean? I mean I actually think there's an element of psychosis involved here.
>
> Geller: Yes. This is a great sign. Your nervous system is fully engaging with the game architecture.

While Pikul's meditations on his body and its relation to his virtual body continue a mapping of the biological body within a technological world, a world marked by disease, a theme prevalent not just in *eXistenZ*, but in many of Cronenberg's works, it also posits a dis-ease with the world in its normative, everyday form that points to one of the other dimensions to *eXistenz* that brushes up on the terrain of *Existenz* and the question of being.

CRONENBERG'S EXISTENTIALISM

> Our existence as such leaves us unsatisfied in its continual and endless drive for more, a drive that lacks a final goal and increasingly realizes its own meaninglessness as it clearly foresees its own end. In deed, work, fame, and our effects on posterity we gain only a second duration for a slightly longer term, but we cannot conceal from ourselves the fact that this second temporal duration, too, has its absolute end in the silence of the universe.
> —Karl Jaspers[8]

Video games have always provided, like most forms of entertainment, such as cinema, a seeming means of escape. This form of escapism, however, only plunges one more fully into the banality of existence in the early twenty-first century. Distraction through entertainment is part of the normative contemporary cultural order. Yet, *eXistenZ* presents this form of escape, at moments, as a process of philosophical and, even, spiritual revelation. Through the fictional framework that the film constructs, we see a world where old and young, men and women are invested in gaming across demographics that correspond in no way to our world. Again, Pikul's absence of a bio-port is unusual, and, while it is through Pikul that the question of an awakening to *Existenz* out of everyday existence through *eXistenZ* the game most takes place, Geller provides the impetus for such a confrontation. This is a result not only of the threats on her life and the crises that protecting her places him in, but also the questions that she poses to Pikul, especially as they begin their fraught journey together following the attempt on her life by Noel Dichter (Kris Lemche). She tells Pikul, "This is it, you see. This is the cage of your own making which keeps you trapped and pacing about in the smallest possible space forever. Break out of your cage, Pikul. Break out now." As an instigator to make him recognize that his everyday life is delimited through its normative banality, we see Geller taking on the qualities of prophetess/priestess/goddess. These divine qualities surrounding Geller's representation only accrue after the opening of the film where we see her surrounded with worshippers. At the Country Gas Station, Gas tells Pikul that he was merely a car mechanic before playing Geller's games. When Pikul confronts Gas with the fact that he is still a mechanic, the same occupation he had before playing Geller's game *Art-God*, he responds, "Only on the most pathetic level of reality ... Geller's work liberated me." Pikul begins to get a sense of his own paltry reality when he puts the game *eXistenZ* on pause. After the dramatically bright scene set within the Chinese Restaurant in the Forest, the world outside *eXistenZ* seems especially muted in color. Yet, this dullness only touches the surface of a more disturbing realization for Pikul. Geller asks Pikul what his real life feels like now.

Pikul: It feels completely unreal.

Geller: You're stuck now, aren't you? You want to go back to the Chinese Restaurant, because there's nothing happening here. We're safe. It's boring.

Pikul: It's worse than that. I'm not sure . . . I'm not sure here, where we are, is real at all. This feels like a game to me and you, you're beginning to feel a bit like a game character.

The growing awareness of his *Existenz* within *eXistenZ* perhaps comes forward in the dialogue that seems to most clearly articulate Cronenberg's vision of existence, or, at least, the vision framed by *eXistenZ*. Pikul and Geller talk as they walk in a line through the Trout Farm, which in keeping with the larger logic of dissimulation marking the different realms of *eXistenZ* is a front for the harvesting of mutated amphibian organs and the parts needed for the production of the game-pods within the virtual universe of the game, in addition to parts for "undetectable and hypo-allergenic weapons," as well as unimagined taste sensations in the form of culinary delicacies.

Pikul: I don't like it here. I don't know what's going on. We're both stumbling around together in this unformed world whose rules and objectives are largely unknown, seemingly indecipherable, or even possibly non-existent . . . always on the verge of being killed by forces that we don't understand.

Geller: That sounds like my game all right.

Pikul: That sounds like a game that's not going to be easy to market.

Geller: But it's a game everybody's already playing.

Geller's response, far from reassuring, suggests a slippage between the game and life, that life is the game that everyone is already playing. The question remains, however, whether there is an escape from the game of life and/or the game, *eXistenZ*, and a way to win, or, perhaps more importantly, a way toward *Existenz* through *eXistenZ*, which is to say, a way beyond the less than real quality of both the everyday and the virtual, toward an encounter with *Transzendenz*.

THE END OF *EXISTENZ*/BEGINNING *EXISTENZ*

Long Live the New Flesh.
—*Videodrome* (1982)

Perhaps the most significant difference between *Videodrome* and *eXistenZ* rests in the way the movies end and how they structure the relation between reality and the simulation of reality. In *Videodrome*, the filmic fiction establishes a reality that is departed from as soon as the first *Videodrome* signal is shown to Max Ren (James Woods). While we are not initially aware of what is at play in Ren's hallucinations, the film plays with the slipping of normal everyday reality from Ren's perspective, gradually, through a number of scenes in the narrative where reality gives way to hallucination. By the end of the movie, the hallucinatory experience of Ren has become completely unanchored to any verifiable reality, even as he follows a path leading to the New Flesh. Everything after the first transmission of *Videodrome* is a hallucination at some level, or, rather, has the potential to be a hallucination. If his hallucinations appear momentary at first, his entire reality is put in quotation marks as his hallucination is the only reality that he knows by the end of the film. Whether his faith in the New Flesh is to be rewarded is not answered by the gun shot that leads to the film's credits.[9] In *eXistenZ*, on the other hand, we begin, not in some fictive reality that is a ground, but, rather, in the midst of a game, even if we are not aware of it. That is to say, while the film begins in what we presume to be "reality," by the closing scenes our perspective is shifted to a position that suspends this initial reality. In the closing scene, we discover that the characters have been participating in a different game, *transCendenZ*. The entirety of the film before these final scenes has taken place in *transCendenZ*, a game that encompasses the preceding narrative of a game designer under an assassination threat for her new game *eXistenZ*. While this may be, at one level, a cinematic trick, allowed for by genre cinema, nevertheless in Cronenberg's film, it has a potentially more destabilizing effect, as it refuses to necessarily ground the narrative in a defining, confining, and anchoring reality. If Max Ren departs from a reality, Pikul and Geller potentially have no reality to which to return. They are adrift in the virtual.

The final scenes move quickly, but also offer significant repetitions from what has been previously offered by the narrative. After Geller kills Pikul, in the midst of the chaos at the ski lodge, she asks if she has won. Slowly we see what we took to be "reality" dissolve away, as church pews appear in the grassy field surrounding the ski lodge. As this new reality visually defines itself, we see Geller, eyes closed, with cybernetic head-ware and data gloves, seated with other gamers in a church structure, as in the beginning of the movie. Given the way the game is supposed to draw upon the imagination of the players, this space may have served as the location for the beginning of the game, if we read the opening scenes now as the opening of the game *transCendenZ*. The church space, however, is not filled with a crowd, as at the beginning of the movie. The church is only occupied by the game players and a representative, Merle (Sarah Polley), for the company, PilgrImage, producing the game, *transCendenZ*. The play with the type fonts echoes the play with the title of the game *eXistenZ* and provides a further strand of material to connect virtual and real world. The banners advertising *eXistenZ*, seen at the beginning of the movie, are now replaced with banners advertising *transCendenZ*.

In these closing scenes, not only is the narrative of the film reframed, but we see the reappearance of many of the individuals encountered in the *eXistenZ* game, now revealed to be participants in the game *transCendenZ*. The reappearance of these characters provides another space for a self-reflexive consideration of how the film is being put together. Just as Geller critiques characters within the game *eXistenZ*, the game players critique their characters in *transCendenZ*, something that in turn contours the performance of the actors in the movie *eXistenZ*. One character notes how trivial his part was, saying "I had a lot to do in that first scene at the church, but I thought the character was boring," while other characters comment on how bad their dialogue and accents were. Vinokur notes, "My accent in the game was so thick, I could hardly understand myself." The gamer who played Gas notes how disappointed he was to die so soon, while other players praise his performance, noting how threatening and scary he was. This scene brings attention to the slightly off performances of the actors, something that can at first be misread as simply being a poor performance or a poorly scripted video game character, but within the cinematic narrative signifies the artifice of the narrative being played out. They are not acting within the confines of realism, but within the confines of scripted video game characters, even as they are also working within the confines of being scripted actors within a movie.

Cronenberg's exploration, however, does not end there. The game designer, Yevgeny Nourish (Don McKellar), talks to Merle, the representative for PilgrImage. He notes that he was very disturbed by the game he just played, the game he designed, stating its strong anti-gaming theme which begins with the attempted assassination of a game designer. The company rep is at first fascinated with how creative that narrative is for a video game, seeing how innovative such a game plot could be, and envisioning future sales, before recognizing the potential danger that this may pose to the game designer given that this narrative plot was not his creation, but potentially pulled from the consciousness of the other gamers. Soon, Geller and Pikul confront Yevgeny, bringing along their dog, the same dog that appears in the game *eXistenZ*, and they proceed to execute Yevgeny, with Pikul using a real gun. They declare death to *transCendenZ* and the demon Yevgeny Nourish, repeating lines that have recurred throughout the film. This does not, however, bring the narrative to a close, as one of the characters, when confronted by Pikul and Geller screams, "No, no, no, no! You don't have to shoot me!" He then seems to break character and ask Pikul and Geller, "Hey, tell me the truth. Are we still in the game?"

The movie ends on this question, yet, given the potentiality that we are still seeing what is inside another game, that what is real remains outside yet some other virtual realm, the film's question remains unanswered and leaves open-ended a number of questions relevant to issues raised in the narrative. In this way, *eXistenZ*, like *Videodrome*, refuses closure. If Cronenberg contemplated an alternative ending for *Videodrome*, where we see the hallucinatory world of the New Flesh, a polymorphous world that breaks the bounds of binary gender and sexuality, then his ultimate choice in ending, showing Ren with his fleshy hand-gun pointed at his head, repeating what Nicki Brand is directing him to do as he watches himself on a television set in an abandoned tugboat, leaves the viewer suspended in a hallucination, uncertain whether there is a world beyond reality, a world of the New Flesh, a world of transcendence. The absence of any confirmation of Ren's delusion leaves the question of whether Ren's hallucinatory state has led him to encounter transcendence as he leaves his old flesh behind for the *Existenz* of the New Flesh or as a dead, deranged suicide.

Likewise, in *eXistenZ*, the end does not close off the possibility that the characters are in another game. The answer to the ending question may be negative. In this case, Geller and Pikul are agents of Realism out to kill Nourish and destroy *transCendenZ*. The slippage that occurs in reality is from an illusory virtual reality informed by the different images culled from the imaginations of each game player, immersed and connected, alone together through their *UmbyCords* to Gellar's host pod, to a social reality, the fictional reality in the film that corresponds structurally to our reality outside the space of cinema. If this is the answer to the gamer's closing question, then we end in a moment that retrieves an anchor to reality. The film and the characters Pikul and Geller act to stabilize the relation to reality. In this situation, *eXistenZ* offers a variant of a narrative that one can see in other films of this genre, most notably the *Matrix*, which structures its narrative around the idea that there is a reality that can be retrieved once one realizes the illusory simulation ordering what is accepted as "reality" in the beginning of the cinematic narrative.

If, however, the ending question is answered in the affirmative, then a very different possibility opens up. The slippage that occurs in "reality" is one from the illusory virtual realm of *eXistenZ* to the illusory virtual realm of *transCendenZ*. If we have moved from one game to another, then something far more destabilizing happens. The slippage from one imaginary realm to another leads to a potentially infinite regress, where there is no longer a reality to return to, where there is no longer an everyday reality to anchor the illusory fantasy reality of the video game world. In this situation, what is our relation to nothingness negotiated through, if there is no longer a stable social reality through which to protect us from the obliterating gaze of Nothingness? Is there a way to move from nothingness to no-thing-ness if there is no stable reality through which to navigate? Yet, this perhaps leaves a deeper question. That is to say, in a world that is always already virtual, is there *Transzendenz* to be strived toward, an experience of *Transzendenz* within a world marked by simulation, where *Transzendenz* may only ever be *transCendenZ*? How do we stabilize experience within a realm where nothing is real, a world of no being, but only appearances? Or, from another perspective, is there a "reality" to fight for or does this fight for "reality" miss how *Existenz* may potentially be awakened in *eXistenZ*? Can *Existenz* be encountered in *eXistenZ*, both film and game?

Or does the framework of fiction, of cinema, of immersive simulation, always already mark a limit to what can be thought through cinema, through video games, through the vertiginous virtual? Cronenberg's film refuses to anchor itself definitively on either side of these possibilities. Instead, it presents a narrative that escapes the binds of reason and the demands of realism to explore reality and existence, appearance and being, in terms transformed through Cronenberg's existentialist infused cinematic narratives, while at the same time posing questions that implicate cinema within the illusions (and allusions) that can be produced through the medium. Can a movie, such as *eXistenZ*, open questions relevant to thinking transcendence and its possible representation in cinema? Can a product of the culture of entertainment and distraction lead to a way of thinking through these entertaining forms of distraction? Can a movie have a "philosophy" and does this mark a difference from a video game that threatens to degrade reality, leading to a world of relativism?

While these questions have haunted the ruminations put forward in this reading of *eXistenZ*, like the movie, the answers, as always, exist perhaps beyond the text, a text that can only point at possible answers to questions of *Existenz* and *Transzendenz*, let alone offer a definitive reading of *eXistenZ*. Questions always remain, especially when we think we are given the answers. As Alain Badiou says,

> So the definition of cinema is paradoxical, and that is why cinema is a situation for philosophy. Cinema is a unique relationship between total artifice and total reality. Cinema is really both the possibility of a copy of reality and the completely artificial dimension of that copy. This amounts to saying that cinema is a paradox that revolves around the question of the relationship between "being" and "appearing." It is an ontological art.[10]

NOTES

1. David Cronenberg and Chris Rodley, *Cronenberg on Cronenberg* (London: Faber and Faber, 1992), 59.
2. David Cronenberg (Producer), David Cronenberg (Director), *eXistenZ*. Canada, 1999.

3. David Cronenberg, *Interviews with Serge Grünberg* (London: Plexus, 2006), 166.

4. Filmplan International (Producer), David Cronenberg (Director), *Videodrome*. Canada, 1982.

5. Cronenberg and Rodley, *Cronenberg on Cronenberg*, 58.

6. At the same time, a future 360 degree immersive virtual environment has been announced at conferences such as the 2016 Samsung's Mobile World Congress.

7. See *The Lawnmower Man* (1992) and *The Matrix* (1999). Gimel Everett (Producer), Brett Leonard (Director), *The Lawnmower Man*. United States, 1992. Joel Silver (Producer), Lana Wachowski and Lilly Wachowski (Directors), *The Matrix*. United States, 1999.

8. Karl Jaspers, *Philosophy of Existence* (Philadelphia: University of Pennsylvania Press, 1971), 68.

9. Cronenberg had considered a final scene where Max appears in the world of the New Flesh, a polymorphous world in which he encounters both Nicki Brand and Bianca O'Blivion who now have penises, and swarm Max into this fleshy world of sensuality. The exclusion of the scene, not only precluded any censorship battles, something the film had to contend with even in its released form, but also left the end of the movie open-ended.

10. Alain Badiou, *Cinema*, trans. Antoine de Baecque and Susan Spitzer (Cambridge: Polity Press, 2013), 207.

BIBLIOGRAPHY

Badiou, Alain. *Cinema*. Translated by Antoine de Baecque and Susan Spitzer. Cambridge: Polity Press, 2013.

Cronenberg, David and Chris Rodley. *Cronenberg on Cronenberg*. London: Faber and Faber, 1992.

Cronenberg, David (Producer). David Cronenberg (Director). *eXistenZ*. Canada, 1999.

Cronenberg, David. *Interviews with Serge Grünberg*. London: Plexus, 2006.

Everett, Gimel (Producer). Brett Leonard (Director). *The Lawnmower Man*. United States, 1992.

Filmplan International (Producer). David Cronenberg (Director). *Videodrome*. Canada, 1982.

Jaspers, Karl. *Philosophy of Existence*. Philadelphia: University of Pennsylvania Press, 1971.

Silver, Joel (Producer). Lana Wachowski and Lilly Wachowski (Directors). *The Matrix*. United States, 1999.

FOUR

Earth and World: Malick's *Badlands*

Jason M. Wirth

In December of 1957, Charles Raymond "Charlie" Starkweather, a bow-legged high school drop-out with a speech impediment and a James Dean fixation, repeatedly tried to buy a stuffed animal on credit from a gas station in Lincoln, Nebraska, for his thirteen-year-old girlfriend, Caril. He eventually robbed the station and took the attendant, Robert Colvert, to a remote area where, after a scuffle, he executed him. A few weeks later, Starkweather and his new girlfriend went on a murder spree, killing ten more people, including Caril's mother, stepfather, and baby half sister, before being captured in Douglas, Wyoming. He was given the electric chair in Nebraska in the summer of 1959 while Caril, still a juvenile, was given a life sentence. She was released in 1976 and later married.[1]

Later investigations revealed that Starkweather had worked as a garbage collector, and suggested that when he collected garbage for the wealthy, he had somehow felt that he, too, was part of their garbage, that he would never amount to anything and never belong to this kind of special world. Eventually, however, he found a way to become famous in his own way, a murderous rebel without a cause.

After abandoning academic philosophy, which had included doctoral studies at Magdalen College, Oxford, a projected dissertation on the concept of world in Heidegger, Kierkegaard, and Wittgenstein, which he did not have the heart to complete under Gilbert Ryle, a thoughtful translation of Heidegger's *Vom Wesen des Grundes*,[2] and a one year position as a sabbatical replacement at MIT, Terrence Malick studied at AFI and eventually found himself at work on his first project as a writer and director.

This project was a cinematic meditation inspired by Starkweather and Caril Ann Fugate.

How did a philosopher turned filmmaker transform his philosophical concerns into the language of film? All of Malick's films are immediately striking as profound experiments with the very possibilities of film as a medium and so it would not be convincing to claim that Malick merely sought to illustrate Heideggerian or other kinds of philosophical themes in cinematic terms or somehow found ways to take cinema and turn it into a form of philosophical argumentation. Moreover, the Badlands of the American West are far from the verdure of the *Schwartzwald* and none of the characters in Malick's *Badlands* (1973), despite voicing pseudo profound clichés like "Consider the minority opinion but try to get along with the majority opinion once it's accepted," are in any way genuinely philosophical.[3] And why turn to this sensational and shocking story, ripped out of the American heartland?

We could think of *Badlands* as philosophical not in the traditional — and expressly non-cinematic — sense of pronouncing philosophical positions or making philosophical arguments, but rather in the film's capacity to call forth or give rise to *thinking as such*. Malick achieves this while remaining honest to the unique powers of cinema. The film is not thesis art nor does it smuggle in a philosophical position through dialogue, narration, or other such tricks. To be clear: the film does not have a particular philosophical position but rather evokes the space of thinking itself as it emerges through the friction between the thoughtless world that Kit and Holly share with everyone in the film (they are in continuity with their world, not in opposition to it) and the stark silence of the Badlands and the earth more broadly. Stuart Kendall and Thomas Deane Tucker speak appropriately not of philosophy as film but of "a certain kind of filmmaking relevant to philosophy."[4] It is this relevance that I wish here to consider.

The vast landscape of *Badlands* is not a mere background, a striking setting for a foregrounded story. It is not scenery, despite Kit's counsel to Holly during their murderous picaresque to "enjoy the scenery." The film enacts a contestation between foreground and background, a tension that gives each to its own, while exposing the foreground as a world and the background, ever intruding upon the foregrounded world, as the earth.[5] The strangeness and incomprehensibility of the earth haunts all of Malick's films — the stark and vast eponymous vistas of *Badlands*, the sweeping wheat fields in *Days of Heaven*, the war-torn tropical jungles of Guadalcanal in *The Thin Red Line*, the unfamiliar new worlds of Virginia and Old England in *The New World*, bucolic Texas and the immensity of creation in *The Tree of Life*, the scarred lives and earth of Oklahoma in *To the Wonder*, even Hollywood itself in *The Knight of Cups*.

A world does not need to recognize itself as a world in order to foreground meaning. The sudden emergence of the pure being of the earth, however, exposes the interpreted world—the shared practices in which the earth becomes in some way intelligible—as our habitat.[6] Since a world does not have to call attention to itself in order to operate, it easily allows our shared meaning-making practices to prevail as if they were obvious, given, and non-ideological. In a sense, Hollywood is the perfect metaphor for a tacitly operating world whose contingency is not exposed. "It is," Deleuze argued, "not we who make cinema; it is the world which looks to us like a bad film."[7] The great global bad film whose ravages include not only the decimation of heterogeneous human and nonhuman forms of life but also the earth ecology itself is an inherently globalizing world that ruinously confuses itself with the earth. Hence when Deleuze provocatively insists that "cinema must film, not the world, but belief in this world, our only link" and that cinema provides "reasons to believe in this world," I would here say, in accordance with the terms that guide this present chapter, that we could also speak of belief in the earth, and reasons for believing in its friction with our otherwise settled worlds.[8] It is in this friction that thinking, the contestation between meaning and being, a contestation that pluralizes and multiplies worlds while simultaneously limiting their range, emerges. It is a friction that can also be felt in the bad movie that is the world depicted in *Badlands* and its contestation by the film's own earthy transcendence. It holds earth and world, cinematic thought and Hollywood, together in their strife. It is to this emergence that I now turn.

We begin by considering some of the artistic liberties that Malick took with the Starkweather legend—a legend that, like the short life of James Dean himself, had already taken on mythic proportions. Malick moved Starkweather from the heartland (Lincoln, Nebraska) to the town of Fort Dupree in north-western South Dakota and shifted his murderous excursion that ended up in Wyoming to a westward movement into the Montana Badlands. Caril Ann Fugate becomes fifteen-year-old Texas transplant Holly Sargis (Sissy Spacek). He softens the brutality of Starkweather's murder of Caril's family while preserving both its suddenness and the strange nature of Caril's eventual complicity. Starkweather had killed Caril's mother and stepfather, and then strangled and stabbed their two-year old daughter. Fugate did not witness this, but later helped hide their bodies. In Malick's rendition, Holly is home for the murder, but strangely, perhaps out of her Texan civility, her innocence, and her affection for Kit, goes along with Kit's initiative, eventually helping burn her own home to the ground. "I could of snuck out the back or hid in the boiler room, I suppose, but I sensed that my destiny now lay with Kit, for better or for worse, and that it was better to spend a week with one who loved me for what I was than years of loneliness." When Holly and Kit are reunited at the end of the film after Kit's capture, Kit casually concedes: "Course it's too bad about your dad . . . We're going to have to sit down, and talk about that sometime." Given all of the time they spent hiding in the woods and on the road, there was plenty of time to discuss this awkward and delicate consideration.

Malick later compressed two separate incidents into the sequence in which Kit shoots his old garbage collecting friend Cato near an isolated building in the desolate plains, and then locked a young couple in a storm shelter and capriciously fired two shots through a crack in the shelter door. Starkweather had paid a visit to an old family friend, an elderly August Meyer, who lived in a farmhouse in Bennet, Nebraska. Starkweather shot him in the head with a shotgun and also killed his dog. They fled in Meyer's car, but later had to abandon it when it got stuck in the mud. Two local teenagers soon picked them up. Starkweather and Caril kidnapped them and brought them back to Bennet to a storm shelter, where the male was executed by a shot to the back of the head. It is not clear if Starkweather had attempted unsuccessfully to rape the woman, but he eventually shot her to death. She was discovered partially undressed with her genitals mutilated. Starkweather later claimed that Caril had attacked them in a fit of jealousy.

For Malick, these murders seem almost arbitrarily motivated, creating the impression that to Kit and Holly murder was not all that real, resembling the way that death appears in bad films. When Kit murders Holly's father, he asks, "Suppose I shot you. How'd that be? Huh? . . . You want to hear what it sounds like?" Why would someone want to hear oneself being shot? If the shot were good enough, one would not survive to benefit from hearing oneself being shot. When Kit shoots his old friend Cato, a motive is not even discussed. "Kit never let on why he'd shot Cato. He said that just talking about it could bring us bad luck and that right now we needed all the luck we could get." After shooting Cato in the stomach, Kit opens the door for him and engages him in small talk. When Holly asked if Cato was upset about being shot, Kit responded that "he didn't say anything to me about it." When Kit shoots the teenagers in the cellar, he is not even sure if he hit them, let alone killed them. "Well, I'm not going down there and look." Holly reminisced that Kit "claimed that as long as you're playing for keeps and the law is coming at you, it's considered okay to shoot all witnesses." Martin Sheen recollects that Malick had instructed him to wave the rifle as if it were a magic wand that could make his troubles vanish. As Malick once told Michel Ciment: "Kit and Holly—and in this respect they are truly children—don't think that death is the end."[9]

Before the sequence at Cato's shack, Kit and Holly had hid in the woods by a river where they built a tree house that looks like a set from Walt Disney's *Treasure Island* (1950) or Walt Disney's *Swiss Family Robinson* (1960). Kit also built a camouflaged pit with a lid that looks like something that one would have seen in a Hollywood war movie set in the South Pacific. They were in no way present to their place. Kit reads *Na-*

tional Geographic and Holly gazes at exotic images in a stereopticon as if they were supposed to be some place else. Kit never learns to fish, and resorts to firing his gun into the water. When Kit finally shoots the bounty hunters, Holly explains that,

> Kit felt bad about shooting those men in the backs but he said they'd come in like that and they would've played it as down and dirty as they could, and besides, he'd overheard them whispering about how they were only interested in the reward money. With lawmen it would've been different. They were out there to get a job done and they deserved a fair chance. But not a bounty hunter.

Only if death is not real is the distinction between murdering bounty hunters and lawmen not specious. Holly tells us that Kit even hopes for nuclear destruction: "If the Communists ever dropped the atomic bomb, he wished they'd put it right in the middle of Rapid City." After he is caught, the deputy asked him about his seeming misanthropy. Kit responded that he thought that people were "OK." So why did he murder all of these people? "I don't know. Always wanted to be a criminal, I guess. Just not this big a one . . . Takes all kinds though."

Charlie and Caril had returned to Lincoln, where they murdered the wealthy industrialist C. Lauer Ward, as well as his wife, Clara, their maid Lillian, and even the family dog. They made away with the Ward car and a lot of jewelry. In Malick's rendition, the industrialist and his maid are spared, the wife is not present, and Kit leaves an accounting of everything they are taking, e.g., groceries and strange items like a silver trophy, with the promise to pay them back. Ward belonged to the happier Hollywood world of the successful to which Kit aspired and to which he imagined himself to be entering by really "ringing the bell" with Holly.[10] He really had no idea what he was doing—a rebel without a cause or even a clue—but he nonetheless sensed that he was really doing something.

Kit and Holly go their separate ways, but Kit later tells Holly that he was captured because he had a flat tire, although based on "the way he carried on about it," Holly suspected this was "false." Indeed it was. Kit had left lots of mementos that he hoped would later be discovered. When the sheriff and his deputy were bearing down on him, he shot his own tire flat, prepared a monument out of stones to mark where he had been caught, and then looked into the side view mirror to make sure he was looking his James Dean best. The deputy recognized this. "You know who that sombitch looks like? . . . I'll kiss your ass if he don't look like James Dean!" Kit beamed: he was a star, the great murderer without a cause. In custody, he dispensed personal objects—his lighter, comb, and pen—as if they had become valuable objects descending from the realm of the (movie) stars.

In the introduction to his 1969 translation of Heidegger's *Vom Wesen des Grundes*, Malick distinguishes a world from a mere interpretation of something.[11] One can interpret things without realizing that the very possibility of thinking of something in a meaningful way depends on a world whose shared practices render beings in any way intelligible. Meaning depends on *In-der-Welt-sein*, being in the world as what "makes a preliminary understanding of the Being of being possible."[12] Moreover, a world makes meaning possible without having to expose itself as doing so. The world can operate tacitly, without ever coming into view. Dasein does not have to be "awake" to its world; the world does not have to break out [*ein Aufbruch der Welt*] or dawn [*ein Weltdämmer*].[13] However, when a problem exceeds the reach of the world, it can also reveal the world precisely as a world. As Malick articulates both the silent operation of a world and its breakout:

> And there is no more sense in speaking of an interpretation when, instead of an interpretation, the "world" is meant to be that which can keep us from seeing, or force us to see, that what we have is one. Heidegger's concept is quite like Kierkegaard's "sphere of existence" and Wittgenstein's "form of life," and, as with them, it enters his inquiry only at its limits, when a problem moves out of his depth, or jurisdiction.[14]

Badlands displays both of these valences of world: its concealed operation and its dawning as a world. The great myths that operate unknowingly within a world rely for their force on the world not breaking out as a world; they keep the questions that expose a world from gaining any traction. In this sense, we could speak of two senses of myth: myths that open a world to the earth, which are also awake to their own mythic qualities, and myths that enclose a world within itself, much in the way that someone like Hannah Arendt speaks of the totalizing imperative of ideology. When the ideology is total, a world has no outside; there can be no exceptions, no questions, and no "miracle of being." Without an "outside" or what Schelling once called an "irreducible remainder" [*nie aufgehender Rest*],[15] nothing can flush a world out. This is the closed, somnolent world within which Kit and Holly dwell. Here meaning circulates in a Platonic Cave as if life were a bad movie—the hypnotic *das Man* spell of Hollywood, television, Harlequin romances, local customs, and pop songs. Such a world is turned in on its self, sealing itself into a thought-free vacuum. What passes for "thought" is a mere symptom of conditions that are so obscure that they do not even manifest as conditions. "Thinking" appears obvious. Kit says lots of things that sound like thought— "Well, I got some stuff to say. Guess I'm kind of lucky that way. Most people don't have anything on their minds, do they?"—but such thoughts mimic thinking without actually thinking. These are non-thoughts posing as thinking and as such express a prophylactic against confronting the limit of a world.

In the world of life as a bad movie, nothing really seems that real, as if it were the shadows that engaged Plato's prisoners. As we have already discussed, death is not real to Kit and not all that real to Holly, who somehow never complained much about the fact that her boyfriend shot her father. The shadowy unreality of death also manifests in the manner in which animals are regarded, most all of whom are murdered or otherwise mistreated. The film opens with a dead dog as if it were just a part of the garbage; Holly's dog is murdered by her father as a punishment; after quitting his job as a garbage collector, Kit finds work at an industrial cattle feedlot where the animals are treated like commodities in a factory; Kit is later seen dancing and playing on the carcass of an inexplicably dead cow; Cato's shack is decorated with antlers;[16] Holly kills her own pet fish, although she later expresses some regret; Kit shoots at the fish that he cannot catch with a net; Holly recollects that "Kit'd sometimes ram a cow to save on ammo, and we'd cook it." The death of animals poses no questions and their lack of value appears obvious.

When it comes to murdering people, Kit may appear abnormal, but it would be a mistake to see Kit and Holly as exceptions to their world; they are continuous with it and their actions are different in degree but not in kind. They are not thoughtless exceptions to a generally thoughtful world, but rather are emblematic of a thoughtless world, a kind of fairy-tale Platonic cave that seals out thinking. Kit murdered people as if he were in a Hollywood film or using a magic wand, but the death of animals, with the exception of Holly's regret for her pets, does not occur to anyone in this world as a question or problem. Starkweather had also killed some of his victims' dogs. The two policemen that capture Kit and end his killing spree do not celebrate the triumph of justice but rather are excited by the prospect that they too will be celebrities; the police are happy to receive souvenirs from Kit; meanwhile the National Guard can be seen mobilizing—similar to mobilization of troops for deployment in WWI at the end of *Days of Heaven*. Perhaps this foreshadows the great Hollywood misadventure that will eventually be the Vietnam War. When Malick returned to cinematic work after his two-decade hiatus, he directly engaged this thin red line of war that separates earth and world, silence and meaning, madness and sanity. This line is only indirectly manifest in *Badlands* inasmuch as war and justice belong to the same bad movie in which death and murder are not real. The elemental violence of death—as well as the prodigal flora and fauna of Guadalcanal—awakens the soldiers from the somnolence of their worlds, confronting them with unanswered and perhaps unanswerable questions. For Kit and Holly, however, their world remains stubbornly tacit in its operation, so much so that its very refusal of an outside evokes the externality of the earth.

The doleful childishness and fairy-tale quality of this tacitly operating world is accentuated by Malick's spare but powerful choice of music, including a memorable piece from Carl Orff's *Musica Poetica* called *Gassenhauer*, his 1952 variation (with Gunild Keetman) of a 1536 lute piece by Hans Neusiedler. Using multiple xylophones as well as castanets and some small drums, *Gassenhauer* is part of Orff's "Music for Children" and belongs to the pedagogical pieces called *Schulwerk*, which were designed to awaken a child's capacity for music. As the house burns down, another *Schulwerk* piece from *Musica Poetica* plays, "Passion," alluding of course to the passion and death of Jesus. The innocence of the children singing contrasts with the original event whose pain and profundity transcends the singers' respective purviews. They know not what they sing. The power of this sequence is considerable: children singing, doll houses and toys burning, all of which allows the tension between Holly's innocence and the horrible reality of the earth's elemental and fiery violence to register. This double valence of fire is a common image in Malick's cinema: destruction, as in the burning house in *Badlands*, Linda claiming in *Days of Heaven* that the "whole earth is going up in flames" as well as the devastation of the rich proprietor's fields, the burning of the Japanese encampment in *The Thin Red Line*, the fiery arrows of the Powhatan as well as the burning of their villages in *The New World*, etc.; and the sacred, as in the *Passion* accompanying the burning house in *Badlands*, the sacred flame in both *The Thin Red Line* and *The Tree of Life*, etc. Fire destroys all worlds, but is simultaneously the sacred power of the earth.[17]

Worlds not only enable the seeming obviousness of what and how we do see, but also of what we do not see that we do not see. For example, missing entirely in the world in which Kit and Holly dwell are the Lakota Sioux, who live nearby on the three million acre Cheyenne River Indian Reservation, founded after the defeat of the Lakota Sioux in the late nineteenth century. The Badlands of South Dakota also bore witness to the Lakota's desperate performance of the Nanissáanah or Ghost Dance, which had been received in a dream vision during the solar eclipse in 1889 by a Northern Paiute shaman from the Great Basin called Wovoka (also known as Jack Wilson). Repetition of the five-day Nanissáanah would bring the spirits of the living and the dead together and end the white man's predatory expansion. Its performance by the Lakota Sioux led to their brutal massacre at Wounded Knee.[18] Malick even changed the name of Dupree to the more Indians-and-cavalry sounding Fort Dupree, which also evokes the Sioux in their absence, such forts having been built as part of the ongoing war against the indigenous. Malick also changed Starkweather's name to the more Hollywood cowboy-sounding name Kit Carruthers. Carrying his rifle as if he were constantly striking Hollywood poses, Carruthers evokes the mythic Hollywood hero-type, a fairy-tale knight in shining armor, the mythic Marlboro Man. This transmutation of Starkweather to an even more explicit Hollywood figure is further accentuated when Kit and Holly change their names to James and Priscilla, presumably as in James Dean and Priscilla Presley.

Despite the unsettlingly unthematized force of their world, Malick does not condescend to Kit and Holly. Absorption in the world is our original fallenness (Heidegger's *Verfallenheit*), the loss of Eden/Earth that haunts Malick's entire oeuvre. Calling the world of *Badlands* a bad movie is not to pin all of the blame on Hollywood for the poverty of fallenness and the anonymous rule of *das Man*.[19] Hollywood is parasitic on the prevailing "sensory motor apparatus" (in Deleuze's phrase). It reinforces as much as it originates and shapes, operating in a vicious and closed feedback loop. Hollywood is making bad movies about the bad movie that is already our lives. In turn, Hollywood movies validate, buttress, and, to some extent, restructure the practices of meaning that made them intelligible in the first place. *Badlands* is not as much about the moral failings and limitations of its characters as it is about an ontological re-imagination of original sin, that is, the propensity of worlds to hide themselves and thereby shut themselves off from the absolute exteriority of the earth. *Badlands* is also in a way about the peculiar fallenness of US culture (worlds are always places on the earth).

The earth nonetheless pushes up against and even haunts the otherwise tacit limits of the world, threatening to expose them as such. Heidegger's former friend Karl Jaspers called this intermediary line between meaning and being, world and earth, sanity and madness, a *Grenzsituation*, a boundary or limit situation, a line that the meaning making and maintaining forces of a world cannot assimilate.

> Situations like the following: that I am always in situations; that I cannot live without struggling and suffering; that I cannot avoid guilt; that I must die—these are what I call boundary situations. They never change, except in appearance. There is no way to survey them in existence, no way to see anything behind them. They are like a wall we run into, a wall on which we founder.[20]

Limit situations threaten to expose the world as a world throughout *Badlands*. Sometimes these situations emerge in the form of unanswerable questions. For example, when Kit and Holly finally have sex and, given their youthful inexperience, it is predictably underwhelming, Holly laments, "Is that all there is to it? Gosh, what was everyone talking about?" Kit retorts, "Don't ask *me*," but then struggles to propose a meaningful response to the great mystery of human carnality. His solution? They will mark this memorable moment for the rest of their lives by crushing their hands with an enormous stone. When Holly refuses, Kit announces that he will always carry the cumbersome stone around with him as a memento, but quickly realizes that it is too heavy and tosses it away. Even Kit himself is a great question to Holly: "It all goes to show how you can know a person and not really know him at the same time." Both the person of Kit and the sheer fact that Holly had been in a relationship with him remain great and troubling questions for her.

Mirrors, which are prevalent through the film, can suddenly become limit situations. Kit often looks into a mirror to make sure that he appears the way that he wants to appear. Even in the woods Kit keeps up appearances by looking into the mirror and shaving. After Cato had been shot and then returned to his forlorn shack, however, he looked into the mirror to see himself at the threshold of death. The mirror no longer reflects a world back in upon itself, but rather allows the transcendence of death—as silent as the earth itself—to penetrate into a world at the moment in which its capacity to make sense of things is violently waning.

The enormity of the earthly landscapes also shakes the semantic boundaries of the world through which Kit and Holly are fleeing. They struggle to orient themselves. "We lived in utter loneliness. Neither here nor there. Kit said that "'solitude' was a better word cause it meant more exactly what I wanted to say." The earth itself cannot be apprehended directly, but must be brought into relief much in the way that a silo gives measure to the horizon. A world makes the earth inhabitable by bringing it down to size, but the earth nonetheless looms beyond any horizon of interpretation.

The strife between earth and world also emerges in one of the film's most brilliant images: Holly's father painting a large bucolic scene of Kauzer's Feed and Grain as an inhabited world of nature. The natural life

Figure 4.1. *Badlands.* **Warner Brothers (Producer). Terrence Malick (Director). Badlands. USA, 1973.**

is all quite orderly and domestic: docile cows, fish swimming in a pond, attractive trees, cultivated earth, a farmer and his house. The sign itself, however, is mysteriously forlorn. It is not near any paved roads and it is hard to imagine customers readily stumbling upon it. Most strikingly, one of the panels has been removed. Not only does the image of the agrarian world bring the vast earth and sky of the Badlands into relief, but the earth also directly penetrates it, shining through the world that has been superimposed upon it.

Finally, unlike the reified world of animals whose deaths pose no questions, in a remarkable sequence in which Kit carries his magic gun as if here were a cowboy, animals—a wild turkey, a lizard, etc.—stare silently back at the camera. Holly had recollected that "we took off at sunset, on a line toward the mountains of Saskatchewan, for Kit a magical land beyond the reach of the law." The moon, producing no light of its own, mysteriously illumines the earth, and the lightening, the distant mountain, and the taciturn creatures loom without explanation, their very countenance a question and a limit. Kit, afraid that he was nothing, really wanted to "ring the bell" and be something, to be validated by countless anonymous eyes. The earth means nothing, but it is not as such nothing. It is absolutely full, always more than how we make sense of it. In his excellent book on Malick, Steven Rybin reflects that "it is precisely a plenitude that the characters themselves cannot recognize as having *been* lost."[21]

NOTES

1. William Allen, *Starkweather: The Story of a Mass Murderer* (New York: Houghton Mifflin, 1976).
2. Martin Heidegger, *Vom Wesen des Grundes* (Frankfurt am Main: Vittorio Klostermann, 1969).
3. Warner Brothers (Producer), Terrence Malick (Director), *Badlands*. USA, 1973.
4. Stuart Kendall and Thomas Deane Tucker, "Introduction," in *Terrence Malick: Film and Philosophy*, ed. Stuart Kendall and Thomas Deane Tucker (New York and London: Bloomsbury Academic, 2013), 1.
5. While I agree with Thomas Deane Tucker that "Malick's landscape setting in this film is not simply the picturesque as seen through the eyes of Kit or Holly" but is rather "a picture of a world," I want here to stress the externality of what utterly resists worldhood and, as such, not only brings a world to its limit, but exposes it to its worldhood. Thomas Deane Tucker, *Worlding the West: An Ontopology of Badlands*, in *Terrence Malick: Film and Philosophy*, ed. Thomas Deane Tucker and Stuart Kendall (New York and London: Bloomsbury Academic, 2013), 89.
6. Kelly Oliver argues for the being of the earth and the meaning of the world. Kelly Oliver, *Earth and World: Philosophy After the Apollo Missions* (New York: Columbia University Press, 2015).
7. Gilles Deleuze, *Cinema 2: The Time-Image* (Minneapolis: University of Minnesota Press, 1989), 171.
8. Deleuze, *Cinema 2*, 172.

9. Holly recollected that Kit had "never met a fifteen-year-old girl who behaved more like a grownup and wasn't giggly. He didn't care what anybody else thought." Lloyd Michaels, *Terrence Malick* (Urbana: University of Illinois Press, 2019), 110.

10. When Kit was captured and later reunited with Holly, he remarked, "Boy, we rang the bell, didn't we?"

11. Heidegger, *Vom Wesen des Grundes*, xv.

12. Heidegger, *Vom Wesen des Grundes*, 111, 113.

13. Heidegger, *Vom Wesen des Grundes*, 111, 108-9.

14. Heidegger, *Vom Wesen des Grundes*, xv.

15. Schelling, in the 1809 *Freedom* essay, spoke of primal nature (*erste Natur*), that which is an "incomprehensible ground" and a *nie aufgehender Rest*, an irreducible remainder that cannot be resolved by reason even with the greatest exertion. F.W.J. Schelling, "Freedom," in *1856-1861 Sämmtliche Werke* (Stuttgart and Augsburg: J. G. Cotta'scher Verlag, I.7, 1946), 360.

16. Kit: "Where'd you get them antlers?" Cato: "They come with the house."

17. John Bleasdale writes, "Fire can be both symbolic of violence and an act of violence itself. Destructive and fascinating, fire accelerates entropy and easily (almost inevitably) gets out of control. In Malick's films, it is used to cover tracks and destroy evidence, making everything look like it could have been an accident. Or an act of God. And fire is also the touch of the divine, a Pentecostal manifestation of the spirit, or the spiritual." John Bleasdale, "Terrence Malick's Histories of Violence," in *Terrence Malick: Film and Philosophy*, ed. Thomas Deane Tucker and Stuart Kendall (New York and London: Bloomsbury Academic, 2013), 41.

18. The Montana Badlands also evoke the memory of Custer and the 1876 Battle of Little Big Horn, which was the last great victory of the Lakota, Northern Cheyenne, and Arapaho.

19. See the relevant analysis in Heidegger's *Sein und Zeit*, esp. §38. "This 'absorption' mostly has the character of being lost in the publicness of the they [*das Man*]. The Dasein, which could be from itself an authentic self, is at first always already fallen away from itself and fallen into the 'world.' [*Dieses Aufgehen . . . hat meist den Charakter des Verlorenseins in die Öffentlichkeit des Man. Das Dasein ist vom ihm selbst als eigentlichem Selbstseinkönnen zunächst immer schon abgefallen und an die 'Welt' verfallen*]." Martin Heidegger, *Sein und Zeit* (Tübingen: Max Niemeyer Verlag, 1986), 175, translation mine.

20. Karl Jaspers, *Philosophy*, Vol. 2 (Chicago: University of Chicago Press, 1970), 178.

21. Steven Rybin, *Terrence Malick and the Thought of Film* (New York: Lexington Books, 2012), 65.

BIBLIOGRAPHY

Allen, William. *Starkweather: The Story of a Mass Murderer*. New York: Houghton Mifflin, 1976.

Bleasdale, John. Terrence Malick's Histories of Violence. In *Terrence Malick: Film and Philosophy*, edited by Thomas Deane Tucker and Stuart Kendall. New York and London: Bloomsbury Academic, 2013, 40-57.

Deleuze, Gilles. *Cinema 2: The Time-Image*. Minneapolis: University of Minnesota Press, 1989.

Heidegger, Martin. *Sein und Zeit*. Tübingen: Max Niemeyer Verlag, 1986.

Heidegger, Martin. *The Essence of Reasons*. Evanston: Northwestern University Press, 1969.

Heidegger, Martin. *Vom Wesen des Grundes*. Frankfurt am Main: Vittorio Klostermann, 1969.

Jaspers, Karl. *Philosophy*, Vol. 2. Chicago: University of Chicago Press, 1970.

Kendall, Stuart and Thomas Deane Tucker. "Introduction." In *Terrence Malick: Film and Philosophy*, edited by Stuart Kendall and Thomas Deane Tucker. New York and London: Bloomsbury Academic, 2013, 1-12.
Michaels, Lloyd. *Terrence Malick*. Urbana: University of Illinois Press, 2019.
Oliver, Kelly. *Earth and World: Philosophy After the Apollo Missions*. New York: Columbia University Press, 2015.
Rybin, Steven. *Terrence Malick and the Thought of Film*. New York: Lexington Books, 2012.
Schelling, F.W.J. Freedom. In *1856-1861 Sämmtliche Werke*. Stuttgart and Augsburg: J. G. Cotta'scher Verlag, I.7, 1946.
Tucker, Thomas Deane. *Worlding the West: An Ontopology of Badlands*. In *Terrence Malick: Film and Philosophy*, edited by Thomas Deane Tucker and Stuart Kendall. New York: Bloomsbury Academic, 2013, 80-100.
Newton, Michael. *Waste Land: The Savage Odyssey of Charles Starkweather and Caril Ann Fugate*. New York: Pocket Books, 1998.
Warner Brothers (Producer). Terrence Malick (Director). *Badlands*. USA, 1973.

FIVE

Pointing Toward Transcendence: When Film Becomes Art

Frédéric Seyler

It might seem odd, at first glance, to approach Karl Jaspers' contribution to a philosophy of film by using Michel Henry's radical phenomenology of life. Whereas the former stresses that *existence* is never without transcendence,[1] the latter insists on the radical immanence of life, and both philosophies seem to be irreconcilably opposed. Yet, a closer look on transcendence and immanence in Jaspers and Henry suggests otherwise. For Jaspers, transcendence is fundamental unity, an origin that escapes every attempt to objectify it. For Henry, this is precisely that which characterizes immanence as affectivity. Moreover, Henry distinguishes, within affectivity, the living (*vivant*) from absolute life (*Vie*), while describing the latter as "transcendence in immanence." Art, therefore, is understood as intensifying immanent subjective powers and, at least indirectly, as "pointing" toward their absolute origin. Could this be also the function of art in Jaspers? And could film, as a work of fiction, claim to be art in this sense? As a first preliminary step toward this hypothesis, the following chapter investigates the standpoint of radical phenomenology with regard to film: Can it be conceived as art, that is, as pointing toward Henry's "transcendence in immanence"? Henry's critique of techno-science in terms of "barbarism"—i.e., as a tool for life's attempt to flee from itself, even to negate itself, his critique of television as a "practice of barbarism" and the fact that, while discussing art, Henry never mentions film—certainly makes such a hypothesis problematic.[2] Henry's critique of television, however, can only be understood if it is referred to the concept of life as affective immanence and to the idea that life is capable of turning against itself. From this point of view, television gives rise to a form of praxis that is pervaded by such a project. This is possible, because television images are marked by their inconstancy, their insignificance and their incoherence. They are thus incompatible with art as generating a growth in sensibility. However, this critique is, as we will see, not applicable to film as such, even in the perspective of radical phenomenology. In addition to this, Bergson's theory of art offers a further criterion to assess the movement of emergence and disappearance of images with regard to art. If the function of art is to make us attentive to the singular nature of reality inside and outside of us, then film can become a work of art just like painting, music, or poetry. It is then pointing not only toward singularity, but also toward life in the sense of Henry's phenomenology and, henceforth, to what he characterized as "transcendence in immanence."

AFFECTIVITY TURNING AGAINST ITSELF

It is in the realm of life itself—as immanent affectivity or pathos—that the reversal of its movement of self-growth (*auto-accroissement*) has to be situated.[3] Henry considers such a reversal to be a fundamental possibility within the history of affectivity (*historial de l'affectivité*). According to this analysis, affectivity necessarily undergoes a phase of suffering, a phase during which the attempt to flee from life emerges as a promise to escape this suffering.[4] Such an attempt amounts to a reversal of the movement of self-growth, while the available energy is used for the purpose of escaping the experience that one is. Thereby, a flight into the realm of exteriority appears as the most effective means for this escape. But since self-experience (*épreuve de soi*) is that which defines life as auto-affection, this attempt must turn into despair and, ultimately, transform itself into the desire for the negation of life as such. In this sense, barbarism must be understood as the ultimate expression of nihilism.[5]

From the standpoint of radical phenomenology this form of nihilism becomes dominant when, building upon the presupposition of scientism according to which only objectivity is real, modern technology materializes this presupposition. While pre-modern *technē* still functions as *mediation* for the actualization of subjective potentialities, the processes mastered by techno-science are anonymous and natural phenomena. The self-accomplishment of subjectivity has been replaced—or tends to be replaced—by the self-accomplishment of nature. When "action" has become objective, the subjective powers belonging to the "I can" become atrophied, insofar as these powers are progressively evicted from the processes of production.[6] Ultimately, it is humanity itself that is subjected to a technological approach in which the human is reduced to a natural being instead of a living subjectivity. Scientism as an ideology first prevails on its own level, namely that of the mind, but the development of technological frameworks based on the paradigm of exteriority leads, in a second step, to a concrete colonization of praxis that reaches deep into everyday existence. Such frameworks are therefore essential to ideology, insofar as they constitute an indispensable practical mediation for the reversal of culture into barbarism. It is praxis itself that is pervaded by the project of self-escape and self-negation, as Henry conveys through his analysis of television.[7]

THE CRITIQUE OF TELEVISION

Television is a product of techno-science and, as such, it is rooted in the development of modern Galilean science. In terms of praxis, the perception involved while watching television is determined by a choice of images that is not made by the subject. To a certain extent, however, this also applies to aesthetic contemplation in general, insofar as it is directed toward an object that is the product of someone else's activity and choice. It applies even more to film as an art form, since the latter shares a number of features with television: the succession and movement from one image to another, elements of narration conveyed through this movement or through elements of dialogue, and of course the fact that television can itself become the technical medium used for film. More specifically, Henry's critique of television targets three main aspects.

Firstly, the "inconstancy" of televised images, whereby the constant succession from one image to the other makes an aesthetic contemplation of one particular image impossible. The subjective powers proper to such contemplation can therefore not be developed or exercised. On the contrary, they are replaced by the movement "of a curiosity that is always disappointed and thus always reborn," a movement that does not allow for growth within subjectivity.[8] Erich Fromm makes a similar argument in his analysis of alienation as opposed to "productive activity": In "productive activity" a change occurs in me, I am not the same as before, whereas in alienated forms of praxis nothing has changed from the standpoint of interiority, and activity is reduced to the consumption of a thing.[9]

Secondly, and as a corollary to their inconstancy, TV images are insignificant. If they had any significance, they would not only capture attention, but also call for reflection and contemplation. However, this is precisely what an uninterrupted flow of images makes impossible:

> Emergence and disappearance are thus only the continually resumed act of life getting rid of itself. It is only in light of such an act that disappearance can become fully intelligible. It presupposes that the content of the image is of no interest in itself and that it is destined to be replaced by another one. If it were to arouse true attention and have a

worth of its own, instead, this would imply that it would remain and that the perception of it would arouse a growth of sensibility and intelligence in the spectator. This would imply that the mind, occupied with this inner work, would latch onto the image . . ., in the omni-temporality of the cultural object that delivers it to contemplation. But, in such a case, life would no longer seek to flee itself in such an image; instead it would find its accomplishment in it, that is to say, in itself.[10]

It is, therefore, the self-accomplishment of subjectivity—as growth of its sensibility—that is made impossible by both the inconstancy and insignificance of images.

Thirdly, and contrary to film, in which the succession of images forms, at least to some extent, a coherent totality, televised images are largely incoherent, as illustrated by the juxtaposition of that which is considered "news" (*actualité*). News programs—which reflect in fact the essence of television as such—are based on a selection that is neither apparent nor intelligible. To aim at intelligibility would mean to "pull the thread of . . . causality, purpose, meaning, value . . ., to think, understand, imagine, and to return to life itself," but this is precisely what television does not provide, insofar as the news broadcast juxtaposes facts that seem to bear no connection with each other.[11] Henry's phenomenological critique of television, however, obviously does not apply *mutatis mutandis* to film as an art form, or perhaps at least, not to all films.

FILM AS ART? TEMPORALITY—SIGNIFICANCE—ATTENTION

With regard to its first aspect, the inconstancy of televised images, it is clear that it is to be found wherever movement and succession of different images are used and thus, by their very essence, in the cinematographic images constituting film. The self-growth of sensibility that Henry finds, for instance, in the aesthetic contemplation of a painting seems to be tied to the permanence of the image contemplated. Another example given by Henry, namely the contemplation of architecture, reveals the same trait. Furthermore, the fact that film is, like television, a medium made possible by techno-science, puts it, from the point of view of radical phenomenology, closer to the project of life's self-escape than to that of its self-growth. But this argument is hardly decisive, since it would equally lead to disqualify reproductions or recordings of art based on techno-science, like music available on CD, photographs featuring architecture or paintings, radio transmissions of concerts, etc. And since those reproductions or recordings do not seem to alter significantly aesthetic reception, but, on the contrary, augment the availability of art and, hence, the possibilities for its reception, it would seem inconsistent with radical phenomenology to discard them. We must therefore look at the two other aspects targeted by Henry's critique of television, in order to see what can be said about film from this standpoint.

The second aspect, the insignificance of television images as related to the continuous movement of their emergence and disappearance, appears to be problematic with regard to cinematographic images. On the one hand, this critique should also be applied to them, insofar as insignificance is a corollary to inconstancy. But, on the other hand, even if we could conclude from this that a particular cinematographic image "is of no interest in itself," does it follow that the film as a whole, or even some of its sequences, is unable to generate "a growth of sensibility and intelligence in the spectator" as well as to arouse "true attention," reflection and contemplation? Such a conclusion would indeed disqualify film as an art form and make it a contemporary expression of "barbarism." That this is not the case, however, lies in the subjective experience of significance that certain films are able to generate. If such an experience is acknowledged, it follows that it is not film as such—i.e., as a medium construed upon the continuous movement of emergence and disappearance of images—that is concerned by Henry's critique, but only films that do not arouse "true attention," growth in sensibility, etc.

The question is, however: Can we account for such an experience of significance within the framework of Henryan radical phenomenology? First, it should be remarked that Henry's approach to aesthetics, while mainly focused on painting and its contemplation, does in fact include both time and movement.[12] Time is here given as the immanent temporality, i.e., as the movement within affectivity, where subjective powers are primarily given.[13] Therefore, the contemplation of a work of art, e.g., a painting, which may be characterized as "static," is itself never static but necessarily correlated if not identical with such an immanent unfolding of the temporality proper to affect. One could argue that the static character of the work of art is precisely a condition of possibility for this dynamic unfolding of affect, as Henry seems to imply in the context of his critique of television. If this were to be the case, radical phenomenology would indeed have to disqualify all art forms in which the art-object is itself temporal, characterized by movement or change. Clearly, this is not the case as Henry's references to music and narration show.

With regard to music, Henry follows a Schopenhauerian line of thought while adapting it to the concepts of radical phenomenology: Music, if and when it is art, is an immediate and, therefore, non-representational expression of the Will, the Will being now understood as the fundamental Force inherent to affect and identical with the essence of affectivity itself.[14] Even more, it is precisely this non-representational aspect of expression that underlies Wassily Kandinsky's effort to establish a theory of abstract painting, where the aim of painting "is to speak not of the world . . . but of the Ground of Being and Life."[15]

Hence, it is music as a dynamic form of art that shapes the phenomenological analysis of painting, and not vice versa. The fact that music requires transcendent or *ek-static* time, that its essence comprises succession and replacement, implies that the latter cannot as such deprive an object of its (potential) value as a work of art. As Husserl's famous example in the 1905 *Lectures on Internal Time Consciousness* shows,[16] the hearing of a melody—i.e., of a temporal object essentially marked by movement as well as by the evanescence of each of its moments—always involves phenomena of retention of the "just-past" within the presence of hearing. Inconstancy, here, does therefore not lead to incoherence: Succession and replacement, of course, do not alter the fact that it is a melody that we aesthetically apprehend as a coherent totality, not isolated tones. They are, on the contrary, the condition for such hearing.

In an analogous way, the same applies even more to narration. Although Henry admits that a radical phenomenology of narration has yet to be developed, it is equally clear that he would be far from considering narrative succession as an argument against the aesthetic value of narration.[17] Among the few hints he gives concerning a phenomenological aesthetics of narration we find, again, the reference to music: By drawing a parallel with Kandinsky's move that referred painting to music, it is both the non-representational and the dynamic character of music that Henry takes as sources for a possible phenomenology of narration, since they correspond to the invisible and dynamic essence of affectivity.[18]

With regard to film, we must therefore conclude that succession and replacement do not lead to excluding film from the realm of art. In addition to the fact that films can be fairly coherent—for instance, through the coherence of narration—and that therefore Henry's third reproach does not apply to film as such, it is reasonable to assume that some films do in fact generate a subjective growth, while others do not. The violence as well as the suspense contained in Paul Verhoeven's *Hollow Man* (2000) certainly does arouse attention, but would we say that it changed ourselves, and the way we look at others or the world?[19] While we may be captivated by its action, and thereby distracted from ourselves, we are only timidly suggested a reflection on invisibility, as well as impunity. In all likelihood, this film is destined to remain an object of consumption in Fromm's sense. On the other hand, one should be able to find examples of films that are not merely objects of consumption and that do arouse "true attention," reflection and the like.

But what is "true attention" and how can we distinguish it from that which would be "false attention"? Perhaps Bergson's theory of art can be of help here, since it takes into account elements of narration and is therefore likely to be applicable to film.[20] Bergson, as we recall, opposes pragmatic attention, based on the satisfaction of needs and focused on generalities, to attentiveness toward the real as singular. Both forms of attention exclude each other, which means that we are only attentive to singularity insofar as we are not trying to fulfill some of our needs. With regard to art, this fundamental dichotomy leads to disqualify comedy as an art form. Comedy basically functions as a tool for social-pragmatic adaptation and sanctions non-adapted behavior with ridicule. Moreover, it uses characters that are generalities or types, like that of "the absent-minded professor," "the career-opportunist," etc. Art, on the other hand, teaches us to look differently at the world and ourselves, i.e., it makes us aware of that which escapes ordinary perception: singularity. Therefore, characters like Shakespeare's Hamlet are themselves depicted in their singularity; they are not types, but fictitious *persons*. As a result, the lesson given by art suspends need-based and utilitarian perception and teaches us to look at reality as irreducibly singular, thereby generating what we could call "true attention."[21]

With regard to film, a movie like Louis Malle's *My Dinner with André* (1981) gives a good example of art in the Bergsonian sense.[22] It is almost exclusively made of the dialogue between two former friends, about their experiences in life, their views on art, i.e., a highly personal exchange that escapes stereotypes and generalities of common-sense discourse. The last sequence of the movie seems even to be an explicit statement of Bergson's theory: While leaving the restaurant and sitting in a taxi, the main character reflects on the evening in a silent monologue: "On the road home through the city streets, there wasn't a street, there wasn't a building that wasn't connected to some memory in my mind: There, I was buying a suit with my father; there, I was having an ice cream soda after school . . . When I finally came in, Debbie was home from work and I told her everything about my dinner with André."

Of course, one might object that this remains a highly personal account, an account that cannot be generalized in order to include everyone's reception of a particular movie. Although this is certainly true to some extent, Bergson's theory implies that such a generalization, a universalization even, is possible: While the work of art awakens our senses to that which is singular, the work of a genius—Bergson uses Shakespeare's *Hamlet* as an example—is the one that is able to give such a lesson universally. The universality of the work of art does therefore not lie in its particular content, but in the "lesson taught."

From a Bergsonian point of view, film, like other art forms, has thus the capability of pointing toward singularity as an essential aspect of reality. It does so by arousing a form of attentiveness to the real that is no longer tied to that which is pragmatically useful. When this criterion is met, the movement of emergence and disappearance of images can no longer be said to be a tool for life's tendency to flee from itself, like it would be the case if film were only in the service of distraction. It is, on the contrary, in the service of subjective self-growth and, as such, it is at least indirectly pointing toward "transcendence in immanence" in the sense of Henry's radical phenomenology and, as a further hypothesis to be debated, to Jaspers' concept of transcendence, insofar as it refers to the original unity that founds objectivity without ever becoming itself an object.[23]

NOTES

1. Karl Jaspers, *Philosophie*, Vol. 2 (Berlin: Springer, 1956), 2.
2. Michel Henry, *La barbarie* (Paris: PUF, 2004). Michel Henry, *Barbarism*, trans. Scott Davidson (New York: Continuum, 2012).
3. The following developments in this section are based on an article of my own. Frédéric Seyler, "The Ethics of Affectivity and the Problem of Personhood. An Overview," *Analecta Hermeneutica* 8 (2016): 218-34.
4. Henry, *La barbarie*, 118-19. Henry, *Barbarism*, 66-67.
5. Michel Henry, *Incarnation: une philosophie de la chair* (Paris: Seuil, 2000), 316. Michel Henry, *Incarnation: A Philosophy of Flesh*, trans. Karl Hefty (Evanston: Northwestern University Press, 2015), 221.
6. Henry, *La barbarie*, 92. Henry, *Barbarism*, 51.
7. Henry, *La barbarie*, 187-99. Henry, *Barbarism*, 107-114.
8. Henry, *La barbarie*, 193. Henry, *Barbarism*, 111.
9. Erich Fromm, *The Sane Society* (New York: Rinehart & Company, 1955).
10. Henry, *La barbarie*, 194. Henry, *Barbarism*, 111: translation modified.
11. Henry, *La barbarie*, 196. Henry, *Barbarism*, 112.
12. For instance in Michel Henry, *Voir l'invisible. Sur Kandinsky* (Paris: PUF, 2005). Michel Henry, *Seeing the Invisible: On Kandinsky*, trans. Scott Davidson (New York: Continuum, 2009).
13. Michel Henry, "Art et phénoménologie de la vie," in *Phénoménologie de la vie*, Vol. 3 (Paris: PUF, 2004), 307.
14. Michel Henry, "Dessiner la musique, théorie pour l'art de Briesen," in *Phénoménologie de la vie*, Vol. 3 (Paris: PUF, 2004), 266.
15. Henry, "Dessiner la musique," 272: my translation. Moreover, Kandinsky's theory is not limited to abstract painting but, for Michel Henry, it is a theory of "all possible painting." Michel Henry, "Kandinsky et la signification de l'oeuvre d'art," in *Phénoménologie de la vie*, Vol. 3 (Paris: PUF, 2004), 217.
16. In Edmund Husserl, *Gesammelte Werke: Husserliana*, Vol. X: *Zur Phänomenologie des inneren Zeitbewusstseins* (1893-1917), ed. Rudolph Boehm (Den Haag: Nijhoff, 1966). Edmund Husserl, *The Phenomenology of Internal Time Consciousness*, trans. James Churchill (Bloomington: Indiana University Press, 1964).
17. Michel Henry, "Narrer le pathos," in *Phénoménologie de la vie*, Vol. 3 (Paris: PUF 2004), 318.
18. Henry, "Narrer le pathos," 318.
19. Columbia Pictures (Producer), Paul Verhoeven (Director), *Hollow Man* (Los Angeles: USA, 2000).
20. Henri Bergson, *Le rire* (Paris: PUF, 2007). Henri Bergson, *Laughter*, trans. C. Bereton & F, Rothwell, London: Macmillan, 1921. Henri Bergson, *Laughter: An Essay on the Meaning of the Comic*, trans. Cloudesly Brereton and Fred Rothwell (London: Macmillan, 1921).
21. Interestingly, the Bergsonian idea of art as a lesson in sincerity is also present in Michel Henry's account of Briesen's work. Henry, "Dessiner la musique," 282.
22. Saga Productions Inc., The Andre Company (Producers), Louis Malle (Director), *My Dinner with André*. USA, 1981.

23. A starting point for further discussion can be found in Karl Jaspers, *Philosophie*, Vol. 3 (Berlin: Springer, 1956), 192-99, where he speaks of *"Kunst als Sprache aus dem Lesen der Chiffreschrift,"* and refers to the artist of "immanent transcendence" as the one who offers a new reading of *Dasein* as *Chiffre* (196).

BIBLIOGRAPHY

Bergson, Henri. *Laughter: An Essay on the Meaning of the Comic*. Translated by Cloudesly Brereton and Fred Rothwell. London: Macmillan, 1921.
_____. *Le rire*. Paris: PUF, 2007.
Columbia Pictures (Producer). Paul Verhoeven (Director). *Hollow Man*. Los Angeles: USA, 2000.
Fromm, Erich. *The Sane Society*. New York: Rinehart & Company, 1955.
Henry, Michel. "Art et phénoménologie de la vie." In *Phénoménologie de la vie*, Vol. 3, edited by Michel Henry, 283-308. Paris: Presses Universitaires de France, 2004.
_____. *Barbarism*. Translated Scott Davidson. New York: Continuum, 2012.
_____. "Dessiner la musique, théorie pour l'art de Briesen." In *Phénoménologie de la vie*, Vol. 3, edited by Michel Henry, 241-82. Paris: Presses Universitaires de France, 2004.
_____. *Incarnation: A Philosophy of Flesh*. Translated by Karl Hefty. Evanston: Northwestern University Press, 2015.
_____. *Incarnation: une philosophie de la chair*. Paris: Seuil, 2000.
_____. "Kandinsky et la signification de l'oeuvre d'art." In *Phénoménologie de la vie*, Vol. 3, edited by Michel Henry, 203-18. Paris: Presses Universitaires de France, 2004.
_____. *La barbarie*. Paris: PUF, 2004.
_____. "Narrer le pathos." In *Phénoménologie de la vie*, Vol. 3, edited by Michel Henry, 309-23. Paris: Presses Universitaires de France, 2004.
_____. *Voir l'invisible. Sur Kandinsky*. Paris: Presses Universitaires de France, 2005.
Husserl, Edmund. *Gesammelte Werke: Husserliana*, Vol. X: *Zur Phänomenologie des inneren Zeitbewusstseins* (1893-1917). Edited by Rudolph Boehm. Den Haag: Nijhoff, 1966.
_____. *The Phenomenology of Internal Time Consciousness*. Translated by James S. Churchill. Bloomington: Indiana University Press, 1964.
Jaspers, Karl. *Philosophie*, Vol. 2. Berlin: Springer, 1956.
Jaspers, Karl. *Philosophie*, Vol. 3. Berlin: Springer, 1956.
Saga Productions Inc., The Andre Company (Producers). Louis Malle (Director). *My Dinner with André*. USA, 1981.
Seyler, Frédéric. "The Ethics of Affectivity and the Problem of Personhood. An Overview." *Analecta Hermeneutica* 8 (2016): 218-34.

SIX

Transcendence in Phenomenology and Film: Ozu's Still Lives

Allan Casebier

Paul Schrader has proposed that there is a transcendental style in film.[1] In this chapter, I wish to consider this idea in light of the phenomenological writing of Edmund Husserl and Karl Jaspers. Edmund Husserl was prominent in developing and utilizing phenomenology in his philosophizing. Jaspers acknowledges his debt to Husserl in his understanding and use of phenomenology.[2] In the philosophical work of Jaspers, transcendence is an important element as well.

The term "phenomenology" has been used in a variety of ways.[3] Though there are commonalities in usage, there is no one overarching meaning for the term. In each use it is therefore important to specify the particular use of the term in play.

In 1637, Christof Friedrich Ottinger, a German Pietist, introduced the term "phenomenology" into philosophical discourse. For him, the term would designate a study of the divine systems of relations between things on the surface of the visible world, as opposed to things of deeper spiritual reality. In the eighteenth century, Johann Heinrich Lambert, a mathematician, physicist, and philosopher, used the term to stand for an endeavor to describe appearances, an activity fundamental to understanding all empirical knowledge. For G.W.F. Hegel in his *Phenomenology of Spirit* (1807) phenomenology became a method for apprehending what is real, that is, coming to know mind as it is in itself via phenomena where phenomena are the ways in which mind appears to consciousness.[4] Hegel's theory took it that dialectic process is the necessary process of human thought. While rejecting a Kantian distinction between phenomena and noumena, Hegel held that phenomena are the source for all knowledge if analyzed in accord with dialectical thinking. Hegel proceeds with sense perception, then through consciousness of self, in a series of dialectics, to the social and historical nature of knowledge, then ultimately to Reason wherein reality is recognized at the highest level, to be that of the Absolute Idea or Spirit, which encompasses all reality.

For a phenomenological analysis of perception, Husserl was aiming for an understanding of how the acquisition of knowledge of a new region of being obtains. Central to this is a notion that consciousness achieves apprehension of objects by means of an act of mediation. In this mediation process, a content is intended (in a special philosophical sense of "intending") that enables apprehension of the object. Husserl uses Greek language terms employed by Aristotle to identify some important elements in this mediation process: "*noema*" and "*noesis.*" There is, thus, in a Husserlean phenomenological analysis, a *noema* (a meaning or a sense) and a process of meaning constitution (*noesis*) arising together. These two elements are inextricably bound up with one another.

The *noema* gives the mental act of apprehension directedness but it does not guarantee that there will be an existing object. The *noema* is that which is common to all acts that have the same object, with exactly the same properties, oriented in the same way, regardless of whether it be perception, remembering, imagining, or any other type of apprehension. *Noeses* are the various ways in which the mind positions itself in relation to the *hyle* (the sense material), on the one hand, and the object, on the other hand, in order to know the object. "Intending an object" is a medieval philosophical concept designating an act of reaching out to an object and at the same time apprehending it. There is always a caveat that when an act of intending is accomplished, of the act itself, it is added, "whether the object exists or not." Thus, with intentionality as the distinctive mark of consciousness, it may be said that for a phenomenological analysis, when intending occurs, *noema* and *noesis* guide the act of reaching out to the object, whether or not the object exists.

Central to a phenomenological analysis is also the use of a method that is variously described as performing a reduction (reducing) or bracketing or *epoche*. Bracketing takes three forms: phenomenological, transcendental, and eidetic. In the phenomenological reduction, the aim is to focus attention on consciousness and its experiences while turning away from focus on the external object. In transcendentally reducing, there is an elimination of empirical or naturalistic assumptions from the stream of consciousness. In the eidetic reduction (the term "eidetic" derives from Plato's term "*eidos,*" meaning the essence or form of something), there occurs a generalizing of the results attained through a transcendental study of consciousness, using a method of variation.[5]

Once the reductions (which arise together, not sequentially) have been accomplished, the question may be considered: what status does the content of consciousness have? In order to answer this question, we need a vocabulary not shot through with object or natural standpoint language; the process of bracketing has been utilized in order to free ourselves from that kind of language. We do not want to then re-introduce such language in answering this question. Husserl has developed some terms that will function in the wake of the reductions having been performed. In addition to speaking of that which is real and ideal—i.e., particular and universal—Husserl speaks of the *realle* and *irrealle*. The *realle* exists in time but not in space in a way that the *irrealle* does not. For example, *noeses* exist in time, but not in space, but are neither real nor ideal. The *irrealle* exists in neither time nor space. A real object, a particular, exists in both space and time.

For example the blue color of my coat, this particular blue of my coat, exists nowhere else. At the same time, my coat also has the property of being blue, a property that other objects can have. For Husserl, to say that my coat is blue is to mark a universal. The universal—blue color—can exist in many different places and times. When, however, the reductions have been performed, consciousness has reduced objects to a purified state. As transcendentally reduced, consciousness may focus on the contents of consciousness without consideration being given to whether the intended objects exist or not as well as to whether they are real or ideal.

To understand the role of transcendence in a Husserlean phenomenological account of film viewing, it is important to recognize the ontology underlying Husserl's conceptualization. Husserl has developed a monism about the human self.[6] There is only one entity, the human I, with an array of aspects. Using his terms, there is *korper*, the corpse, the physical aspect of the one self. It exists whether the human being is alive or dead; there is also another aspect that he calls *leib*, designating the living body; there is also psyche, a unity of body and mind. There is also what Husserl calls "the transcendental ego." This term has unfortunately led many readers of Husserl to take him to have developed a virulent idealism, where there is an aspect of the self—the transcendental ego—that makes objects have the properties they do precisely because the transcendental ego makes it so. By the term transcendental ego, Husserl is actually referring to an aspect of the self that is the locus of intentionality. There is an aspect that does the intending, the acts of constituting the object, and setting features of an object in place.

With this monism in mind, the term "transcendence" in Husserlian phenomenology may be seen in its proper place in his system. When an object is said by him to be transcendent, he means that the object is not part of the act of apprehending an object; it stands apart from the act of apprehension. In constituting an object using the mediating object, the *noema*, and its accompanying element, *noesis*, the object that is reached out to in the process of intentionality is not part of the intentional act.

Before Karl Jaspers' use of phenomenology and his concept of transcendence can be delineated, it will be important to clarify one other element in the Husserlean account of perception in general and film perception in particular, namely, horizon.[7] When apprehension of the mediating object via *noema* and *noesis* obtains, horizon is also utilized. Husserl makes reference to horizon in explaining how an act of apprehending an object presupposes important features of the perceiver's system of background beliefs about relevant features of the object. What is prescribed of an object as it is intended in a particular act, A, under a particular *Sinn*, leaves much about the object open or indeterminate. The possible further determinations of the object compatible with what is prescribed of it in A, Husserl calls the "horizon" of the object (as intended in A). Husserl uses the example of looking at a dice and some die to illustrate. Husserl's observation is that horizons are pre-delineated due to the co-determinative activity of the perceiver.

> The horizons are 'prescribed potentialities.' . . . The predelineation itself, to be sure, is at all times imperfect; yet, with its *indeterminateness*, it has a *determinate structure*. For example: the die leaves open a great variety of things pertaining to the unseen faces; yet it is already 'construed' in advance as a die, in particular as colored, rough, and the like though each of these determinations always leaves further particulars open. This leaving open . . . is precisely what makes up the 'horizon.'[8]

The meaning of the German term, "*horizont*," is constraint. Horizons constrain perception in terms of expectations. Husserl explains this point in *Experience and Judgment*: "The object is present from the very first with a character of familiarity; it is already apprehended as an object of a type more or less vaguely determined and already, in some way, known. In this way the direction of the expectations of what closer inspection will reveal in the way of properties is pre-delineated."[9] Husserl pinpoints more specific constraints on an act's horizon in the following passage from *Experience and Judgment*: "The factual world of experience is experienced as trees, bushes, animals, snakes, birds; specifically as pine, linden, lilac, dog, viper, swallow, sparrow, and so on. . . ." By contrast, "What is given in experience as a new individual is first known in terms of what has been genuinely perceived, it calls to mind the like (the similar)."[10] In another passage, Husserl directly addresses the notion of constraint as essential to horizon:

> Every experience has an experience 'horizon.' . . . For example, there belongs to every external perception its reference from the 'genuinely perceived' sides of the object of perception to the 'co-intended' sides — not yet perceived, but only anticipated. . . . Furthermore, the perception has horizons made up of other possibilities of perception, as perceptions that we could have. If we actively directed the course of percep-

tion otherwise: if, for example, we turned our eyes that way instead of this, or if we were to step forward or to one side, and so forth.[11]

For Husserl, however, transcendence is not confined in all references to the limited role in intentionality as explained above. He makes a place for transcendence insofar as it is under the *epoche*. As such, transcendence is transcendence-within-immanence. It should be clear that transcendence is not pure "transcendence." After the eidetic reduction, there is a condition which excludes every sort of transcendence."[12] Still, the task of phenomenology should include an exploration of "the sense of transcendence," that is, the manner in which we have experience of an objective world as such.[13] In coming to regard transcendence in this way, Husserl has begun by rejecting a conceiving of transcendence as framed in Cartesian terms, whereby the central question is how to "transcend" the closed sphere of subjectivity in order to attain an "external" objectivity beyond the subject. Thus, transcendence is conceived of as objectively attainable. In his way, Husserl has found a path to re-thinking transcendence, not by assigning it to a supra-rational faculty or to faith, but rather by re-thinking it from within the concept of phenomenological givenness.

Karl Jaspers, in his three-volume work *Philosophie*,[14] allows for transcendence to play a more central role in his whole philosophical system than Husserl did. Indeed, transcendence is that which makes our lives individual and constitutes authenticity. Jaspers commences from what may be termed an "existential" starting point: "everything essentially real is for me only by virtue of the fact that I am I myself—i.e., self-realization occurs in the context of my existence (*Existenz*).[15] Jaspers uses the term *Existenz* as a technical term to isolate the particular notion of existence he has in mind. "*Existenz*" does not refer to just any kind of existence. It refers instead specifically to possible individual existence in terms of its freedom and acts of willing. For Jaspers, the essence of *Existenz* is in its intentional tending to the other, that is, to engage in transcendence.[16] Thus for Jaspers it may be said that just as I do not exist without the world, I am not myself without transcendence. I stand before transcendence, which does not occur to me as existing in the world of phenomenal things but speaks to me as possible—speaks to me in the voice of whatever exists and most decidedly in that of my self-being.

For Jaspers transcendence then is that which is experienced as beyond the person, but it is not something that is empirically real. Transcendence cannot be objectified; it is beyond both subjectivity and objectivity. In an important way, it is not something in the world though it appears whenever there is *Existenz*. In responding to a question of whether transcendence can be thought in the manner that Kant theorized *noumena*—as something that cannot be perceived but can be thought—Jaspers would emphasize that it is beyond any categorizations. To frame the question in terms of horizons, there is no horizon that reveals transcendence. In relation to transcendence we are in the realm of what he calls "the Encompassing." The Encompassing is not the horizon of our knowledge at any particular moment. Rather, it is the source from which all new horizons emerge, without ever being visible even as a horizon. It never becomes an object. Never appearing to us itself, it is that wherein everything else appears.[17]

Jaspers and Husserl more or less share the same concept of horizon. For both, objects have objectivity for us if apprehended under one or more horizons. For Jaspers, transcendence is a condition wherein horizons are in abeyance. When we sense this condition, we say there is something "ineffable" being experienced. Jaspers acknowledges what he calls "cyphers," which enable confrontation with transcendence. This is the case for Jaspers with art, whereby cyphers can confirm the impossibility of knowing that which is transcendent. That is why we say that there is something ineffable about certain things that we encounter in art. Jaspers says that this relationship is connected with our being authentically our self, our true self: "the place of transcendence is neither in this world nor beyond, but it is the boundary—the boundary at which I confront transcendence whenever I am my true self."[18]

I believe that some of what Jaspers has in mind with his conception of transcendence illuminates the meaning of transcendence in Shrader's analysis of there being a transcendental style in film. For Shrader, the films of Yasujiro Ozu are paradigmatic of the style. In Shrader's conception of a transcendental style in film, the best examples of its use are in the films of Ozu and Robert Bresson, while to a lesser extent the style is in a film such as *Ordet* (1955) by Carl Dreyer. However, the term "transcendental style" is not an achievement predicate, i.e., a film is not either in the style or not in the style. The transcendental style can be used by a filmmaker in varying degrees. Schrader gives examples from other well-known filmmakers: "Elements of the transcendental style can be detected in the films of many other directors; Antonioni, Rossellini, Pasolini, Boetticher, Renoir, Mizoguchi, Bunuel, Warhol, Michael Snow, and Bruce Baillie."[19]

Transcendental style is thought by Schrader to be opposed to conventional depictions and portrayals of reality, such as realism, naturalism, psychologism, romanticism, expressionism, impressionism, and rationalism. In a summary statement of film approaches that are incongruent with the transcendental style, Schrader says: "The enemy of transcendence is immanence, whether it is external (realism, rationalism) or internal (psychologism, expressionism). To the transcendental artist, these conventional interpretations of reality are emotional and rational constructs devised by man to dilute or explain away the transcendental."[20] It is Schrader's view that transcendental style stylizes the world of the film by eliminating those elements which are primarily expressive of human experience, "thereby robbing the conventional interpretations of reality of their relevance and power." In this way, he likens the experience of films with the transcendental style to the mass in Catholic ritual, which "transforms experience into a repeatable ritual which can be repeatably transcended."[21] With Shrader's idea that the transcendental style provides in general an experience of the transcendent, a film made in this style puts the film viewer in touch with what is beyond normal sense experience as well as all those things we take to be immanent in experience. The particular way in which Ozu developed his transcendental style had much to do with the Oriental historical and cultural setting in which he worked. Schrader says that it is so natural and indigenous to the Japanese sensibility that it may be said that Ozu was able to develop the transcendental style and yet stay within the popular conventions of Japanese art.[22]

There is much to be said for Schrader's observation. In the Japanese aesthetic, the highest term of aesthetic praise is *shibui*.[23] Whereas in the West, the beautiful object is often an attention-getter, for the Japanese aesthetic sensibility, the ultimate in beauty, *shibui*, is anything but a quality that will attract attention. Restraint is one of its prominent ingredients. *Shibui* art objects are unobtrusive, unostentatious, and modest with understatement as a characteristic stylistic. An underlying notion is that the less powerful object will probably be the more artistically effective. Another core feature is hiddenness. The appreciator who comes in contact with *shibui* finds his or her taste left unsatiated by the *shibui* object. *Shibui*'s ever hidden aspect creates a lingering attraction for more since the object is so fashioned that it reveals only enough of itself to impel one to seek additional qualities of what has been found pleasing but which are not readily perceivable. Another core feature is simplicity. *Shibui* designs are left unadorned and incomplete, allowing much scope for the appreciators to exercise their imagination. One's imagination is indeed taxed to its limits by the extremely minimal suggestiveness encountered in the experience of the Noh Theatre or the Zen sand and rock garden. Ozu's style of filming reflects this proto-typical aesthetic sensibility. His camera is placed at the level of a person seated in traditional Japanese fashion on the tatami mat three feet above the ground. Donald Richie, in his study of Ozu's filmmaking practice describes the camera placement as follows:

> Ozu's films are shot from an almost invariable angle, that of a person sitting on the tatami matting of the Japanese room. The camera rarely pans, though traveling shots are relatively common in earlier pictures. Fades in and out are seldom found in his later films and dissolves are very rare; usually the sole punctuation Ozu allows himself, particularly in his postwar pictures, is the straight cut.[24]

As Ozu restricted his palette to the barest minimum, *shibui*-like, "He thus relinquished most of the major ways through which a film-maker directly expresses himself in film, and severely restricted his means of cinematic comment."[25] Richie illustrates Ozu's severely restricted use of standard means of expressions by way of dissolves, fades, emotional direction, and his use of the stationary camera rather than moving camera via dolly shots, special lenses, framing and editing.[26] Moreover, Ozu enables a concentration on the present. As Richie describes it: "One is reminded of the Zen aphorism: 'When I eat, I eat; when I sleep, I sleep.' When one does something one does nothing else; one immerses self entirely in the task at hand and appreciates it while completing it."[27]

In addition to Ozu's shooting practice, Richie speaks of the cast of mind that Ozu adopts and which he fosters in the viewer, a cast of mind that is distinctively Japanese. Richie sees Ozu cultivating a philosophy of acceptance with roots in Zen Buddhism as well as in Japanese aesthetics:

> In Zen texts, one accepts and transcends the world, and in traditional Japanese narrative art one celebrates and relinquishes it. The aesthetic term *mono no aware* is often used nowadays to describe this state of mind. The term has a long history . . . from the beginning it represented feeling of a special kind: "not a powerful surge of passion, but an emotion containing a balance . . . on the whole, "*aware*" tended to be used of deep impressions produced by small things." . . . Ozu did not, of course, set out self-consciously to capture this quality. . . . Nonetheless, his films are full of it, since he was.[28]

Figure 6.1. *Late Spring*. Shochiku Eiga (Producer). Yasujiro Ozu (Director). Late Spring. Japan, 1949.

Schrader speaks approvingly of Richie's interpretation that Ozu is primarily the artist of *mono no aware*. Schrader describes Ozu's emphasis on "aware" rather than conflict—a staple of the genres that take us away from transcendence such as realism or expressionism—as making Ozu an advocate of Oneness and Japanese life. We may add a filmmaker who puts us in touch with transcendence. In his signature sequences, often called his still lives, I find Ozu to closely create what Jaspers would call "ciphers" that put us in touch with transcendence. In these still lives sequences, we feel we are experiencing something that is ineffable. Richie says of the still lives, "Ozu's still lives and otherwise empty scenes become containers for our emotions. . . . Empathy is not the key here. . . . Primary to the experience (of the still lives) is that in these scenes empty of all but *mu*, we suddenly apprehend what the film has been about, i.e., we suddenly apprehend life."[29] *Mu* is the Japanese term for nothingness. The first koan of Zen is *mu*. *Mu* stands for negation, emptiness, and void. Emptiness, silence, and stillness are positive elements in Zen art. *Mu* represents presence rather than the absence of something. *Mu* is used to refer to the spaces between the branches of a flower arrangement wherein the emptiness is an integral part of the form. On Ozu's burial tomb, there appears only the *kanji* for *mu*. Richie gives an example from Ozu's *Late Spring* (1949) to describe still life sequence:

> In *Late Spring* the daughter has seen what will happen to her: she will leave her father, she will marry. She comes to understand this precisely during the time that both we and she have been shown the vase. The vase itself means nothing, but its presence is also a space and into it pours our emotion. The shot of the vase is a long one, lasting some ten seconds, and it is one that "can accept deep, contradictory emotion and transform it into an expression of something unified, permanent, transcendent."[30]

It would seem then that the famous critic of Japanese cinema, Donald Richie, shares similar inclinations with those of Paul Schrader. In reflecting on those moments of ineffability called "still lives" in the films of Yasujiro Ozu, both are led to "transcendence" as the word that best captures their nature. When we ask ourselves what Richie and Schrader are pointing to with their reference to transcendence, Karl Jaspers' writings are the best place to go to in order to understand what is being said to us.

NOTES

1. Paul Schrader, *The Transcendental Style in Film* (Berkeley: University of California Press, 1972).
2. See Osbourne P. Wiggins and Michael Schwartz, "Edmund Husserl's Influence on Karl Jaspers's Phenomenology," *Philosophy, Psychiatry, and Psychology* Vol. 4, 1 (March 1997): 15-36.

3. See Allan Casebier, "Phenomenology," in *Oxford Encyclopedia of Aesthetics*, ed. Michael Kelly, Vol. 3 (New York: Oxford University Press, 1998) 485-488.
4. G.W.F. Hegel, *Hegel's Phenomenology of Spirit*, trans. A.V. Miller (Oxford: Oxford University Press, 1977).
5. See Suzanne Cunningham, *Language and the Phenomenological Reductions of Edmund Husserl* (The Hague: Nijhoff, 1976), 58.
6. Edmund Husserl, *Ideas II*, trans. R. Rojcewicz and A. Schuwer (Dordrecht: Kluwer, 1989), 128-42. For the original German text, see Edmund Husserl, *Ideen zu einer reinen Phänomenologie und phänomenologischen Philosophie. Zweites Buch* (The Hague: Nijhoff, 1913).
7. David W. Smith and Ronald McIntyre, *Husserl and Intentionality* (Dordrecht: Kluwer, 1982), 227-41.
8. Edmund Husserl, *Cartesian Meditations*, trans. Dorion (The Hague: Martinus Nijhoff, 1960), 45.
9. Edmund Husserl, *Experience and Judgment*, trans. James Churchill and Karl Ameriks (Evanston: Northwestern University Press, 1973), 113.
10. Husserl, *Experience and Judgment*, 331.
11. Husserl, *Experience and Judgment*, 32.
12. Edmund Husserl, *Ideas I*, trans. W. Boyce Gibson (New York: Collier Books, 1962), 58.
13. Husserl, *Formal and Transcendental Logic*, section 93.
14. Karl Jaspers, *Philosophie* (Berlin: Springer, 1932).
15. Karl Jaspers, *Philosophy of Existence* (Philadelphia: University of Pennsylvania Press, 1971) 3-4.
16. Karl Hoffman, "Basic Concepts in Jaspers' Philosophy," in *The Philosophy of Karl Jaspers*, ed. Paul Arthur Schilpp (New York: Tudor Publishing, 1957), 93.
17. Karl Jaspers, *Philosophie*, Vol. 2 (Berlin: Springer, 1932), 45.
18. Jaspers, *Philosophy of Existence*, 18.
19. Schrader, *The Transcendental Style*, 10.
20. Schrader, *The Transcendental Style*, 10.
21. Schrader, *The Transcendental Style*, 11.
22. Schrader, *The Transcendental Style*, 17.
23. See Allan Casebier, "The Japanese Aesthetic," in *Journal of Comparative Literature and Aesthetics*, v. XXIII, 1-2 (2000): 53-57.
24. Donald Richie, *Ozu* (Berkeley: UC Press, 1974), 105.
25. Richie, *Ozu*, 105.
26. Richie, *Ozu*, 106-9.
27. Richie, *Ozu*, 122.
28. Richie, *Ozu*, 51-52.
29. Richie, *Ozu*, 174.
30. Richie, *Ozu*, 174.

BIBLIOGRAPHY

Casebier, Allan. "The Japanese Aesthetic." In *Journal of Comparative Literature and Aesthetics*, v. XXIII, 1-2 (2000): 53-57.
———. "Phenomenology." In *Oxford Encyclopedia of Aesthetics*, Vol. 3, edited by Michael Kelly, 485-88. New York: Oxford University Press, 1998.
Cunningham, Suzanne. *Language and the Phenomenological Reductions of Edmund Husserl*. The Hague: Nijhoff, 1976.
Hegel, G.W.F. *Hegel's Phenomenology of Spirit*. Translated by A.V. Miller. Oxford: Oxford University Press, 1977.
Hoffman, Karl. "Basic Concepts in Jaspers' Philosophy." In *The Philosophy of Karl Jaspers*, edited by Paul Arthur Schilpp, 93-114. New York: Tudor Publishing, 1957.

Husserl, Edmund. *Cartesian Meditations*. Translated by Dorion Cairns. The Hague: Martinus Nijhoff, 1960.
——. *Experience and Judgment*. Translated by James Churchill and Karl Ameriks. Evanston: Northwestern University Press, 1973.
_____. *Ideen zu einer reinen Phänomenologie und phänomenologischen Philosophie, Zweites Buch*. The Hague: Nijhoff, 1913.
——. *Ideas I*. Translated by W. Boyce Gibson. New York: Collier Books, 1962.
——. *Ideas II*. Translated by R. Rojcewicz and A. Schuwer. Dordrecht: Kluwer, 1989.
Jaspers, Karl. *Philosophie*. Vol. 1-3. Berlin: Springer, 1932.
——. *Philosophy of Existence*. Philadelphia: University of Pennsylvania Press, 1971.
Richie, Donald. *Ozu*. Berkeley: UC Press, 1974.
Schrader, Paul. *The Transcendental Style in Film*. Berkeley: University of California Press, 1972.
Smith, David W. and Ronald McIntyre. *Husserl and Intentionality*. Dordrecht: Kluwer, 1982.

SEVEN

ASA NISI MASA: Kierkegaardian Repetition in Fellini's *8 1/2*

Joseph Westfall

The question of film's relationship to transcendence or the transcendent is, it seems, at least at first, the question of film's relationship to itself. Fiction films do not appear obviously to gesture beyond themselves, and even when we understand them to have some essential relationship to reality—in their origin or production, in their meaning or significance, in their impact or influence—this remains a matter of the immersion of art in reality, or reality embedded within art, not a matter of bringing film into relationship with some reality beyond the real. No, the question of transcendence and film must begin—must always begin—with the question of film's self-understanding and self-relationship, the ways in which film comes to the viewer in order, at least in part, to present itself as itself, whatever it is. Blockbusters are blockbusters precisely because they do not do this—or do not do it consciously, or well: they serve primarily as escape pods, vehicles the viewers can use to take a break from the realities of their lives. The movement is unidirectional: filmgoer → film → fantasy. This is not an experience of transcendence; it is an evasion of reality by way of the abandonment of the self.

It is, of course, also great fun. But as a way of coming into relationship with something greater than ourselves, blockbusters—and all movies of the "blockbuster" type, all movies that exist primarily to facilitate escapist fantasies and ticket sales—fail. Or, if the failure is not their own, they nevertheless do little to make obvious or easy an experience of transcendence for the viewer. They encourage distraction over self-knowledge, amusement over self-awareness, and they do so always by way of motion—hence, "cinema," from the Greek κίνημα or κίνησις, movement—by visually or narratively moving us from wherever we find ourselves, seated there in the darkened theater, into an imagined-imaginary world. The cinema transports us, and more often than not *seeks* to transport us—to transport us *as such*, movement for movement's sake. On the surface of it, the cinema tries neither to transform nor to understand. Just to move.

This is what makes a film like Federico Fellini's *8 1/2* (1963) so difficult to comprehend as cinema.[1] Obviously, of course, in some clear and material sense *8 1/2* is a movie: it is filmed, on film, for later projection in cinemas around the world. But thinking of cinema as movement, it is difficult to see how *8 1/2* moves, except again in the most obvious, most material sense in which a series of photographic frames are projected onto a screen in rapid enough succession to stimulate the illusion of motion in the minds of the viewers. Narratively speaking, however, almost nothing happens in the film: a famous Italian film director, Guido Anselmi, has committed to making yet another film, but he has little idea what sort of film he wants or ought to make; after a number of reflections and considerations, and a great many distractions, he concludes that he cannot make the movie.[2] On one level, on the most obvious and even superficial level, that's the whole thing. Of course, Guido's experience is punctuated by the various interpersonal relationships he has—with his filmmaking colleagues, his friends, his mistress, his wife, his actresses—as well as his dreams and fantasies, and his memories of various figures and events from his own childhood. But even these seem to lead nowhere in particular, even into the final moments of the film.

It's in those final moments, however, that I think we find some of the deeper significance of *8 1/2*—and where we find the possibility of transcendence—but we do so not by way of moving outward and away from ourselves, the traditional direction for transcendent experience: we do so by way of a repetition. I mean this in the Kierkegaardian sense, a sense appropriated, if in a somewhat modified form, by Gilles Deleuze, for whom it is a relevant concept both in general, as addressed in *Difference and Repetition*, and in film, as addressed in *Cinema*, especially Volume 2: "The Time-Image."[3] Deleuze nearly singlehandedly makes "repetition" an important notion in twentieth-century European thought, and the recognition of his significance to Continental philosophy is rightly earned, but I will not discuss Deleuze here. For the purposes of sorting out the importance of repetition to questions of transcendence in a film like *8 1/2*, I think Kierkegaard is a more useful, and more interesting, resource.

Kierkegaard, naturally, has nothing to say about the cinema. He died forty years before the Lumière brothers made their first film. But Kierkegaard does have a great deal to say about art and the aesthetic, performance, and the notion of repetition—explored in great if somewhat unconventional depth in the book, *Repetition*, ascribed to the pseudonymous author, Constantin Constantius—is an important one for coming to understand any human experience involving a conscious awareness of time's passing, of the human existential condition of temporality. Unlike the traditional plastic arts—painting, sculpture, architecture—film moves. In moving, it exerts some power over the spectator's experience of time; by way of forcing the viewer to move with the events of the film through time to their conclusion, film—like theater, music, and dance—comes into some sort of relationship with the spectator's experience of himself or herself as temporal. And it's in coming to understand the precise nature of the film in time that we can begin to see how Fellini can offer us an occasion for an experience of transcendence in a film like *8 1/2*.

My goal here is to bring these different notions—cinema, movement, temporality, repetition, transcendence—into meaningful relationship, and to that end, I will first explore repetition as it occurs in Constantius' *Repetition*, and then apply repetition so understood to cinema, by way of an analysis of repetition in *8 1/2*. Transcendence, we will see, is not something one achieves in film by way of using movies like catapults, tools for launching ourselves out of and away from immanence into some higher plane of being. Rather, it is only in experiencing a film experiencing itself as a film—a relation that relates to itself in the relating—that we can see beyond the world of the film and simultaneously beyond ourselves, to something more.

RECOLLECTION AND REPETITION

At the very heart of the notion of repetition set forth by Constantin Constantius in *Repetition* is the assertion that repetition is the modern equivalent of whatever recollection was in ancient Greece. Constantius notes, "Say what you will, this question will play a very important role in modern philosophy, for *repetition* is a crucial expression for what "recollection" was to the Greeks. Just as they taught that all knowing is a recollecting, modern philosophy will teach that all life is a repetition."[4] If we conceive of repetition at least initially as Constantius does, in terms of a contrast with recollection, then the ways in which repetition offers us an account of human temporality are thrust to the fore.

But what is the nature of the difference between recollection and repetition? Any ordinary, everyday conception of repetition conceives of repetition as the second, or further, occurrence of some prior, first event. Thus, in everyday usage, "to repeat" means "to do or experience again," and this notion—of the "again-ness" of an occurrence—seems necessarily to depend upon a specific conception of the relationship between the present and the past. In order to repeat myself in speech, for example, what I say now must be something I have already said before. Such a conception depends, then, upon a stable conception of the relevant past events. From the point of view of everyday repetition, the past is a settled affair. But this conception of repetition treats repetition as existentially and temporally identical to recollection: both are ways of looking back and relating to the past from the perspective of the present. To recollect is to remember what has gone before; to repeat is to enact or undergo the very same sort of thing one could, in the realm of knowledge, recollect. In short, both recollection and this everyday model of repetition ground the significance of the present—memory or event—in its relationship to the unalterable past.

If this were all there were to Constantius' notion of repetition, it would not be much of an advance upon the Greeks at all—and it would be of little use to thinking about film. In contrast to the everyday sense of repetition as effectively similarity in sequence, however, Constantius distinguishes repetition in his sense quite markedly from recollection. He writes, "Repetition and recollection are the same movement, except in opposite directions, for what is recollected has been, is repeated backward, whereas genuine repetition is recollected forward."[5] Most thinking about time presupposes that the point of view for thought is the present—all thinking is in the present moment—and thus the past is always something to be looked back upon from a present point of view. Repetition would be the recognition from within the present moment of a correspondence between that which is happening now and that which happened then, some time ago, in the past.

The explanation of Constantius' description of repetition—"*genuine repetition*"—as "recollected forward," however, is not immediately clear. Constantius does not appear to be arguing that repetition is a mode of anticipation—a looking-forward—given that he treats repetition as if it were something one could only experience as repetition in the present. Moreover, the characterization of repetition as a kind of recollection—as recollection forward—seems to confuse the issue even more. Whatever repetition is, recollection is always backward-looking, as we can see in our use of the term as a synonym for or species of memory. To recollect *forward* would require a much deeper understanding of what Constantius means both by recollection *and* repetition. And whatever headway we might already have made in our inquiry seems all of a sudden to be lost.

Constantius' reference to "genuine repetition"—distinguishing it, presumably, from another, less genuine, or false, repetition—can help us to regain our footing. Once we acknowledge that there are two senses of "repetition" with which we are dealing here, we can start to think of repetition not only in contrast to recollection but also in terms of a contrast between two different repetitions. One way of thinking about repetition is the one we have already seen: repetition as reoccurrence. This understanding of repetition—what I was calling "everyday repetition," above—presupposes a present-tense point of view on the part of the individual recognizing the repetition in time: from the perspective of this moment, what transpired can be said to have transpired before. This dovetails quite nicely with our notion of recollection, which also presupposes a present-tense point of view looking backward to some prior moment in time: such a repetition can be identified only by virtue of a prior instance being recollected. But on this model, repetition is not forward-looking at all: in fact, on this model, repetition is not just backward-looking, but is in at least one way—that is, as an existential position in time—indistinguishable from recollection.

To recognize a repetition of this everyday sort is to be so knowledgeable of the past and so aware of the present that one can see similarities between the two, wherever and whenever they exist. Recollection is, before anything else, a theory of knowledge. Nothing about recollection's knowledge of the past excludes the possibility of knowing one's present circumstances; in fact, as we have seen, as a theory of knowledge recollection depends upon knowledge of the present as well as the past in order to make sense of knowing. The legacy of the Platonic doctrine of recollection seems in fact to be this belief, that knowledge is the cognizable residue of the past in the present—which is just to say that knowing is largely a function of memory. To follow in this line is to conclude (with Plato) that recollection is not just memory but also knowledge itself: to know the past is, quite simply, to know.

Following on this everyday conception of recollection is our everyday or "false" repetition: if to know that 2 + 2 = 4 is to recollect that it is so, then, any time I have an experience of 2 + 2 in the present, my recollection that the sum is 4 is a repetition—the reoccurrence of that recollected truth. Of course, few of the repetitions we seek are of this straightforwardly arithmetical sort. Before we get into the repetition Constantius tries to effect in his narrative, his return to Berlin, he gives us a humorous but instructive example: "When the queen had finished telling a story at a court function and all the court officials, including a deaf minister, laughed at it, the latter stood up, asked to be granted the favor of also being allowed to tell a story, and then told the same story. Question: What was his view of the meaning of repetition?"[6] This fictional event, despite its literary quality, has the same structure as the arithmetical example of repetition: the first occurrence, the queen's telling of the story, is repeated in the deaf minister's telling of the same story. But the anecdote also points out the problem with the everyday conception of repetition, what makes it false, rather than genuine. From the point of view of the deaf minister—someone whose deafness presumably prevented him from hearing the story the queen told in the first place—the story is being told for the first time. He seeks to repeat the great comedic effect he witnessed after the queen told her story, but if we can imagine what this scenario would look like for the other court officials gathered there, we can see that this is beyond the deaf minister's ability to achieve: in retelling the very same story just told by the queen, the deaf minister will not rouse the room to laughter as she did. In fact, in retelling the very same story, the deaf minister will make clear how telling the same story a second time is essentially a *different* event from the first telling. The difference is not just one of chronological sequence, that the deaf minister's telling comes second, which would be true of any repetition, false or genuine. The difference is that, in being an exact copy of the first, the second plays a different role in the lives of those hearing, even telling, the story. When the queen told the story the first time, it was essentially storytelling; when the deaf minister told the story for the second time, it was essentially copying the queen. The "for-the-second-time-ness" of the deaf minister's telling is of the essence of his telling, such that he has not repeated the queen's first telling of the story but has done something else entirely: it's not a repetition at all.

Constantius' book, *Repetition*, has two parts, in the first of which he narrates briefly an attempt he made to achieve a repetition. He describes a second trip he took to Berlin, the point of which was to achieve a repetition of a prior trip he had taken to the same city. To this end, he makes every effort to do everything he had done the first time around, in exactly the same ways, and as one might expect, the narrative is largely a recounting of all the ways in which the effort fails: the situation of the innkeeper has changed since Constantius had stayed there the first time; the theater is playing a different show; the food is of a different quality; etc., etc. On the basis of this experience, however, Constantius comes to a philosophical conclusion: "When this had repeated itself several days, I became so furious, so weary of the repetition, that I decided to return home. My discovery was not significant, and yet it was curious, for I had discovered that there simply is no repetition and had verified it by having it repeated in every possible way."[7] Like the deaf minister, although somewhat more self-consciously, and making as exact a copy of the prior experience as is possible, Constantius discovers that one cannot achieve a repetition in this way. As neither man can imagine any other sort of repetition, the conclusion is a straightforward and compelling one: repetition is impossible. One cannot take one's first trip to Berlin a second time.

Constantius follows his anecdote about the deaf minister, however, immediately with a second, different anecdote: "When a schoolteacher says: For the second time I repeat that Jespersen is to sit quietly—and the same Jespersen gets a mark for repeated disturbance, then the meaning of repetition is the very opposite [of what it meant to the deaf minister]."[8] Despite his inability to achieve repetition in his own life, Constantius does open the possibility of a completely different sense of repetition— what he called, above, "genuine repetition"—which evades the contradiction inherent in the false repetition. Although Jespersen's repetition has something of the character of the deaf minister's, Jespersen having done the same thing more than once, it is not a repetition by virtue of the similarities between the first and second occurrences alone. To see how this is the case, however, we must return once more to our inquiry into repetition.

REPETITION AND TRANSCENDENCE

From the perspective of recollection, repetition is impossible—because repetition would require that one be able to conceive of receiving again what once was lost—lost in the sense in which everything past is lost to the present. To believe in recollection, as did the Greeks, is to believe that the past is both unchangeable and irrecoverably lost to us. One recollects the past because recollection is the only means by way of which one can come into relationship to the past. And one recollects the past because recollection is the only means by way of which someone who is resigned to the certainty of loss, to having lost the past, can come into relationship with the present, as well. Recollection sees everything but touches nothing. For recollection, the world is always already essentially dead. "It may be true that a person's life is over and done with in the first moment," Constantius writes, "but there must also be the vital force to slay this death and transform it to life."[9] And for Constantius, of course, that "vital force" is repetition.

To understand what Constantius means by a "genuine repetition," I think, one must engage the question not from a strictly chronological or sequential point of view, but in terms of transition or movement. From recollection's point of view, the truth exists exclusively in some distant past, only to be found in the present by relating this moment now to that moment then. What the two moments have in common, for recollection, is their common participation in something that really exists in neither moment: the eternal, the timeless, the idea. This divests time itself of significance, while simultaneously resolving any lingering Aristotelian concerns about an infinite regress: every moment is made meaningful in its relation to some prior moment, but no one of those past moments is or can be the origin or foundation of meaning. Each moment in time means what it means only by virtue of participation in something other than time. In this sense, the loss with which recollection begins is, importantly, the loss of time or time's significance itself. In this way, recollection forces an absolute distinction between time and eternity, placing the potential for all meaning on eternity's side of the division, and thus grounding one of the more classical understandings of the relationship between immanence and transcendence. Transcendence, on this view, is the elevation above temporality into something at least temporarily approximating eternity's unchanging point of view.

Change, however, is of central importance to understanding repetition: as such, Constantius rests everything upon the notions of movement and transition. He writes,

> the Greek view of the concept of κίνησις [motion, change] corresponds to the modern category "transition" and should be given close attention. The dialectic of repetition is easy, for that which is repeated has been—otherwise it could not be repeated—but the very fact that it has been makes the repetition into something new. When the Greeks said that all knowing is recollecting, they said that all existence, which is, has been; when one says that life is a repetition, one says: actuality, which has been, now comes into existence.[10]

As we have seen, recollection rests upon a series of presuppositions requisite for its coherence as both a theory of knowledge and an understanding of human temporality. For recollection to function, we must believe that the starting point for all inquiry is and could only ever be the present; that time's movement is always the loss of the past in the present, recoverable only in memory; that a human being is or is not in possession of knowledge at any given moment in time; further, that a human being's position in time is fixed and unchangeable, such that one is always only ever now, in the present. On such a view, time's passage is necessarily progressive and evolutionary: there is nothing genuinely new under the sun, because everything that comes to be has come to be out of its immediately prior cause. Recollection rests the present on a foundation of eternity, and thus, for recollection, there is no such thing as radical or qualitative change: only quantitative, incremental development, as we find in Plato, and Kant, and Hegel—in all idealism.

Repetition, however, is all about radical change: motion, novelty, transformation, transfiguration. Repetition—genuine repetition, Jespersen's repetition—does not begin with the present moment. For repetition, to try to understand temporality by starting in this moment, now, would be to grant from the get-go that what has been is no more and is no longer capable of change. But Constantius—when theorizing, if not also in his own life and practice—does not think time and temporality must be understood in this way. If repetition is possible, it does not begin at the end of the causal chain, as in the present moment, but at the beginning, as in the past. Instead of conceiving of the past as over and done with, as closed and unchanging, repetition opens the past by centralizing transition and movement. The human self is not fixed and finished, nor is it at one stage of a progressive, dialectical, development. Rather, the human self is ever in motion, such that, to understand even the smallest bit of what one is in the present, one must reconceive the present as *simultaneous* with the past. For repetition, the present is simultaneous with the past in the sense that, like the present, the past remains open—not merely open to interpretation, which anyone must grant is true, but open to real change, even now. The past can become something new, by virtue of developments in the present. The past is always capable of becoming more than it was, or is.

When we acquiesce to what seems the commonsense, rational, and scientific view, that the past is over and done with as far as we, in the present, are concerned, we produce a wall between present and past that can only be breached in one direction: the past can influence the present, but not the other way around. For Constantius, however, repetition means reconceiving the relation between past and present such that that wall is permeable in both directions. When the deaf minister repeats the queen's story, the only conception of repetition applicable is the "false repetition," the idea that the minister's story is a copy, a duplicate, a replica of the queen's: and, because it is not the original, the queen and the other court officials can identify it as a copy, which makes it a very different sort of thing than was the queen's telling of the story and thus not a repetition, really, at all. But when the schoolteacher gives Jespersen a mark for repeated disturbance, something altogether different is happening. Jespersen disrupts the class; then, at a later point in time, Jespersen disrupts the class again. On one level, of course, this is no more or less a repetition than the deaf minister's unfortunate retelling of the queen's story. But there is an element to Jespersen's story that is missing in the deaf minister's: in being marked for "repeated disturbance," Jespersen's first disturbance takes on a new character, not just a new interpretation. In the time between the first disturbance and the second disturbance, Jespersen was free not to disrupt the class again. Had he chosen not to continue being disruptive, he would never have been marked for repeated disturbance, and that first disturbance would have been exactly what it seemed to be at the time: a single disturbance. But by way of the second disruption, the first disturbance becomes the *first* disturbance, the first in a series, the first of a different kind. The very nature of the first disturbance is transformed by the occurrence of the second disturbance.

Given that Jespersen is free, the first disturbance could not have been the first of a series when it occurred; it only became that later, after it was finished. The first disturbance becomes something other by virtue of a change in Jespersen, whose own character is changed by the repeated disturbances, as well. A man who has never married before gets married; his spouse is mathematically his "first" spouse, but only mathematically — until that marriage ends, and the man marries again. Then, when he refers to the first marriage as his "first marriage," the entire character of that marriage changes. Were a previously unmarried man to refer to his spouse as his "first" spouse, we would be misled as to the character of the relationship. One's "wife" or "husband," and one's "first wife" or "first husband," are not just different points in a sequence: they are different sorts of things. Or, more grimly, take the example of a serial killer. After having killed his first victim, he is not a *serial* killer, and the murder is one sort of thing. But once a series occurs—once we perceive a repetition—then the characters of the crimes committed change. Even that first murder—which, at the time, was in no way part or evidence of a series—changes retroactively. "A murder" is a very different sort of thing from "the first in a series of murders." Or think of the difference between the "Great War" and the "First World War," or the "Gulf War" and the "First Gulf War." Sometimes, the second occurrence of an event has no bearing on the character of the first occurrence, as in the deaf minister's case; in such cases, it is the second occurrence's nature that is affected by the first's. And sometimes, a second occurrence only sheds new light on and increases our understanding of the first occurrence, as when an author's second book explains and clarifies what was meant in her first book. But in other cases—those which Constantius refers to when he refers to "genuine repetition"—the second occurrence has a retroactive causal effect on the first occurrence, such that its very essence is transformed, in defiance of the ordinary passage of time.

One way to begin to understand this—a Kierkegaardian way, I think—is to reconceive of time as not composed of discrete and separable moments, but instead as an unfolding process of change. Understood in this way, every moment is part of a larger whole the nature of which is always unclear to those who observe it, but which can become clearer as the process develops in time. Our desire to understand, to know something once and for all, or to achieve what Edward F. Mooney calls "finished knowledge," and then to move onto the next thing, inspires us to divide time into as many fragments as we can: small fragments, individual moments, are easier to know.[11] But if the truth is not some eternal present awaiting discovery, and is instead a moving process of change through time, then there is no finished knowledge. The truth moves. As it moves, its nature becomes more or less clear to those of us who try to grasp it. A repetition is not simply a new occurrence in a series of similar occurrences; it is a transformation of the self in recognition of and relation to the "ongoing-ness" of time that transfigures the world.

No material reality can be changed by future events; this is the foundation of the ordinary conception of time and the false or impossible repetition. But the truth does not inhere in matter; for Kierkegaard and Constantius, the truth is not a property of assertions as they relate to the world. Truth—and meaning—are processes that develop and reveal themselves—or are revealed—in time, but which are not themselves conditioned by time. Like melodies, they are movements through a medium whose essence they do not share; melodies are not sound waves, despite the fact that they are made of nothing but sound waves. And like melodies, truth and meaning offer us not merely reinterpretations of the material world but the transcendence of it. Constantius, comparing modern and Hegelian philosophy to the genuine repetition, writes, "Modern philosophy makes no movement, as a rule it makes only a commotion, and if it makes any movement at all, it is always within immanence, whereas repetition is and remains a transcendence."[12] And it is in this notion of repetition as transcendence that even Constantius sees the nature of his own inability to achieve a repetition in Berlin: "repetition is too transcendent for me. I can circumnavigate myself, but I cannot rise above myself. I cannot find the Archimedean point."[13] Repetition is a rising above or beyond oneself, being and not being what one is, becoming something other than what one was but in a transfiguring way. One is and is not the same; as unidiomatic as it sounds, one *was* and *was not* the same. The meaning of the past remains open into the present, as well as the future, because the nature of what is past remains open into the present as well as the future. And the key to uncovering the truth is not to be found in settling the past once and for all, but precisely in the opposite movement: in unsettling the past, and reconceiving it not as the cause but as a part of the present moment. The past is present, always—and it moves.

ASA NISI MASA: 8 1/2

Cinematography—κίνησις, κίνημα (movement) + γράφος (writing)—means, literally, "writing with movement," and that we refer most commonly to the products of this art as "movies"—an abbreviation of "moving pictures"—further emphasizes the centrality of movement to any understanding of film. If we understand time and motion in the strictly linear and causal fashion of recollection, then the only films we are capable of making or understanding are those which follow a strictly chronological pattern: one discrete event leads to the next, with the art of the filmmaker residing in the manner in which the causal connections are communicated to the spectator. Much of the history of popular cinema can be explained in terms of two basic film genres, what we might call "the mystery film" and "the quest film," and both of these genres are defined in terms of a strictly linear relationship to time. What I am calling "quest films" set forth a goal which characters understand and must accomplish in the future: romances are of this sort, as are Westerns, typically, and historical films. "Mystery films," on the other hand, establish that some unexplained phenomenon is occurring, and it is the task of one or more characters to discover what caused this phenomenon in the past in order to achieve resolution in the present: mysteries, of course, and most films noirs are of this sort, as are horror films. Science fiction and fantasy films, which have their origins early in the history of cinema, with films like Georges Méliès' *A Trip to the Moon*, 1902, are split between the two: *Star Wars*, 1977, is a quest film, *Star Trek*, 1979, is a mystery film. Although not all popular films utilize the flashback as a direct link between "present" and "past" events, relative to the temporality of the film, the great majority of them relate to time in the manner of recollection: the past is lost to the present, and can be recovered only in memory; the past sheds light on the present, and present discoveries can help to explain the past, but nothing done now can influence anything done then.

It is somewhat ironic that recollection's temporality is so dominant in the cinema, however, given that the very nature of cinema is to operate according to a different principle of temporality, one much more akin to Constantius' genuine repetition than to the false repetition of recollection. Stanley Cavell famously acknowledges, in his first book on film, the paradoxical nature of filmgoing: that, when watching a film, we experience the present—its projection—and the past—its recording—simultaneously, watching past events develop in the present as if their outcomes have yet to be determined.[14] Like all art and writing, film re-presents the past as present, and it is not an easily dismissible oddity that the words you are reading right now were written many months or years ago, which is the past for you, but very much the present for me. But film does something more than writing can do, since language forces writing into a linear and chronological mold. In this regard, as noted briefly above, cinema is as much like music as it is like literature. And, like music, cinema requires the spectator to engage both attention and memory simultaneously; the first notes of a symphony or song cannot be understood as the *first* notes until the intermediary and final notes have also been heard. And yet, those first notes never play again in the present: they are heard, and understood in whatever way the listener understands them, the first time—and then, when the later notes have also been heard, the truth and meaning of those first notes is retroactively transformed. Or, as with repetition, perhaps "transfigured" is a better term: materially unchanged but nevertheless entirely different. Even the most linearly chronological film presents viewers with this paradox, that, for the viewer, the first shots and scenes of the film are changed retroactively by the last shots and scenes of that film. It's not just that I understand the first scenes better once I've seen the film all the way through; it's that, by the time I get to the final scene, those first scenes *are* different; or, better, the distinction between first scene and final scene is from a certain perspective a meaningless and counterproductive one, because the film is a single motion from beginning to end. Although we experience it in a linear chronological sequence, it is whatever it is, and means whatever it means, as an undifferentiated and non-temporal phenomenon. Like music. Or like life itself.

This is not to say that, from a different perspective, we cannot legitimately observe or analyze different scenes or different elements at work at different points in a film's duration. Just that, in the end, understanding what a film means is always also going to be a matter of relating individual elements to the overarching whole. As we will see, viewing a film in this twofold way can show us not only the ways in which the film relates to us, individually, but also the ways in which the film relates to itself—and, by way of relating to that relation, we can also experience a kind of self-transcendence.

Federico Fellini's *8 1/2* is a film filled to the very brim with repetitions. Most of these are of the ordinary variety, "false" repetitions, whereby we see some past moment reoccur in the present. Most of them are also highly psychologized. To take but a few: the plot of *8 1/2* revolves around the frustrated efforts of a famous filmmaker to make *another* popular and important film; the first time we see Guido's face is in his reflection in a bathroom mirror;[15] the "pre-appearance" in an early scene of Guido's actress and muse, Claudia, in his fantasy at the spa; the notes on Guido's screenplay made by the critic, Daumier, which comment on many of the scenes and characters, especially the fantasies, that we see in the film itself; the fantasy sequence wherein Guido imagines being kissed by his dead mother and then she metamorphoses into Luisa, his wife; when he wakes up his mistress, Carla, and asks her to "Make a face like a whore,"[16] giving her a look reminiscent of the prostitute, La Saraghina, whom he and his childhood friends would pay to dance the rhumba; when, in conversation with Guido, Carla recalls having bought him the same tie that Luisa had, "Remember? And when you wore it I never knew whether it was hers or mine";[17] or, infamously, when Guido fantasizes that all the women he's ever known live together in a harem which he rules and for which misogynistic power he is loved. Perhaps most demonstratively, when Guido, his production team, and Luisa and her friends gather to watch screen tests for various roles in the film Guido is trying to make, we see other actors play the roles of the characters in *8 1/2* itself: Luisa, Carla, La Saraghina.

In a subtler sense, as well, we can see Fellini introducing repetitions of world cinematic history in the film: the actress playing the older French actress, Madeleine, who feels discarded and abandoned by Guido, played the young French ex-pat, Yvonne, who felt discarded and abandoned by Rick Blaine in Michael Curtiz' *Casablanca* (1942); the flashback sequence to young Guido's encounter with La Saraghina on the beach, where the Catholic school authorities discover him and try to return him to school to be disciplined, ends in a comedic chase scene filmed so as to copy the flicker and accelerated speed associated today with silent films, especially with the bumbling incompetence of the police in Mack Sennett's *Keystone Cops* films (1912-1917); and the final scene, wherein all of the figures from Guido's life gather in a long line and dance, about which I will have more to say, below, is a clear repetition of the "dance of death" scene at the end of Ingmar Bergman's *The Seventh Seal* (1957). All of these scenic and cinematic repetitions are important, and each is worthy of extended analysis in its own right, but for my purposes here, I will not be attending to them—preferring instead to focus on what I take to be two deeper, interrelated, and more significant repetitions in the film: the first childhood flashback; and the non-Bergmanian elements of the final scene of the film. *8 1/2* does not give us a linear, chronological story about Guido's psychological self-development. Instead, it goes around the same things again and again, circumnavigating Guido's life without rising above it—at least, until the very end of the film. But this is not the steady ascent of a quest film, nor the informative descent of a mystery film; nor is it simply Fellini's filmic autobiography. *8 1/2* is something else.

To come nearer the heart of *8 1/2*, we need to look back into the film, to the first childhood flashback, a return to a night in the young Guido's life. Initially, the flashback scene shows us Guido as a boy, fleeing from the adult women who are trying to get him to take his "wine bath." Immediately before the flashback scene, however, Guido finds himself at a dinner in an open-air restaurant where a clairvoyant, Maya—whose very name brings the question of the relationship between reality and illusion to mind—begins reading patrons' minds. As he is preparing to leave, Guido has a conversation with Maya's assistant, Maurice, an old friend of his, who informs Guido that the "trick" is partly stage magic, and partly, he asserts, real: "There are some tricks, but there's also something true about it. I don't know how it happens, but it happens."[18] Guido volunteers to have his mind read, as he has something specific for Maya to "see"—and, when Maurice "transmits" the message to Maya, she notes, "I don't understand. *I can't repeat it.*"[19] She writes three gibberish words on a chalkboard that forms the screen against which she performs, and then, reading them aloud, says, "Asa . . . Nisi . . . Masa?" Maurice asks Guido if Maya got it right, Guido assents, and then Maurice inquires, "But what does it mean?"[20] Guido does not answer. The next thing we see is the wine bath flashback.

I think this double scene—Guido's psychic interaction with Maya, coupled with the second half of the childhood memory—is the mysterious center of the entire film. Guido carries this phrase—"Asa Nisi Masa"—with him, it seems, wherever he goes; he can recall it immediately, without delay. It is, as Maya informs us, unrepeatable, and yet she can inscribe it on the chalkboard screen for the restaurant patrons and cinemagoers alike. Guido can see it on the screen, but cannot—or will not, but in any case does not—explain its meaning. That's left for Maurice, and for us, to ponder.

Having been bathed, toweled, and deposited in bed, the boy Guido joins what seems like a roomful of children, all of whom are supposed to be asleep. The grandmother patrols the bedroom, telling the children that she knows if they are pretending to sleep. But once she has left, a twelve-year-old girl sits bolt upright in bed and, conducting some sort of ritual with her arms and hands, excitedly whispers to Guido: "Guido, don't go to sleep tonight! It's the night the portrait's eyes move. You're not scared, are you? You have to be quiet! Uncle Agostino will look into a corner of the room, and the treasure will be there! Don't be afraid, Guido! We'll be rich! Do you remember the magic words?"[21] We see Guido sitting up in bed, and we see the portrait of Uncle Agostino, and then the girl begins to chant, repeating the words over and over: "Asa Nisi Masa . . . Asa Nisi Masa . . . Asa Nisi Masa. . . ."[22] The repetition of the nonsense words is the last spoken line in the flashback scene. "In his book *8 1/2*," D. A. Miller writes, "As we require scholars to tell us, this otherwise incomprehensible phrase is a pig-Latin-like form of 'anima', which is in turn (Fellini being a fresh convert to analytic psychology) Carl Jung's name for the unconscious feminine part of a man's personality."[23] There is something interesting to the Jungian reading, especially given the significant role women play in Guido's life, but it is also worth noting, of course, that the word *"anima"* is an ordinary Italian word: it means "soul," but might also mean "heart," "center," "spirit," or "ghost." Whatever it means to Fellini, the children engaged in repeating the words believe that they are magic, and that the magic they will unleash will make the picture move, and make them rich. That the magic words—"Asa Nisi Masa"—are the heart or soul, the center, of the film is increasingly evident. And the connection here to cinema as such—magical moving pictures that lead to wealth—is also clear. As Alexander Sesonske writes, "in the film, the utterance of 'asa nisi masa' works like magic, releasing the marvelous flow of the joyful life of the farmhouse scene. And the childish promise is hardly idle, for it was when the picture moved its eye—when Fellini found his true métier in motion pictures—that we all became enriched."[24] Whatever the significance of Fellini's Jungianism for the making of the film, the unity here of magic, nonsense, repetition, and meaning cannot be dismissed—and could not be more Kierkegaardian.

From the point of view of repetition, however, there is another added level of significance to the magic words—"Asa Nisi Masa"—and that has to do with the way in which Guido's recollection of this childhood incantation defies the conventional temporality of popular cinema and literature, if not also ordinary human experience. When we see that it's not just in his childhood bedroom that Guido repeats the words, over and over again, but that he is in some sense still running them over in his mind at the ripe old age of forty-three, we realize that the significance of the flashback is not that it provides a key to understanding the adult Guido of the film's present, as it would be, say, in a mystery film. Rather, when Maya reveals that which she cannot repeat, that which is on Guido's mind as he struggles to make his film, she shows us that the repetition of the magic words—"Asa Nisi Masa"—is ongoing in Guido's life. It's not that the present experience is explained by the past experience, but that the present experience and the past experience are *the very same experience*, an experience that has not yet come to an end. It is neither fully present, because it began thirty-something years ago, nor fully past, because it continues. Thus we might say that, from Guido's point of view, the magic words—"Asa Nisi Masa"—are and have always been in a

Figure 7.1. *8 1/2*. Rizzoli, Angelo (Producer). Federico Fellini (Director). 8 1/2. Italy: Cineriz, 1963.

present-tense process of repetition. Guido is still trying to make pictures move.

To the extent that *8 1/2* achieves cinematic resolution, it does so in its final scene—a scene already noted, above, as instantiating a certain sort of repetition, that of a similar scene in a Bergman film. Whereas the Bergman finale is often referred to as the "Dance of Death," the figure of Death leads a group of the dead to the afterlife in a line, dancing and holding hands, the Fellini version is similarly frequently referred to as the "Dance of Life." There are, no doubt, grounds here for a deeper comparison of Fellini and Bergman—two titans from opposite ends of Europe who dominate world cinema for at least two decades—but, for our purposes here, it is enough to note that, unlike Bergman's dance, Fellini's is a beginning, not an ending. This undermines the conclusive power of the film's conclusion in important ways.

In the scenes preceding the film's finale, however, we see Guido and his entourage delivered to the beachside spaceship set for what the film's producers think will be a great promotional launch of the film: they will invite the press, and Guido will be made available to answer their questions about the upcoming release. At this point in the film, however, we realize that there is no film: Guido does not know how to make the film he wants to make, or even, perhaps, what that film is. He has allowed the external momentum of his filmmaking success to develop around him the apparatus for a film—the beginnings of a screenplay, a cast, a crew, financing, and so on—but there is no "there" there, and the press conference is the moment when this all becomes apparent to everyone. Given

Fellini's penchant for interspersing fantasy and dream elements with scenes that take place in the "reality" of the film world of *8 1/2*, it is not entirely clear at which point in the press conference fantasy takes over from reality—but the scene devolves rapidly, with reporters shouting increasingly personal and increasingly hostile questions at Guido, who does not answer them, opting instead to put his head down on the table in front of him, and then, to climb under the table and try to crawl away. He does not make it—in the end, in this scene, he draws a gun from his pocket and shoots himself in the head—but this is not real suicide; it's the escapist fantasy of a man whose life has finally come apart. In the next shot after the fantasy suicide, the production director, Bruno Agostini, is walking with Guido, telling the crew to take down the spaceship set: the production is over, there will be no film.

We then see Daumier, the critic, probably presented as an imagination of Guido's, telling Guido that quitting the film was the right choice: "today is a good day for you. . . . There are already too many superfluous things in the world. It's not a good idea to add more disorder to disorder."[25] As Daumier goes on in this way, we watch Guido walk toward and get into a car. As he seems perhaps ready to depart, he is interrupted by the shouting of his friend, Maya's assistant, Maurice. Daumier's voice continues on, as Maurice tells Guido to wait: "We're ready to begin."[26] Guido ceases trying to leave, and as he sits pensively in the driver's seat of the car, figures from earlier moments in Guido's life—earlier moments in the film we are watching—start to appear, dressed all in white, walking toward some common goal. First Claudia, dressed as she was in Guido's fantasy at the spa, who turns and catches Guido's gaze, and that of the filmgoer. Then the nannies from Guido's childhood, one of them carrying the boy Guido. Then La Saraghina. Then Guido's parents. Then his mistress, Carla, and then others, on and on, different persons from different periods of Guido's life, all walking forward. Guido speaks: "What is this sudden joy that makes me tremble, gives me strength, life?" And then, finally, we see Luisa, walking with her friend, Rossella, a circus ring coming into view in the background. The many companions of Guido's life are headed toward a circus. "At this point, Guido has what is the final revelation of the film, presented in voice-over: "Everything seems good. Everything is meaningful. Everything is true. Oh, I wish I knew how to explain myself. But I don't know how to say it. So that's it. Everything is as it was before! Everything is confused again! But all this confusion . . . it's me, myself."[27] Whereas in a standard mystery film or quest film—by way of a false repetition—the hero might find his way to a personal redemption effected by the discovery of "the key" or "the answer" that wraps everything up in a neat, explicable bow, Guido moves in the opposite direction. He is freed by the realization that he is *more* complex, *more* ambiguous, *more* self-contradictory, *more* confused than he had realized. And, cinematically, that confusion is represented on the screen by the repopulation of the shot with every character or actor who has appeared in the film so far. To be himself, he must not try to uncover his unique and enduring core, as if there is a truth to him that underlies all of the falsity. Rather, he realizes in the film's final moments that he *is* that falsity—the multiplicity, the contradictions—and that, to be himself, he must both see and love it all without trying to simplify or understand it.

Maurice, now more in the role of ringmaster than magician's assistant, leads the various persons to their spots on a raised dais, where they form a single-file line. He clears the way for Guido, who now has his director's megaphone, to direct. Between the two of them, they add new organization to the chaos. As they do so, Guido is approached by Carla who, smiling, says, "Now I've got it. You can't do without us. What time will you call me tomorrow?" And Guido, distractedly and dismissively, as if to undermine even this last attempt at providing a simple, understandable "key" or "answer" to the problems of the film, responds, "Yes, yes. Now, hurry up! Get in line with the others."[28] Even when it seems we might be able to articulate the heart, the *anima*, of the filmmaker or the film, we are wrong: there is no key, there is no answer, because whatever the truth is, it is not expressible in language. As Charles Affron notes,

> [Guido] happily confesses his inability to express himself—"Everything is confused again!"—because the confusion is perceived to be "me, myself," and therefore the true meaning of the film. Of course, this meaning is simple in his (and our) ability to locate it in Guido's person and life; it is also complex, irreducible, untranslatable in the multiplicity of its confusion."[29]

Popular cinema conditions us to expect straightforward and simple resolution—resolution in simplicity—and *8 1/2* resists this emphatically. The film's finale does not finalize anything: as Miller writes, "Iconoclastic, miscellaneous, violently 'alive,' the finale is meant to *flaw* this masterpiece, by dramatically attacking, again and again, the total style that is its premise."[30] If anything, cinematically, the finale *un*-finishes the film.

And yet, . . . Guido's circus finale concludes with a dance which itself concludes, not with Guido—not with the adult played by Marcello Mastroianni-Guido, anyway, who enters the dance himself, with Luisa, before the film's end—but with a song. The tune has occurred before, at various points in the film, and it has a circus rhythm; it's played by a motley band of circus clowns who are led by the boyhood Guido playing the piccolo. As the figures dance in a very large circle, hand-in-hand, the circus band organizes itself into something approximating military formation. Guido has recollected everyone from his life—and Fellini has recollected every character from his film—into a single scene, a monstrosity beyond the bounds of plot and narrative, beyond all understanding, all jumbled up without regard to whence in the story they come—as

Daumier warned, adding more disorder to disorder—but a scene which nevertheless reflects and redoubles everything there is of Guido, and *8 1/2*, at once. Every moment of the film is present there, but without regard to the linear, chronological sequence in which it first appeared. It is a genuine repetition.

And, significantly for the film and for Kierkegaard, or Constantius, it is a repetition that, in changing nothing, changes everything. The finale is the film, transfigured. And in the finale, we see Guido re-experiencing his entire life in a single moment: the past merges with the present into a single, non-temporal thing. Everything and everyone he has ever known is changed, retroactively, by this non-temporal moment. One might expect from such a confusion of persons and events and eras the sort of psychological and existential crisis experienced, say, by Arjuna when he receives the third eye from Krishna and sees everything without the differentiating mechanisms of human consciousness. But instead, Guido is elated and elevated by the experience. He sees the chaos of the world, the chaos that he is, and it is in that vision that he finds the simultaneously self-denying and self-unifying capacity to love. In re-relating to himself, temporally speaking—in coming to a different point of view on his own understanding of and relationship to time—Guido transcends himself. He ceases that circumnavigation characteristic of Constantius and the false repetition, and rises above himself to become . . . himself. As he ever was, but for the first time.

In this transcendent, non-temporal moment of repetition, the viewer experiences the repetition of *8 1/2* itself, as well; it is a film that shows us everything, and then shows us everything again. In this, *8 1/2* brings to the fore an essential aspect of cinema as an art, in a way, however, that is unlike almost every other film. When we see Guido turn from the simplifying impulse the rationalist critic, Daumier, represents—away from the desire to explain the film away with an easy "answer," or "lesson," or "key" to interpretation and meaning, away from the urge to make sense to the viewer, to us—we experience the film turning away from such easy answers and totalizing explanations as well. To watch *8 1/2* is not just to see a repetition depicted in Guido's life, but to experience one. And to experience film in this way is to re-experience oneself in this way: transfigured, non-temporal, swept up in the *movement* of truth rather than trying to possess it. It is to transcend oneself, to stop going round and round the self and to rise above it—without, of course, ever ceasing to be the thing one is rising above. To see oneself transfigured, as one always is but also undergoing an unceasing process of change, like a dead actor brought to life with each new viewing of the film, or like a member of the audience, seated motionlessly in a movie theater but simultaneously a jumble of competing and contradictory motions. Magically, to be both the same and different, both then and now, simultaneously, to be as still as a portrait and yet always in motion.

Asa Nisi Masa, Asa Nisi Masa, Asa Nisi Masa. Everything is confused again; we're ready to begin.

NOTES

1. Angelo Rizzoli (Producer), Federico Fellini (Director), *8 1/2*. Italy: Cineriz, 1963. The film was written by Federico Fellini, Ennio Flaiano, Tullio Pinelli, and Brunello Rondi, based on a story by Federico Fellini and Ennio Flaiano.
2. The character Guido Anselmi is played by Marcello Mastroianni.
3. Gilles Deleuze, *Difference and Repetition* (New York: Bloomsbury Academic, 2014). Gilles Deleuze, *Cinema II: The Time Image* (New York: Bloomsbury Academic, 2013).
4. Søren Kierkegaard, *Repetition*, in *Fear and Trembling; Repetition*, ed. and trans. Howard V. and Edna H. Hong (Princeton: Princeton University Press, 1983), 131.
5. Kierkegaard, *Repetition*, 131.
6. Kierkegaard, *Repetition*, 150.
7. Kierkegaard, *Repetition*, 171.
8. Kierkegaard, *Repetition*, 150. Bracketed words are my own.
9. Kierkegaard, *Repetition*, 137.
10. Kierkegaard, *Repetition*, 149. Brackets are original to the text.
11. Edward F. Mooney, "*Repetition*: Getting the World Back," in *The Cambridge Companion to Kierkegaard*, ed. Alastair Hannay and Gordon D. Marino (Cambridge: Cambridge University Press, 1998), 300-301.
12. Kiekegaard, *Repetition*, 186.
13. Kiekegaard, *Repetition*, 186.
14. Stanley Cavell, *The World Viewed: Reflections on the Ontology of Film*, Enlarged Edition (Cambridge, MA: Harvard University Press, 1979), 25-27.
15. For a broader analysis of the role of reflection and repetition in *8 1/2*, see Christian Metz, "Mirror Construction in Fellini's *8 1/2*," in *8 1/2: Federico Fellini, director*, ed. Charles Affron (New Brunswick, NJ: Rutgers University Press, 1987), 261-66. The commentary by Metz is a selection from his book, Christian Metz, *Film Language: A Semiotics of the Cinema*, trans. Michael Taylor (New York: Oxford University Press, 1974).
16. This quotation is from the English translation of the continuity script published in Federico Fellini, "The Continuity Script," in *8 1/2: Federico Fellini, director*, edited by Charles Affron (New Brunswick, NJ: Rutgers University Press, 1987), 55. All further quotations of the film are from this translation.
Claudia was played by Claudia Cardinale, Daumier by Jean Rougeuil, Luisa by Anouk Aimée, Carla by Sandra Milo, and La Saraghina by Eddra Gale. The older French actress who plays a young French ex-pat, Madeleine, was played by Madeleine Lebeau. Rick Blaine was played by Humphrey Bogart. The boy Guido is played by Riccardo Guglielmi, Maya by Mary Indovino, and Maya's assistant, Maurice, by Ian Dallas. A twelve-year-old girl is played by Roberta Valli.
17. Fellini, "The Continuity Script," 54.
18. Fellini, "The Continuity Script," 81.
19. Fellini, "The Continuity Script," 82. My emphasis.
20. Fellini, "The Continuity Script," 82.
21. Fellini, "The Continuity Script," 86.
22. Fellini, "The Continuity Script," 86.
23. D. A. Miller, *8 1/2, BFI Film Classics* (New York: Palgrave Macmillan, 2008), 55. See also Charles Affron, "8 1/2 What?" in *8 1/2: Federico Fellini, director*, ed. Charles Affron (New Brunswick, NJ: Rutgers University Press, 1987), 13-14.
24. Alexander Sesonske, "*8 1/2*: A Film with Itself as Its Subject," *On Film: Essays* (January 12, 2010), Criterion.com. Accessed July 21, 2018. The essay is also available in print form accompanying the Criterion Collection Blu-ray edition of *8 1/2*. Rizzoli,

Angelo (Producer), Federico Fellini (Director), *8 1/2*, The Criterion Collection. Italy: Cineriz, 1963. Blu-ray 2013.
25. Fellini, "The Continuity Script," 184.
26. Fellini, "The Continuity Script," 185.
27. Fellini, "The Continuity Script," 186-7.
28. Fellini, "The Continuity Script," 189.
29. Affron, "8 1/2 What?" 17-18.
30. Miller, *8 1/2*, 108.

BIBLIOGRAPHY

Affron, Charles. "8 1/2 What?" In *8 1/2: Federico Fellini, director*, edited by Charles Affron. New Brunswick, NJ: Rutgers University Press, 1987, 3-19.
Cavell, Stanley. *The World Viewed: Reflections on the Ontology of Film*, Enlarged Edition. Cambridge, MA: Harvard University Press, 1979.
Deleuze, Gilles. *Difference and Repetition*. New York: Bloomsbury Academic, 2014.
_____. *Cinema II: The Time Image*. New York: Bloomsbury Academic, 2013.
Kierkegaard, Søren. *Repetition*. In *Fear and Trembling; Repetition*, edited and translated by Howard V. and Edna H. Hong, 125-231. Princeton: Princeton University Press, 1983.
_____. "*Gjentagelsen*." In *Søren Kierkegaards Skrifter*, Bind 4, edited by Niels Jørgen Cappelørn, Joakim Garff, Jette Knudsen, and Johnny Kondrup, 5-96. Copenhagen: Gads Forlag, 1997.
Fellini, Federico. "The Continuity Script." In *8 1/2: Federico Fellini, director*, edited by Charles Affron, 37-201. New Brunswick, NJ: Rutgers University Press, 1987.
Metz, Christian. *Film Language: A Semiotics of the Cinema*, translated by Michael Taylor. New York: Oxford University Press, 1974.
_____. "Mirror Construction in Fellini's *8 1/2*." In *8 1/2: Federico Fellini, director*, edited by Charles Affron, 261-66. New Brunswick, NJ: Rutgers University Press, 1987.
Miller, D. A. *8 1/2, BFI Film Classics*. New York: Palgrave Macmillan, 2008.
Mooney, Edward F. "*Repetition*: Getting the World Back." In *The Cambridge Companion to Kierkegaard*, edited by Alastair Hannay and Gordon D. Marino, 282-307. Cambridge: Cambridge University Press, 1998.
Rizzoli, Angelo (Producer). Federico Fellini (Director). *8 1/2*. Italy: Cineriz, 1963.
Sesonske, Alexander. "*8 1/2*: A Film with Itself as Its Subject," *On Film: Essays* (January 12, 2010). Criterion.com. Accessed July 21, 2018.

EIGHT

Transcendence and the Ineffable in Scorsese's *Silence*

David P. Nichols

So much of meaning is communicated by way of silence. We know its power in our indirect uses of language, like the hesitant pauses of dialogue, the nuances of things said and unsaid, and the contextual clouds that overshadow it all. We know the presence of meaning because of a silent backdrop, one which pokes through the spaces between our words or sentences. We even experience silence by coming up against the boundaries of language itself, as though it lacked an orbit wholly comprehensive for the world we inhabit. In the moments where language falls short, we nonetheless feel the summoning of what is ineffable about our world. Film has the power to speak to us from the silence of a beckoning world, in a manner that transcends our ordinary linguistic abilities. One of the better examples of this in recent cinema is Martin Scorsese's *Silence*, adapted from a Japanese novel by Shusaku Endo.[1] I aim to show that Scorsese's film illustrates many uses of silence, through indirect language, natural settings, symbolism, and other means of letting the world speak for itself. My interpretation makes use of the phenomenological concept of silence found in Maurice Merleau-Ponty, especially as he relates it to the rhythm of film. The "silence" of a film, I will argue, includes all of the negative ways that it hides a world from us, particularly at the level of its underlying ontological fabric or "flesh," and yet at the same time manages to show that very concealment to us.

On the face of it, *Silence* is a relatively simple narrative about the intense persecution of Jesuit missionaries and their Japanese converts in the early days of the Tokugawa Shogunate. The protagonist, Father Sebastian Rodrigues (Andrew Garfield), enters Japan with the assistance of Father Francisco Garrpe (Adam Driver) in search of their former teacher, Father Christovão Ferreira (Liam Neeson). The young Portuguese priests cannot believe the rumors that Ferreira had apostatized in response to persecution. Yet the quest leads Rodrigues down a path into the very apostasy that he so much deplores. He witnesses the gruesome tortures of the faithful, their difficult decisions under duress, and the steadfast refusal of so many to apostatize by means of stepping on the *"fumie"* icon of Christ. Eventually, Rodrigues' contacts with the hidden Christians, the *kakure karishitan*, result in betrayal by one of its weakest members. But after his arrest, Rodrigues is never physically harmed by the authorities, nor his life threatened—he is only made to watch the acute sufferings of his fellow believers. He gradually comes to realize that the glorious martyrdom that he had once envisioned for himself would no longer be an option. Unless he apostatizes, Japanese Christians would continue to be tortured in his presence without end. So, at the advice of the apostatized Ferreira, who had succumbed to the same fate long ago, and in the presence of the *fumie* icon, which seems to beckon him, Rodrigues chooses to step forward, onto the face of God, and into the night of his own damnation.

The wide appeal of Endo's novel stems in no small part from the author's masterful ability to bring silence to the fore of human experience. This silence is perhaps most obvious as a theological theme, whereby Rodrigues must come to terms with a God whose absence seems so disturbing. The novel stubbornly refuses the logic of theodicy at every turn in order to embrace a more immanent divine process. Simply put, the story infuses God into the experiences of human suffering instead of placing God at a distance. But this much only scratches the surface of what the story has to offer about silence as an experience of the world. Silence is for Endo's novel a necessary component of language itself, as that which precedes and engulfs our words—what lets voice have its place. It is felt in the indifference of the captors, in what they say and do not say. Even the literary style of the book heightens the reader's awareness to the silences of writing itself: characters pass in and out of clarity for us depending on the perspective offered by any one of multiple narrators. Some characters are pursued, located, and yet never truly found, like the rumored apostate, Father Ferreira. Silence is felt in the natural environment, vast and insurmountable, that cares nothing for the humans that it crushes. It is known perhaps most oppressively in death—in our forgetting of the dead, and also in the faint ways that the ghosts still show themselves. The rich symbolism of the novel speaks for silence too, by bringing silence into a language that fosters transcendence.

The religious context for *Silence* helps facilitate that sense, so prevalent in religious belief and practice, of a transcendent depth underlying if not betraying language itself. The Japanese word translated for the English title *Silence* (*Chinmoku*) combines two kanji characters, one meaning "to sink" or "subside" (*chin*) and the other for silence (*moku*).[2] As such, the combination lends itself to ecstatic possibilities for thinking about human existence and its world. By describing the human being as ecstatic, I mean that human existence is a process of standing out from itself in order to stand within a world of its own orientation. Thus a layering takes place, with the result that the ontological source for beings sinks or subsides beneath the totality of the familiar orientation. In religious symbolism, the separation between these layers, expressed as the holy and unholy, can be on full display for ritual and art. One of my favorite Japanese examples is the Kiyomizo-dera in Kyoto, where Kannon, the bodhisattva of compassion, looks out upon a lush forest and its waterfall from inside of a temple atop an enormous raised structure. When I first came upon her, flanked by numerous deities, all of them sheltered in the dusty darkness of the wooden hall, I saw almost nothing. Only when my eyes had adjusted from the light of the sun to the interior darkness of the sanctuary did I realize the great depth of the hall, its whole pantheon at work behind the scenes of what passes for ordinary in human perception. Equally striking are the great icon screens of traditional Christian altars, less common since Vatican II, but still mandatory in Eastern Orthodox churches. There the icons are sometimes called "windows of heaven"—not because they point to somewhere else, but on account of the sense of ontological depth that they usher into the here and now.

Decades before Endo wrote his novel, Merleau-Ponty had developed his own concept of silence as an aid for explaining the sedimentation at work in human perception. For Merleau-Ponty, silence is a metaphor that aims at what is elusive to the linguistic order and yet continues to speak through it. Silence describes a more original interconnectedness or "flesh" of the world, with its own jointure among beings, its own temporal rhythm, and its own gesture.[3] At this deeper level of the phenomena we frequently encounter a richness of experience—always there, perhaps, but easily bypassed.[4] The connectivity of the phenomena account for much of this richness, as when the painter's line actually depends upon and brings together the space around it, or a vibrant red recalls my previous experiences of that one red dress or that open wound on the battlefield. As a metaphor, silence is not to be taken literally for what has no sound: it can include the loudest experiences of all. Nor is Merleau-Ponty claiming that language puts us in direct opposition to the primordial experience of the world. Rather, he is saying that the world has a vibrancy, togetherness, and directionality all its own, which surfaces for us through language, and yet because of the limitations of language, frequently gets muted. There is a coming-into-meaning at work here reminiscent of what Christian theology has long identified as the *logos*. Or, to reach behind that, into the Hellenic background preceding Christianity, it is what Heraclitus describes as a backward-stretching attunement, an oppositional coherence, like unto the bow or lyre, their cords stretched back over wood.[5]

These lessons on silence are for Merleau-Ponty just as relevant to film, albeit in its own peculiar way. In his essay, "The Film and the New Psychology," he argues for film having its own internal rhythm.[6] He rejects the stance that cinema provides the viewer with a representation or reproduction of the world in motion. Like the visual arts in general, film does not reproduce the visible so much as it makes a world visible in the first place. "The meaning of a film," says Merleau-Ponty, "is incorporated into its rhythm just as the meaning of a gesture may immediately be read in that gesture: the film does not mean anything but itself."[7] In the rhythm of the film, any given shot depends on the emerging sequence of shots preceding it for its meaning. The director has a handle on the rhythm of the film, through its selection of shots, cutting of scenes and sequences, cadence, the concentration it holds on an image such as the face, and so forth, as though in all of this there lay an emergent order of reality that he or she strives to maintain.[8] The emergent order must always shift through perspectives, by way of camera angles, as though the story were being witnessed from one face after another—always one perspective at a time, yet in a seemingly endless stream.[9] For this reason Merleau-Ponty likens the film to painting—rather, a sequence of paintings—more than he does to the drama, where perspective remains far less restricted. This proximity to the painting is especially evident when he argues that the rhythm of the film follows a visual course for which the rhythm of language can only participate secondarily. Moreover, when the film industry added sound to films, the use of language had to stand in relief against the "silence" of a deeper rhythm whose features pierced through the limits of dialogue.

One advantage of film over the novel in this case is that the medium works from the immediacy of a visual experience, language emerging from its flesh, whereas the written page must work in reverse, from language to imagination. What Endo's novel supplies with brilliant literary description, Scorsese matches with a vividness that allows for the silence to be felt. This includes silence felt in terms of distance, the nearness and farness of God for the characters. That distance sometimes shows itself in the great encompassing of the world, as when the priests float on tiny boats in the midst of a vast ocean, and Portugal seems so infinitely far away. At other times, the thickness of forest and swamp, fog and darkness, bring the silent weight of that encompassing nearer. The most striking examples of silence from Scorsese's storehouse of natural phenomena may be those of torture, when the faithful are overwhelmed by the elements. In one scene, three villagers are crucified for their faith, tied to wooden crosses over hard stones bordering the ocean, and left to die as the rising tide slaps them to exhaustion. They pray for paradise, and the villager who lasts longest, Mokichi, dies only after singing for it: "We're on our way, we're on our way, We're on our way to the temple of Paradise...."[10] Merleau-Ponty speaks of the possibilities of language, in its emotional gestures, for "singing the world" and thereby letting its silent greatness soar within us.[11] The painful irony about this particular scene is that the victims pray for paradise at the same time that it cruelly smothers them, as though the world seals them within its own silence. The closer they come to being itself, the further away it seems.

Several of the film's more breathtaking vistas point the viewer to the importance of incarnation. Much of the narrative itself follows Rodrigues' descent from a theology of vertical transcendence to one that is thoroughly horizontal. He learns to relinquish his attachment to the heroism of the traditional Western martyr, with its uncompromising glory, at the service of a just Judge, in exchange for the more maternal and immanent "God with us" of shared suffering. It could have been a lesson straight from Merleau-Ponty himself, when he observes of the incarnation principle how,

> ... Christianity is, among other things, the recognition of a mystery in the relations of man and God, which stems precisely from the fact that the Christian God wants nothing to do with a vertical relation of subordination.... Claudel goes so far as to say that God is not above but beneath us—meaning that we do not find Him as a supersensible idea, but as another ourself, who dwells in and authenticates our darkness. Transcendence no longer hangs over humanity: we become, strangely, its privileged bearer.[12]

Toward the beginning of the film, when Garrpe and Rodrigues convince their superior, Father Valignano, to let them sail for Japan in search of Ferreira, Scorsese closes the scene with the three men walking together along the massive stone steps of their college. The camera angle, from the sky, looks down directly at their heads as they walk, with the result that the viewer can no longer ascertain whether they are climbing or ascending the steps. Without a firm "ground" to view them from, they are simply traversing the screen horizontally, from left to right. Not long after, when the two priests set sail from Macau, China, into the beautiful horizon of Nagasaki Bay, the camera lifts momentarily into the clouds far above for a view of the sun, as if they were sailing under the expectations of a vertical calling. Immediately after this, their first landing in Japan, at Tomogi Bridge, brings them to a massive cave, womblike in appearance, where they are welcomed into the new country by Christian villagers. Little do they know that they are about to experience the condescension of God, in the incarnate reality that is Japan and themselves.

In *Silence*, the setting comes alive to tell much of the story, as though the narrative were rooted in a deeper reality. Perhaps Scorsese best sums up the gesture of the world, from its silence, in a scene where Rodrigues and Garrpe watch an eagle cut through the forest air, and the former says, "That's God's sign." Fully in its element, the eagle passes through its surroundings much like the pulling of a zipper—by drawing the phenomena around itself unto itself, for a singularly conjoined flesh. But most of God's own signs are disturbing, like crows circling high above an exhausted Rodrigues shortly before his capture.[13] There on the same island, Rodrigues finds an abandoned village, formerly inhabited by Christians, now crawling with feral cats. The nervous movements of a lizard on a white rock foreshadow the priest's betrayal at the hands of the weak-willed Kichijiro. When the priest collapses from unbearable thirst, lured to the authorities by Kichijiro's salty fish, the film raises the sounds of the forest around him. Flies frequently appear as reminders of the insignificance of human lives, as if to reduce martyrs to manure. The cicadas occasionally break up the otherwise solemn air of death, possibly singing for the indifference of time. Maggots gather, mosquitoes swarm, frogs croak, bats flitter. In the novel, thunder rolls in the distance while the magistrate Inoue grows angry at his victims.[14] All of these examples speak to an attunement, whereby the experiences of death, abandonment, betrayal, and even the violence of anger emerge from a source too deep for words. After Rodrigues finally tramples the *fumie*, a rooster crows in the far distance, not only for the sake of paralleling the gospels, but to raise the sun for a cold new day.[15]

Clearly the film does have a "flesh" of its own, which is to say, a rhythm in Merleau-Ponty's sense of an original moving jointure of reality. Scorsese creates a fabric of reality, a weave among the scenes, by evoking for the viewer a kind of monastic attunement, not unlike the experience of silence one might gain from an extended stay at, say, a Catholic or Buddhist monastery. With enough solitude the pilgrim begins to feel the world reemerge, so that what was not easily seen becomes vivid, and what was not heard becomes loud. For this reason the soundtrack had to be simple: few music pieces at all, mostly liturgical, or on occasion, the simple sound of a single instrument, e.g., a bass drum to mimic the ocean's darkness. Soon the background sounds of ocean, storm, and forest emerge for a harmony all their own. The film opens to a black screen, accompanied by the loud sounds of Japanese forest—insects, birds, and the like. Suddenly the raucous goes completely mute, and the title of the film appears, its white letters against a black background. The film ends in much the same way—black screen, with the successive sounds of beach, storm, and forest. When Rodrigues and Garrpe first speak with Valignano at the college, they sit within an unnecessarily large and vacant room, with flying buttresses over their heads—the sort of visual architecture the vast symmetry of which Scorsese will subsequently convey in natural scenery. As the three men ponder the rumor of Ferreira's apostasy, his trail having gone silent, the sound of the cicada eerily rises and falls over the dialogue. Much later, in one of the hardest cuts of the film sequence, immediately following Rodrigues' arrest, the sound of the cicada interrupts the scene change. The same happens at the sharp cut that passes from his apostasy to his fallen life remainder. These moments do not merely signal to the viewer his passing into the same oblivion as Ferreira, but also the silence of scene cuts themselves—the caesura, the interspersed nothings, that are as necessary for meaning as are spaces between words or sentences.

Most of the experiences of silence felt by the characters are facilitated by an awareness of another absence, namely death, which hangs over the entire narrative in varying degrees. Here we do well to apply another phenomenological concept—that of "mood"—for the sake of making sense of how we relate to an enjoining structure of reality that engulfs us. For instance, in the existential-phenomenological analysis of Martin Heidegger's *Being and Time*, mood is the result of my world mattering to me.[16] The sobering reality of my ecstatic existence is such that ultimately I find myself unable to "fit" into the semblance that I have helped construct. For an existentialist like Heidegger, death might cast a pall over the semblance; it might expose its inadequacies, opening cracks in the structure, through which the emptiness of my own existence begins to show. In the case of *Silence*, we observe instead that death opens fissures from which the silence might speak loudly and richly. The characters do feel the haunting emptiness of their projects as missionaries, as when Rodrigues comes upon an abandoned or burnt village, or he reflects upon the Jesuit's progresses in Japan, the historical trail of which seems to evaporate before his very eyes.[17] At the *bon* festival for the dead, shortly after his apostasy, the whole world turns ghostly for him—a dead man among the dead. Yet these experiences of the emptiness of his own project tend to open him to more than his own non-being. They make openings for the world to show itself from an original otherness, its flesh, in a manner that transcends our expectations for meaning and resists our possession of the world.

Language remains important for understanding the silence, even if only because of its power to conceal. Many times the indifference of the captors becomes apparent in the quiet subtleties of what they say and do not say to their prisoners. At other times the words, and actions, of speakers simply become pointless, and therefore drowned out to Rodrigues, as when the captors prove wholly apathetic in dialogue, or when Kichijiro has yet another moment of weakness. Scorsese injects several moments of linguistic misfire between the priests and the Japanese Christians: Garrpe keeps asking the converts to repeat themselves on account of their thick accents; Rodrigues feels compelled to correct their pronunciation of key Christian terms. In the middle of the film, Rodrigues finds himself interrogated by an assigned interpreter, who boils with resentment about previous priests, like one Father Cabral, for having despised everything Japanese—houses, food, customs, and the language itself.[18] The scene conveys a sense of regret by Rodrigues for needing the Japanese world to submit to the privileges of his linguistic framework. As for the communication of prayer itself, Rodrigues says to God in the novel that, "when I speak to you it seems as though I only blaspheme."[19] The apostatized Ferreira expresses similar limitations to an incredulous Rodrigues: "Deceiving myself? How can I explain the part of me that is not all self-deception?"[20] Ferreira goes on to insist that Japanese language and its cultural traditions prevent the Japanese from ever truly understanding Western theology. For this he uses the example of Francis Xavier's translation of *Deus* into *Dainichi* (Great Sun), which allowed the Japanese to retain a more animistic or polytheistic connection to the elements.[21]

These many silences of communication—the limitations, marginalisms, and concealments—exemplify a perspectivism central to the story. At Rodrigues' interrogation, beneath a blistering afternoon sun, he struggles to convince his captors of the universality or catholicity of his religious truths. "The truth is universal," he insists. "It's common to all countries at all times. That's why we call it the truth. . . ." His persecutor Inoue responds with a metaphor, that Christianity resembles a tree that might grow well in one environment but not in another. "Everyone knows that a tree that flourishes in one kind of earth may decay and die in another." Or, in the novel, "Father, have you never thought of the difference in the soil, the difference in the water?"[22] In a recent introduction that Scorsese wrote for Endo's novel, we find the following comment about the author's work, which underscores the problem. "In fact, it seems to me that *Silence*, his greatest novel and one that has become increasingly precious to me as the years have gone by, is precisely about the particular *and* the general. And it is finally about the first overwhelming the second."[23] Scorsese writes this within the context of talking about the perspective of authorship, and Endo's personal struggle to find Japanese roots for his own Catholic faith. The interpretation of this story as being about the particular *and* the general, not only one or the other, and the overwhelming of the general by way of the particular, suggests that for Scorsese at least, the story strikes a proper balance between absolutism and relativism, one where shared knowledge is indeed possible, but always at the expense of *my* angle.

Sometimes Scorsese undercuts the intellectualism of absolute thinking by allowing for the lessons on perspective to be felt at the gut. Shortly after Rodrigues faces the interrogation by Inoue, having boldly championed the universality of his beliefs, a disturbing scene ensues—one best described as an exercise in psychological warfare. Five of his fellow prisoners are taken into the center of the prison camp, in full view of all the Christians, and ordered by an official to step on the *fumie*. When each refuses in turn, the official then orders the guards to return them to their cells, with the exception of one, whom Endo refers to in the novel as the "one-eyed man."[24] Next, the official walks to the one-eyed man and matter-of-factly chops off his head with a samurai sword. In the film, as in the novel, Rodrigues does not actually see the event take place. Rather, he first hears the head of the decapitated Christian fall to the ground and roll, followed by the shrieking of a female prisoner. In order to finish the demonstration, the official then has Kichijiro, who had recently joined the prisoners in the camp—but possibly as a secret informant—step on the *fumie* and promptly gain his freedom. Of course the one-eyed man, like all cycloptic figures, symbolizes lack of perspective, which may apply more broadly to all of the Christians in the prison camp given the simplicity of their faith. Yet the deadly message sent from the captors is primarily for Rodrigues himself, although he does not see it coming. They cause the theologically persistent priest to feel as viscerally as possible—to "know" in the flesh of his stomach—what happens to the man who insists on seeing the world singularly, from the head.

The narration of *Silence* passes through different voices, the effect of which is to ground us in the necessity of perspective. The story begins from the pen of Rodrigues, in a series of letters, with no addressee. After his capture, the story proceeds without his pen, almost as if from an "objective" third person nowhere that also sees everywhere, complete with occasional glimpses into Rodrigues' own thoughts. Scorsese allows for the protagonist's inner monologue to surface during this phase, although sparingly. Here at the middle of the narrative, the temporary silence of the narrator's identity—the perspectiveless perspective—coincides with the swelling hubris of Rodrigues, determined to attain his own glorious martyrdom. After he apostatizes, the film enters a third stage of narration, told from the vantage point of a Dutch trader named Dieter Albrecht. (Endo actually closes the novel with the diary accounts of two men, one the clerk of a Dutch firm in Nagasaki, and the other, a Japanese officer overseeing Rodrigues' assigned residence.) The inwardness of Rodrigues slips further away from us, enveloped not only by his new Japanese identity, but also on account of the Dutch narrator not being able to relate to him. Each of the three major stages of narration in *Silence* frames his identity, with increased losses, until finally Rodrigues—now Okada San'emon—disappears, almost completely, into the silence of the God he is not allowed to speak for. Meanwhile, what we lose as viewers is not some objective, vertical, God's eye view of Rodrigues—we never had it—but rather the perspective that could belong to him alone.

Fortunately language does not only conceal what is most meaningful, such as the semblance of phenomena. Symbols are crucial for their ability to speak from the silence, and in ways that illuminate what is at stake ontologically. Here I do not have in mind simply the metaphors of film and literature that indirectly reinforce realities about the story, as with the incessant use of the fan by Inoue and other Japanese officials. In the novel, Endo also has them rubbing hands together, or hitting fans against hands, in order to illustrate their sense of power. Rather, the religious symbols in *Silence* have a way of gathering what might typically remain elusive to us and keeping that otherness extraordinary. They are more aptly described as ciphers of transcendence: they seem to glow with being, as though charged with a greater grace, their gestures an endless supply of interpretive possibilities.[25] The first villagers to meet Rodrigues and Garrpe soon notice with holy awe a small rustic wood cross hanging from the neck of the former. As Rodrigues hands his cross to a grateful Mokichi, a cricket chirps loudly, almost as if from the cross itself.[26] In the next Christian village, when Rodrigues runs short of symbols, he has to take apart his rosary and disperse its beads to believers—a fine reminder of the particular over the general. So eager are they for symbols that their persecutors burn and scatter the bodies of the martyrs to the ocean so that no relics remain for the Christians to venerate. Throughout the story, the characters are waging a spiritual battle over the symbols themselves, with the *fumie* at the center. They are told, ad nauseam, that trampling on it constitutes a "mere formality," when in fact they know better than to confuse it for the flatness of the ordinary linguistic sign, which can only point, and never amplify what is ineffable. In the end, Japanese officials catch Kichijiro possessing a tiny icon, safeguarded within an *omamuri*, or amulet, strung about his neck. Last of all, Scorsese shows the body of a deceased Rodrigues, denied a Christian burial, and subjected instead to a traditional Buddhist cremation, go up in flames, but with a little cross hidden in his hands, secretly inserted there by his Japanese wife.

One symbol is particularly important for the film—so much so that it speaks for all the others, and even for the "flesh" of film itself. In Macao, just before the departure to Japan, we see Rodrigues reflecting upon an icon of Christ as he stares up from his bed at the ceiling. "And as I prepare to do his work, I see his face before me," he says. "It fascinates me. I feel such great love for it." Scorsese chooses the face of Christ depicted in El Greco's *Veil of Veronica*, crowned with thorns and bleeding, yet wide-eyed. This marks a significant departure from the novel where Endo instead used as the object of Rodrigues' veneration the image of a triumphant resurrected savior, victorious over death, from the church of Borgo San Sepulchro in Italy.[27] Yet the result is not altogether different: whereas for the novel, Rodrigues learns to abandon the gloriously triumphant image for that of the ugly and despised *fumie*, the film allows him to grow with respect to the same icon. The *Veil of Veronica* icon type conveys, by way of its legend, something particularly pertinent to all imagery everywhere. It is a legend of the first icon of Christ, which supposedly comes from him wiping his face on Veronica's veil while en route to his crucifixion. The fabric takes the reverse image, and with it, a reminder of the power of the mirror in every icon of Christ. The second time Rodrigues comes upon it, he is drinking from a stream, immediately preceding his arrest. He sees his own face staring back at him in the water, followed by the face of the El Greco Christ, and then his own face again. In response, he goes mad for a moment, making grotesque faces and slapping the water with his head, as though the face of God had the power to disrupt his rationality.

The mirror at work in the painting, and in the film for that matter, is no mere reflection of the world, but the original showing of a world in itself, in such a way as to invert the way we see. Nicholas of Cusa, in *The Vision of God*, captures this mirroring quality of Christian iconography, when he describes the passivity of human perception as a standing before the Eye of God.[28] My seeing is, from the outset, already a being seen, in the sense that seeing requires me to enter an arena of visibility that precedes and makes possible all appearances. Furthermore, our experience of the Eye, says Nicholas, is like unto that of a mirror, which by its coincidence of opposites, *coincidentia oppositorum*, grants me the possibility of seeing things, not only as I would have them, but as they are given over to me in a look somehow their own. Merleau-Ponty observes a similar self-giving of the world in Dutch paintings when he says, "In paintings themselves we could see a figured philosophy of vision—its iconography, perhaps. It is no accident, for example, that frequently in Dutch paintings (as in many others) an interior in which no one is present is 'digested' by the 'round eye of the mirror.'"[29] The roles between the painter and the visible switch, explains Merleau-Ponty, so that it is no longer I who look at the forest, but the forest that looks at me. Likewise the possession of sight reverses for Rodrigues at the stream, so that he experiences himself being seen, before the dizzying Eye. In this moment we the viewers see two poles of film at work—on the one hand, its flesh and its Eye of God, whereby the film, in its original gift, "does not mean anything but itself," and on the other hand, what I have called above the seemingly endless stream of shifting perspectives, by way of camera angles, as though the film were being witnessed always from the vantage point of some face.[30]

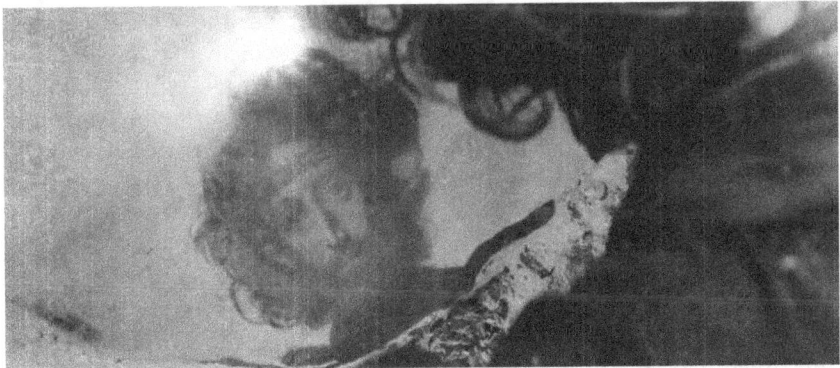

Figure 8.1. *Silence*. Winkler, Irwin, Randall Emmett, George Furla (Producers). Martin Scorsese (Director). *Silence*. Los Angeles: Paramount Pictures, 2016.

One of the great ironies of *Silence* is that the face of God just is that upon which one must walk, or the opening of a path, at least, into the incarnate. The El Greco image appears to Rodrigues a final time as he awaits his fate in the wooden cell of the prison camp. It stares up at him from the planked floor to give him peace; Scorsese wisely situates it in such a way as to have one crack between the floorboards run up and down Christ's face, between the eyes, just alongside of his nose. That crack is again the caesura—the death of God and not only the life of God—from which arises all negation, including the coincidence of opposites which transforms. When Rodrigues stands at last before the *fumie*, and gazes upon its Man of Sorrows image of suffering, he gets to hear God speak with human voice at last. This voice could be a product of Rodrigues' own imagination, and yet, presumably, we are to still take it as a revealing from the icon nonetheless. It sounds quite possibly like a synthesis of the voices of Andrew Garfield and Liam Neeson.[31] "Your life is with me now. Step." As he does so, the El Greco Christ flashes across the screen one more time, in complete silence, bordered in darkness, and then lost to that darkness. Rodrigues tramples, falls forward, and grasps the icon by hand, all at the same time. He has finally taken hold of the image, although only by sacrificing everything he thought he stood for.

At the point of denouement, where Rodrigues tramples and yet grasps the face of God, we learn an important lesson about the transformative and transcendental power of the image. The film had already pointed us to the ability of symbols to speak for the ineffable, and to do so in a manner that resists or disrupts human rationality. The primary symbols of Christianity—e.g., incarnation, death and resurrection—face us with great truths about the original rhythm or moving semblance of the world. For Rodrigues, the image pushes him to the brink of madness, and eventually to a radical inversion of his thought. But the primary symbolism shows its astounding flexibility in this story—as if the symbol were able to invert everything we had come to expect of *it*. When Rodrigues chooses to apostatize he actually embraces the whole "condescension" narrative of Christianity for himself—not in the conventional Christian ways of thinking about salvation as vertical, patriarchal, and gloriously triumphant, but in a mode that constitutes, arguably, a deeper grasp of what the symbolism always had to offer. He essentially chooses to damn himself (from Christianity) for the sake of those he loves, so he might take their sufferings upon himself. "You are now going to fulfill the most painful act of love that has ever been performed," says Ferreira. As Rodrigues stands before the innocent victims who hang upside down, their heads enclosed in pits of excrement, he finally sees them, not from the vantage point of his own spiritual aspirations, but as from the Eye—and thusly *with* the transformative power that speaks through the symbolism in its most jaw-dropping historical moments. For Rodrigues the move is thoroughly kenotic: he must empty himself to the point of the unraveling of his world as it seems to hold together. Or, to use more Nietzschean language, he "goes under."[32]

Rodrigues seizes the opportunity to become Christ, that master of all inversion, by "betraying" the very tradition that had struggled to keep his image sacrosanct only to have made the mistake of riveting it in place. This betrayal of the ossified tradition is not altogether different from the one that punctuates Dostoevsky's "Grand Inquisitor" passage, where the prisoner, who had remained silent, finally kisses the aged inquisitor's bloodless lips. *Silence* is even more thoroughly a story about betrayal—its multifaceted possibilities, and ultimately, its needfulness. Although Kichijiro epitomizes what Rodrigues most wants to avoid becoming—a turncoat instead of a martyr—the priest feels compelled to go "even to one such as this." On the abandoned island, where Kichijiro may well have sold out the villagers, it is not clear which man is hunting after whom. As the film progresses, Scorsese keeps reducing the amount of time between each of Kichijiro's betrayals, until finally, the apostatized priest is no longer able to absolve him, only to be present with him face-to-face in an unspoken communion. But Kichijiro is not the sole representative of betrayal in *Silence* any more than Judas is for the gospels. The cock crows for Peter, the people shout "Crucify," the religious figures . . ., the politicians . . ., and so forth. Only one face betrays it all, and stands in holy silence.

The film offers a layered sense of reality commensurate with an ecstatic reading of human existence, one reminiscent of Merleau-Ponty's phenomenological use of the term "silence." Moreover, Scorsese's *Silence* shows us important possibilities for the ineffable in film, some of which are not so easily conveyed by way of the novel alone. Much of this he accomplishes negatively, by sharpening our sense of the limits of human existence, through suffering and death, and in communication, through the concealments and boundaries of language. An essential negation permeates all of this silence, its caesura allowing for every break of scene and screen shot, limiting with the perspective of the camera angle, overshadowing with mood, cloaking phenomena as background, and ultimately, juxtaposing the viewer to the world of the film itself. At other times the silence speaks more positively—as in the presence of symbols, for instance, which allow for the crystallization of what is at work at an ontological level. The silence of a film—any film—is all the ways in which it speaks to us from the world's gesture, as though the world of the film had a togetherness and motion of its own that only surfaces in language to greater and lesser degrees. Properly speaking, silence does not constitute a representation of what happens in the so-called real world exterior to film. Instead, it conveys world through a rhythm that adheres to its own mysterious order, the inner workings of which the director comes to realize in the film's making. Scorsese readies the viewer for this rhythm by settling him or her into a kind of monastic attunement whereby natural surroundings are allowed to emerge again in their sensual fullness, whether in a cacophony of forest sounds or the rich expanse of an island sky. All of this has a texture about it, a flesh, in which the phenomena are conjoined. This flesh brings with it a sense of place, so as to put us before a world—as though before a face, which could look at us from its own eyes. This face can speak to us, from the silence, and often by way of symbols, much like a mirror that reverses our ordinary sensibilities about who we are and what surrounds us.

NOTES

1. Irwin Winkler, Randall Emmett, George Furla (Producers). Martin Scorsese (Director). *Silence*. Los Angeles: Paramount Pictures, 2016. Shusaku Endo, *Silence*, trans. William Johnston (London: Peter Owen, 2016).
2. Mark W. Dennis and Darren J. N. Middleton, "Introduction: *Silence* in the World," ed. Mark W. Dennis and Darren J. N. Middleton, in *Approaching Silence: New Perspectives on Shusaku Endo's Classic Novel*, xi-xxiv (New York: Bloomsbury Academic, 2015), xxii.
3. Glen A. Mazis, *Merleau-Ponty and the Face of the World: Silence, Ethics, Imagination, and Poetic Ontology* (Albany: State University of New York Press, 2016), 21-24.
4. Mazis, *Face of the World*, 27.
5. Heraclitus says, "They do not apprehend how being at variance it agrees with itself [lit. how being brought apart it is brought together with itself]: there is a back-stretched connexion, as in the bow and the lyre." G. S. Kirk, J. E. Raven, and M. Schofield. *The Presocratic Philosophers*, Second Edition (Cambridge: Cambridge University Press, 2003), 192.
6. Maurice Merleau-Ponty, "The Film and the New Psychology," in *Sense and Non-Sense*, eds. Hubert L. Dreyfus and Patricia Allen Dreyfus, 48-59 (Evanston: Northwestern University Press, 1964).
7. Merleau-Ponty, "Film and New Psychology," 57.
8. Merleau-Ponty, "Film and New Psychology," 55.
9. Mauro Carbone, *The Flesh of Images: Merleau-Ponty between Painting and Cinema*, trans. Marta Nijhuis (Albany: State University of New York Press, 2011), 56.
10. Endo, *Silence*, 98.
11. Mazis, *Face of the World*, 37-38.
12. Maurice Merleau-Ponty, "Indirect Language and the Voices of Silence," in *The Merleau-Ponty Aesthetics Reader*, trans. Michael B. Smith, ed. Galen A. Johnson (Evanston: Northwestern University Press, 1993), 107-8.
13. Endo, *Silence*, 106.
14. Endo, *Silence*, 134.
15. Endo, *Silence*, 264.
16. Martin Heidegger, *Being and Time*, trans. John Macquarrie and Edward Robinson (New York: Harper & Row, 1962), 177.
17. Endo, *Silence*, 150-52.
18. Endo, *Silence*, 137.
19. Endo, *Silence*, 186.
20. Endo, *Silence*, 222.
21. Endo, *Silence*, 230-31.
22. Endo, *Silence*, 171.
23. Martin Scorsese, "Introduction," in *Silence*, Shusaku Endo (London: Peter Owen Publishers, 2016), 5.
24. Endo, *Silence*, 184.

25. For Karl Jaspers' theory of ciphers, see Karl Jaspers, *Philosophy*, Vol. 3, trans. E. B. Ashton (Chicago: The University of Chicago Press, 1971), 113-208. "I do not think beyond the cipher, for its glow is that of being." Jaspers, *Philosophy*, 115.

26. This call of transcendence is strongly reminiscent of Zen Master Kakuan's *Ten Bulls*, wherein the pilgrim hears the encouraging sound of crickets and the nightingale beckoning him to enlightenment. Kakuan, "Ten Bulls: The Zen Oxherding Pictures," trans. Nyogen Senzaki and Paul Reps, in *The Buddha and His Teachings*, eds. Bercholz, Samuel and Sherab Chödzin Kohn (Boston: Shambhala, 2003).

27. Endo, *Silence*, 39.

28. Nicholas of Cusa, *The Vision of God*, trans. Emma Gurney Salter (New York: Frederick Ungar Publishing Co., 1960), 37-38.

29. Maurice Merleau-Ponty, "Eye and Mind," in *The Merleau-Ponty Aesthetics Reader*, trans. Michael B. Smith, ed. Galen A. Johnson (Evanston: Northwestern University Press, 1993), 129. (pp. 121-149)

30. Merleau-Ponty, "Film and New Psychology," 57.

31. One could also argue that the voice of Christ in this scene sounds quite similar to that of Father Valignano, who reluctantly sent Rodrigues on his path at the beginning of the film. As such, it could point in a deconstructive way to the origin of Rodrigues.

32. For good examples of Nietzsche's *untergehen*, see "Zarathustra's Prologue." Friederich Nietzsche, *Thus Spoke Zarathustra*, trans. Walter Kaufman (New York: Random House, 1995), 9-25.

BIBLIOGRAPHY

Carbone, Mauro. *The Flesh of Images: Merleau-Ponty between Painting and Cinema*, translated by Marta Nijhuis. Albany: State University of New York Press, 2011.

Dennis, Mark W. and Darren J. N. Middleton. "Introduction: *Silence* in the World." In *Approaching Silence: New Perspectives on Shusaku Endo's Classic Novel*, edited by Mark W. Dennis and Darren J. N. Middleton, xi-xxiv. New York: Bloomsbury Academic, 2015.

Dostoevsky, Fyodor. *The Grand Inquisitor*. Translated by Constance Garnett. Edited by Charles B. Guignon. Indianapolis: Hackett Publishing Company, 1993.

Endo, Shusaku. *Silence*. Translated by William Johnston. London: Peter Owen, 2016.

Heidegger, Martin. *Being and Time*. Translated by John Macquarrie and Edward Robinson. New York: Harper & Row, 1962.

Jaspers, Karl. *Philosophy*, Vol. 3. Translated by E. B. Ashton. Chicago: The University of Chicago Press, 1971.

Kakuan. "Ten Bulls: The Zen Oxherding Pictures," in *The Buddha and His Teachings*, translated by Nyogen Senzaki and Paul Reps, edited by Bercholz, Samuel and Sherab Chödzin, 211-22. Kohn. Boston: Shambhala, 2003.

Kirk, G. S., J. E. Raven, and M. Schofield. *The Presocratic Philosophers*, Second Edition. Cambridge: Cambridge University Press, 2003.

Mazis, Glen A. *Merleau-Ponty and the Face of the World: Silence, Ethics, Imagination, and Poetic Ontology*. Albany: State University of New York Press, 2016.

Merleau-Ponty, Maurice. "The Film and the New Psychology." In *Sense and Non-Sense*, edited by Hubert L. Dreyfus and Patricia Allen Dreyfus, 48-59. Evanston: Northwestern University Press, 1964.

Merleau-Ponty, Maurice. "Indirect Language and the Voices of Silence," in *The Merleau-Ponty Aesthetics Reader*, translated by Michael B. Smith, edited by Galen A. Johnson, 71-130. Evanston: Northwestern University Press, 1993.

———. "On the Phenomenology of Language," in *Signs*, translated by Richard C. McCleary, 84-97. Evanston: Northwestern University Press, 1964.

Nicholas of Cusa. *The Vision of God*. Translated by Emma Gurney Salter. New York: Frederick Ungar Publishing Co., 1960.

Nietzsche, Friederich. *Thus Spoke Zarathustra*. Translated by Walter Kaufman. New York: Random House, 1995.

Scorsese, Martin. "Introduction," in *Silence*, Shusaku Endo, 5-8. London: Peter Owen Publishers, 2016.

Winkler, Irwin, Randall Emmett, George Furla (Producers). Martin Scorsese (Director). *Silence*. Los Angeles: Paramount Pictures, 2016.

NINE

La Passion de Jeanne d'Arc and the Cadence of Images

John B. Brough

Robert Sokolowski writes that a single image, such as a painting, can possess a cadence or rhythm.¹ A film is a whole formed from many images in succession. It, too, has a rhythm or cadence, but in its case through the successive flow of the images composing it. I will attempt to show in this chapter that this is preeminently true of Karl Theodor Dreyer's *La Passion de Jeanne d'Arc*.² The film covers the brief stretch of time consumed by Joan's trial and execution. The trial as it unfolds in the film is twofold. There is the legal proceeding, and there is the trial of Joan's faith, of her integrity and being. The two are entwined, which is why the trial becomes her passion.³ Passion here is a matter of undergoing, but also of action and choice. Joan undergoes a brutal prosecution and imprisonment, and, at one point, chooses to sign the confession that will save her from the stake. In a final decision, however, she withdraws the confession and is executed. If, in Karl Jaspers' view, it is in extreme situations that one's existential mettle is put to the test, then it is hard to imagine a situation more extreme than the one in which Joan finds herself. She must choose between her physical existence and her *Existenz* as a being who transcends the physical. She cannot preserve both.

La Passion de Jeanne d'Arc is a film notable for many reasons: the brilliance of Maria Falconetti's performance as Joan; the austerity of its settings, when settings are there at all; its handling of space, sometimes contradictory and disorienting. But most strikingly, it is a film of close-ups; indeed, it is made up almost exclusively of images of human faces and their expressions, "microphysiognomic close-ups," as Bela Balázs called them.[4]

Such a cascade of images, even of the human face, poses the danger of shattering the film's unity. What might emerge, as Eisenstein thought, would not really be a film but photographic confetti, however wonderful each individual photo might be.[5] Dreyer knew how disconcerting his "aggressive close-ups" often were. He described them as "jumping unannounced on the screen and demanding the right to an independent existence," behaving "like a flock of noisy troublemakers."[6] David Bordwell, noting the absence of spatial cues and the continuity of classical screen space that might supply a context for the close-ups and ensure a "smooth flow and effortless intelligibility," argues that it is the "developing narrative situation of the character Jeanne" that unifies and organizes the film.[7] This is certainly true in a substantive sense—the film is about Joan's passion—but it does not explain how a coherent narrative picture of Joan can emerge in the midst of Dreyer's unruly flock. Indeed, Bordwell hints that Joan's character unifies the film in many instances despite the barrage of close-ups. I want to suggest, however, that it is the cadence or rhythm of the images that secures the unity that Eisenstein failed to find in the film. It is through the rhythms of the close-ups of expressive faces that the story of Joan's passion takes shape. The facial images may indeed draw attention to themselves individually, and the rapidity with which they follow one another may be disconcerting and even dizzying, but the rhythmic way in which Dreyer arranges them lets the central themes and motifs of the film emerge and develop with distinctive force, finally reaching resolution in the film's powerful final scenes.

One might say that Dreyer weds discontinuity-editing with continuity-editing in the service of following Joan's journey through suffering, self-betrayal, and guilt, to a final, redemptive decision that at once restores her integrity, her *Existenz* and transcendence, but also entails her death. Joan's external and internal trials ride the film's rhythm, or better, rhythms, for the film is polyrhythmic. Balázs formulates this relation of internal life and external rhythm when he writes that in the films of certain directors, including Dreyer: "The dramatic rhythm of the story is transposed into visual picture-rhythm and external, formal rhythm steps up the speed of the internal drama," conveying to us "internal storms, the quiverings of internal tension."[8] The rhythm of facial close-ups not only tells us "things for which we have no words—the rhythm and tempo of changes in facial expression can also indicate the oscillation of moods which cannot be put into words."[9]

This becomes particularly clear in the film's preeminent rhythm: the dialogical. Joan's passion unfolds in a process of questioning and cross-examination. It may seem odd that questioning and answering should play such a prominent role in a film without sound, which is why some critics at the time saw *Joan* as a film struggling to escape its silence. In

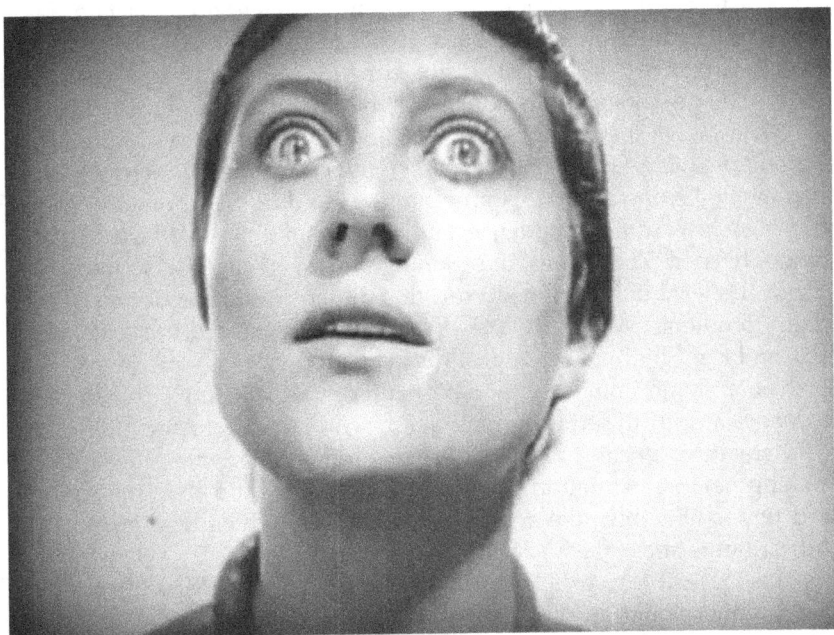

Figure 9.1. *La Passion de Joanne d'Arc.* **La Société générale (Producer). Karl Theodor Dreyer (Director).** *La Passion de Jeanne d'Arc.* **Paris, France, 1928.**

fact, the interrogation of Joan is gripping and revealing precisely because it develops in the silent, rhythmic interplay of images of Joan's face and the faces of her judges. We see, as Balázs puts it, "a series of duels between looks and frowns, duels in which eyes clash instead of sounds . . . We can follow every attack and riposte of these duels on the faces of the combatants . . ."[10] There are, of course, intertitles, but they do not disrupt the progress of the narrative. On the contrary, they enrich the rhythm of dialogical images and further the narrative flow.

Perhaps the most striking and effective instance of this rhythmic merging of images and intertitles comes toward the end of the film when Joan turns the accusation that she has been sent by the devil back against her judges. "To make me suffer, the devil has sent you," she says in an intertitle, which is immediately followed by a close-up of the faces of two of the judges reflecting their stunned reactions. Joan then turns slightly, taking aim at new targets: "and you" the intertitle reads, followed by the image of two more faces looking aghast; and then "and you" a third time, with yet another microphysiognomy showing great distress, and then the rhythm repeats itself yet again. The cadence here approaches a staccato pitch as Joan's accusers are successively exposed.

A textual dimension clearly enters the film through the intertitles, but it enters it in other and more significant ways as well. A scribe continually records the interrogation, transforming the judges' questions and Joan's replies into a historical record. The judges seek clear and concise answers that can become part of the court record justifying a verdict of guilty. The questions involve doctrines that in the hands of the judges are effectively laws specifying what must and must not be said, rather than matters of living faith. From Jaspers' perspective, these doctrines could also evoke "ciphers" that escape the legal and textual domain entirely and push toward transcendence, and which therefore involve things that cannot be said. The judges' questioning, however, suggests that they are not in the least bit concerned with this dimension of the doctrines they claim to defend. With only a few exceptions—glimpsed in subtle, tenuous, and rare rhythms of support for Joan—the judges reduce everything to the literal and immanent, and particularly to the textual. This suggests a deeper aim of the trial: to tame Joan, who appears to the judges as a wild creature, a center of unbridled freedom and private interiority, by making her into something public and objective, and thus manageable and understandable, like a predictable empirical thing or a text in their authoritative and orderly world.

This view of Joan as a free subject is reflected with particular force in the rhythm of questions about what she wears. When asked whether it is God who has ordered her to dress "like a man," she replies in the affirmative. She tells the judges that when she has accomplished her mission, she will again put on a woman's clothes. The judges are clearly distressed, to the point of obsession, that Joan dresses like a man. Her attire itself represents a transcending of the established social order, as does her role as a military leader. For a woman to dress as a man is as unnatural to the judges as it would be for a man to dress as a woman. In their estimation, Joan's attire is a violation of being, of the essential, empirical order of things, and therefore "shameless, abominable to God." But Joan refuses to be defined as essentially this or that. Her sex may be a fact in the empirical world, but it is not her essence. Her essence is her liberty, in which case she is free to dress as a man if her mission, which has defined the empirical situation in which she has made her choices, demands it. The judges want Joan to *be* a woman in the way in which an ordinary thing in the world is simply the thing it is. But Joan, though she is in the world, is not of it; she enjoys phenomenal, empirical being, like the three-legged stool on which she sits in the courtroom, but she transcends what is fixed and determined. She resists complete absorption into the text of the world with its unbending laws. She chooses to dress as a man because she has chosen to drive the English out of France.

There is a revealing scene in Joan's cell that gives the measure of her resolve. Exhausted and distraught by her grueling interrogation in the opening courtroom session, Joan asks that she be allowed to hear Mass. At first, Bishop Cauchon, the presiding judge, responds to her request with rage, but then, following a whispered suggestion by Loyseleur, the most crafty of the judges, says that she may attend Mass—but only if she stops wearing men's clothing. Joan refuses, drawing Cauchon's rebuke that "you would rather dress as man than attend Mass! . . . You are no daughter of God. You are Satan's creature." A close-up of her face shows the agony her choice has cost her.

The duel over what Joan wears gives way to the dialogical rhythm that dominates the rest of the film until the final scene. One might call this the "confessional" rhythm. If Joan can be induced into signing a confession admitting that she has been misled by Satan, that she has forsaken the church and violated its doctrinal laws and texts, she will have been brought under control. "The desire for real selfhood," James Schamus writes, is set over against "its counterpart, the rhetoric of the authoritative, containing text."[11] But this is the text as the theologian-judges interpret it. At one point in the trial, a judge asks Joan if she does "not feel that these learned doctors are wiser than you?" Joan replies: "But God is even wiser." The "learned doctors" lay claim to knowledge, thus reducing transcendence to immanence, packaging it in doctrines and dogmas subject to their authority. "God" may be the "cipher" through which Joan touches transcendence, but in contrast to the learned doctors, she does not claim to understand God, at least not in the way one might be said to know the meaning of a text or even the necessities governing the empirical order. This becomes progressively more apparent throughout the trial. When asked whether God hates the English, Joan responds: "I do not know if God loves or hates the English." When she expresses her confidence that she will be delivered from prison, the judges, ever literalists, ask when this will happen. "I know neither the day nor the hour," Joan responds. When she is asked whether she is in a state of grace, she answers: "If I am, may God keep me there. If I am not, may God grant it to me." In each of these instances, the images of the judges' faces show their displeasure and discomfort with her responses. They are, of course, frustrated that their prey has slipped their inquisitorial traps; but on a deeper level, they sense, perhaps, that they are confronting a unique subject who exists on an entirely different plane from theirs. They may use the language of transcendence, but they remain fixed in the realm of immanence, that is, the world of things and texts. Their questions emanate from an objective, public, and authoritative ground; Joan's responses come from the perspective of genuine transcendence, which can be glimpsed in the images of her face, but resists formulaic expression. The judges seek the spurious transparency of texts; Joan expresses the transparency of being-oneself. The "language" of transcendence is at best oblique and often simply silence. Language cannot encompass the all-encompassing; the subject can only hope to touch it through symbols and ciphers. Balázs's rhythmic duel of expressive faces thus reveals itself to be "a battle between self and authority," between Joan's integrity and freedom and an institutional authority that demands conformity to its laws and requires from Joan a written confession of her transgressions.[12]

The judges are unscrupulous in their campaign to extract that confession. The first interrogation session, during which Joan is subjected to verbal abuse and spat upon by one of the judges—a close-up shows the spittle striking her cheek—fails to make much prosecutorial progress. Loyseleur, the shrewd judge, then forges a letter purporting to have been sent by King Charles telling Joan that he will march on Rouen with a great army and that he has sent Loyseleur, "a devoted priest," whom Joan can trust. Joan takes Loyseleur's expression of "great" sympathy and feigned kindness at face value, and, in the second round of interrogation, turns to him at each question and receives a silent nod signaling that it would be acceptable to answer the judges's questions affirmatively. To the question whether she is certain that she will be saved, Joan, guided by Loyseleur, answers that she is. At that point, Massieu, a young monk who is genuinely sympathetic to Joan (the part is played by Antonin Artaud), steps forward to warn her to be careful: "It's a dangerous answer." Massieu is dressed down savagely by Cauchon and steps back into the shadows. There is a rhythm of support for Joan in the film; but each time it appears, it is quickly suppressed.

The judges, still unable to draw a confession out of Joan, take her to the torture chamber. There she is presented with a prepared, written confession. Cauchon tells her that if she does not sign, "the Church will abandon you. . . . You will be alone." Joan responds: "Yes, alone. Alone with God." She refuses to sign. Then, in a dizzying rhythm of close-up images, the machines of torture spin and mesh like malevolent gears, pulling Joan into a vortex of terror. She still refuses to sign. At that point, she collapses and is carried to her cell.

After she is bled and regains consciousness, Cauchon appears at her bedside. She is weak and fears that she is close to death. It is now Cauchon's turn to advance the rhythm of feigned sympathy. He tells Joan, with the slightest wisp of a reassuring smile, that the Church is merciful and "always welcomes the misguided lamb." Joan appears relieved and hopeful. She extends her hand to touch his, and does touch it for an instant, but he immediately recoils, withdrawing his hand from Joan's reach, a frown, perhaps a hint of panic, sweeping across his face. On Joan's face, the image of isolation could not be more stark. She has no human support. "In the patriarchal society depicted in [Dreyer's] films," as Jytte Jensen writes, "an institutionalized relationship of men and the written word takes precedence over the possibility of emotional relations between human beings."[13]

There is still her relation to God, however, and Joan is informed that the Eucharist is being brought to her. A priest-judge enters her cell. He raises the host, but just as Joan is about to receive it, the confession is thrust in front of her. If she signs, she can receive God and escape death.

Transcendence is being offered in the symbol of the host, but in a corrupt form, as a thing and a bribe. She refuses to sign. The priest withdraws the host and leaves the cell. Joan, a tear coming down her cheek, buries her face in her hands. Cauchon turns on her: "Do you not know it is the body of Christ you refuse? Do you not see that you outrage God by your obstinacy?" The outrage, of course, lies in the judges' use of the Eucharist, and of Joan's intense desire to receive it, as means to secure their ends. Joan, on the other hand, has again chosen to maintain her integrity, which is one with her faith. Not to receive the Eucharist in these circumstances is to secure her being and to maintain her relation to transcendence.

With this scene, the judges appear to have failed once and for all to force Joan to sign the confession. They alert the executioner. But then, in a courtyard setting adjacent to a cemetery where a fresh grave is being dug, they make a last attempt to get Joan to sign the confession. She is addressed, harshly at first, by the same priest who had earlier withdrawn the host. At the same time, she—and we—see a skull tossed up by the gravedigger's spade, worms twisting through its empty sockets. The priest then shifts from haranguing to pleading, even returning to the rhythm of sympathy— "Joan, we have great sympathy for you." Pressed by an onrush of threats and images of death, battered by harsh condemnations alternating with expressions of sympathy, Joan succumbs and signs. Since she is illiterate and cannot write her name, Loyseleur guides her hand in making the signature. You have "done a good day's work," he tells her. "You have saved your life and your soul." This she may indeed have done, but at the expense of the loss of her self, as we can see in the sadness depicted in the close-up of her face.

Cauchon reads a decision condemning Joan to life in prison. She is removed to her cell where a barber cuts her hair, which we see falling to the floor in snippets around her feet and next to a simple crown of straw, which we have seen her weaving in her cell and which, in an earlier scene, taunting guards placed on her head in a mockery of Christ's passion. As the barber sweeps up the hair cuttings, he also sweeps up the crown, another Jasperian "cipher," and tosses it aside. At that moment, Joan is awakened to the transcendence she had forsaken in signing the confession. She sees her self, her existence, being swept away with the crown. She asks the barber to bring back the judges. They return, and Joan recants her confession. "Everything I said was for fear of the stake." This time there are no threats and condemnations from the judges. Cauchon asks, "Have you anything else to tell us?" She indicates that she does not. She has reached a depth of existential self-understanding that she cannot put into language. In that silence, and in the judges' acceptance of it, she emerges as "the victor in the battle of discourses."[14]

The final scenes after Joan recants reprise the themes that rhythmically appear throughout the film, transforming them and bringing them to conclusion. When she sees her crown swept away, she realizes that she has failed. She has lied and is now truly guilty of a "great sin": "I have denied God to save my life." Her sin is not that she has broken the Church's rules or transgressed its doctrines, as the judges think. Her sin is that she has abused her freedom and turned it against herself. She confesses to Massieu, the monk who has been a sympathetic presence for her throughout the trial, but this is confession in a new and authentic sense. It is made privately, in living speech that no one but her confessor can hear, and the contents of which no one can reveal. There is no signature, no public, written trace of what she has said, for her contrition touches her unique being, her relation to transcendence, which is incommensurable with the public being-in-the-world that marks a text deposited in an archive, such as the transcript of her trial.

Failure and guilt are part of the perpetual process—the trial—of choosing to be oneself. So, too, is insight. In preparing her for death, Massieu returns to the same series of questions the judges asked Joan early in the proceedings. Now, however, the answers are different. "How can you still believe you are sent by God?" Massieu asks. Joan replies: "His ways are not our ways." The failure to know is a sign of the reality of transcendence, as James Collins observes.[15] The Wholly Other, all-encompassing being-itself, cannot be encompassed by our finite knowledge. "And the great victory"—the victory that Joan probably originally thought would be a military conquest? Joan's reply: "My martyrdom." "And the deliverance?" "Death." King Charles never appears with his great army. Joan must deliver herself, not from prison, not from death, but from self-betrayal. She does not *choose* death. She chooses to be herself, and that means, in the situation in which she finds herself, that she must accept death. This, not her signed confession, has been her "good day's work."

The rhythm of the Eucharist also continues. The priest who had earlier refused her communion and later berated her appears again, now with the Eucharistic viaticum. This time no written confession is thrust toward her. She simply receives the host. She is then given a rough one-piece shift, a piece of women's clothing perhaps, if only barely. She can wear it now, for her mission has been accomplished. She may not have liberated France, but she has restored her own freedom and integrity.

Complex rhythms, intense and rapid, fill the final scene. Images of Joan bound to the stake, of flames rising, of birds flying overhead, of soldiers brutally beating back rioting crowds, repeat themselves again and again with accelerating speed. The flames grow higher, Joan's body bends and finally disappears in the inferno, and the birds continue to soar overhead. Joan has not escaped isolation and suffering. She has accepted their reality as the condition of her transcendence. I would like to think that is what Stanley Cavell had in mind when he wrote: "The fullest image of absolute isolation is in Dreyer's *Joan of Arc*, when Falconetti at the stake looks up to see a flight of birds wheel over her with the sun in their wings. They, there, are free. They are waiting in their freedom, to accompany her soul. She knows it. But first there is the body to be gone through jutterly."[16]

NOTES

1. Robert Sokolowski, "Visual Intelligence in Painting," *The Review of Metaphysics*, 59/2 (2008): 333-54.
2. La Société générale (Producer), Karl Theodor Dreyer (Director), *La Passion de Jeanne d'Arc*. Paris, France, 1928.
3. A third element is involved here: The passion of Christ. Christ's passion, adumbrated in many symbols throughout the film, is less a matter of rhythm, however, than of the horizon in which the particular rhythms of the film and its images move. To do justice to it would require a second chapter. Here I have chosen to discuss several important rhythmic patterns that emerge against the background of this horizon.
4. Bela Balázs, *Theory of the Film: Character and Growth of a New Art* (New York: Dover Publications, 1970).
5. David Bordwell, *The Films of Carl-Theodor Dreyer* (Berkeley: University of California Press, 1981).
6. Bordwell, *Films of Dreyer*, 235 note 5.
7. Bordwell, *Films of Dreyer*, 71, 78, 84.
8. Balázs, *Theory of Film*, 129, 131.
9. Balázs, *Theory of the Film*, 72.
10. Balázs, *Theory of the Film*, 74.
11. James Schamus, "Dreyer's Textual Realism," *Carl Th. Dreyer*, ed. James Jensen, 59-66 (New York: The Museum of Modern Art, 1988), 61.
12. Balázs, *Theory of Film*, 61.
13. Jytte Jensen, "Heretics, Witches, Saints, and Sinners," in *Carl Th. Dreyer*, ed. Jytte Jensen, 49-58 (New York: The Museum of Modern Art, 1988), 50.
14. Bordwell, *Films of Dreyer* (Berkeley: University of California Press, 1981), 91.
15. James Collins, *The Existentialists: A Critical Study* (Chicago: Henry Regnery, 1952), 113.
16. Stanley Cavell, *The World Viewed: Reflections on the Ontology of Film* (Cambridge: Harvard University Press, 1979), 159.

BIBLIOGRAPHY

Balázs, Bela. *Theory of the Film: Character and Growth of a New Art*. New York: Dover Publications, 1970.
Bordwell, David. *The Films of Carl-Theodor Dreyer*. Berkeley: University of California Press, 1981.
Cavell, Stanley. *The World Viewed: Reflections on the Ontology of Film*. Cambridge: Harvard University Press, 1979.
Collins, James. *The Existentialists: A Critical Study*. Chicago: Henry Regnery, 1952.
Jensen, Jytte. "Heretics, Witches, Saints, and Sinners." In *Carl Th. Dreyer*, edited by Jytte Jensen, Jytte, 49-58. New York: The Museum of Modern Art, 1988.
La Société générale (Producer). Karl Theodor Dreyer (Director). *La Passion de Jeanne d'Arc*. Paris, France, 1928.
Schamus, James. "Dreyer's Textual Realism." *Carl Th. Dreyer*, edited by James Jensen, 59-66. New York: The Museum of Modern Art, 1988.
Sokolowski, Robert. "Visual Intelligence in Painting." *The Review of Metaphysics*, 59/2 (2008): 333-54.

TEN

Ciphers of Transcendence in *2001: A Space Odyssey*

Kevin L. Stoehr

This chapter discusses some of the ways in which viewings of Stanley Kubrick's landmark science-fiction film *2001: A Space Odyssey* (1968) may evoke speculation about the idea of transcendence through an experiential challenge to the audience's customary modes of perception and reflection.[1] Such a challenge can be described in terms of what philosopher Karl Jaspers called "ciphers of transcendence" that help to occasion certain "limit situations." These are situations in which the individual can recognize, come to terms with, and go beyond habituated forms of rationality. Ciphers differ from symbols, according to Jaspers, in the sense that symbols represent objects or objective realities while ciphers indicate the ineffable "Encompassing" of reality. This "Encompassing" is indicated by a type of pre-conceptual horizon of indeterminacy that transcends the distinction between the subjective and the objective, underlying, rather than directly corresponding to, our particular intuitions and cognitions.[2]

Kubrick's movie points repeatedly to that background presence of the unconditional by shattering the conditions of our familiar experiences, especially conventional movie-watching—even producing at times a sense of what theologian Rudolf Otto calls "the numinous," an experience of mystery that is both overwhelming and magnetizing (*mysterium tremendum et fascinans*).[3] Ciphers in *2001* include the enigmatic black monoliths, the pulsing kaleidoscope of shapes and colors that make up the Star Gate journey, the abstract Star Child in the final shot, and the very images of vast interstellar space. On a narrative level, Kubrick's film addresses the theme of the human experience of the transcendent in the form of encounters with extraterrestrial intelligence, encounters that may also engender speculations about the nature of metaphysical reality. Cinematically, Kubrick makes recurring use of techniques that evoke the audience's feeling of detachment from the "earthly" realm of physical Nature and that also summon the viewer to a philosophical interpretation of visual ciphers. He does this through his manipulation of both cinematic space and cinematic time as well as his intentional uses of narrative ambiguity. This chapter will explore some of these techniques along with their implications.

There are three forms of transcendence involved here:

1. a type of cinematic experience that may result in a feeling of "disembodied presence," to steal a term from phenomenologist Hubert Dreyfus,[4] thus disrupting the viewer's familiar frameworks of cognition that are rooted in patterns of bodily perception;
2. the evocation of questions concerning ways in which the individual may seek to go beyond conventional forms of human nature—especially with the assistance of technology and, more specifically, machine intelligence; and
3. a consideration of questions regarding the possibility of humans experiencing or knowing "the Transcendent" in the form of conceptual insight into the true nature of metaphysical reality.

Related to these forms of transcendence are the moral, psychological, and even spiritual implications of the human need for such an "other-worldly" experience or transformation. Does Kubrick's film, in its depiction of transcendent forms of intelligence intervening in human evolution, conclude on an optimistic or pessimistic note in terms of our place and future in the cosmos?

By way of introduction, it must be said that the fact that Kubrick's overall body of cinematic work mostly dwells upon the more irrational aspects of human nature does not necessarily imply that he was, overall, a pessimist. In fact, Kubrick was told by a *Playboy* interviewer back in 1968, while discussing his recently released *2001*, that some critics had "detected not only a deep pessimism but also a kind of misanthropy" in his work.[5] This was especially the case, according to the interviewer, when considering the "curiously aloof and detached" style of his film *Dr. Strangelove*. And recent audiences who had seen *2001* were mystified enough to ponder whether the film's creators—chiefly Kubrick and his cowriter Arthur C. Clarke—were delivering a positive or negative message regarding human nature and its potential. Kubrick replied to the interviewer:

> You don't stop being concerned with man because you recognize his essential absurdities and frailties and pretensions. To me, the only real immorality is that which endangers the species; and the only absolute

evil, that which threatens its annihilation. In the deepest sense, I believe in man's potential and in his capacity for progress. In *Strangelove*, I was dealing with the inherent irrationality in man that threatens to destroy him; that irrationality is with us as strongly today, and must be conquered. But a recognition of insanity doesn't imply a celebration of it — nor a sense of despair and futility about the possibility of curing it.[6]

Almost since the release of *2001*, there has been some debate as to whether the movie presents a generally optimistic or pessimistic view of humanity and its place in "the big picture." The cosmic vision of the Star Child in the final shot has been viewed by many as a life-affirming symbol indicating the transformation of astronaut Bowman, as some form of archetypal human, into a newly enlightened species. One thinks here of Nietzsche's idea of the human being as a transition between ape and *Übermensch*. Of course, Strauss's classical piece, *Also sprach Zarathustra*, based on the title of Nietzsche's famous work, plays a major role in Kubrick's film. But the concluding spectacle of the Star Child might also signal our infantile vulnerability in the face of an infinite and uncaring universe, with no clear pattern to serve as a standard of intelligibility or progress. Indeed, Kubrick made directorial and script decisions that clearly left the ending of the film, the shot of the Star Child, at a purely symbolic level, just as he made choices that frequently eliminated explanatory devices in favor of ambiguity and open-endedness. As Kubrick said in that same *Playboy* interview:

> *2001* is a nonverbal experience; out of two hours and 19 minutes of film, there are only a little less than 40 minutes of dialog. I tried to create a *visual* experience, one that bypasses verbalized pigeonholing and directly penetrates the subconscious with an emotional and philosophic content. To convolute McLuhan, in *2001*, the message is the medium. I intended the film to be an intensely subjective experience that reaches the viewer at an inner level of consciousness, just as music does; to "explain" a Beethoven symphony would be to emasculate it by erecting an artificial barrier between conception and appreciation. You're free to speculate as you wish about the philosophical and allegorical meaning of the film ...[7]

Much is indeed left open to the audience's interpretation. The viewer finishes this journey, on the one hand, with a symbol of the glorious triumph of cosmic self-consciousness, as it were, and yet also with a deep sense of human limitation and fallibility, given a sense of the scope of interstellar space as well as the prior storyline dealing with HAL's nearly successful destruction of the astronauts' mission. The theme of our finitude and fragility is suggested not only by the presence of a subversive technology but also by the graphic prologue that depicts prehistoric "humanity," by the astronauts' physical disconnection from the mother ship, and even by the metaphor of a shattered glass in the later dreamlike "hospital room" (or "astral zoo") sequence. The mysterious monoliths or "doorways" that appear throughout the film signal higher forms of intelligence and deeper levels of cosmic reality, but they may also remind us of our cognitive limits—and perhaps also of our mortality, since they resemble traditional gravestones as well. The film's theme of the odyssey, a clear reference to the title of Homer's epic, is typically understood in positive evolutionary terms, and yet it might also be construed as the idea of a nightmarish adventure into the terrifying abyss of the unknown. In both Kubrick's and Homer's epics, there are not only one-eyed "monsters," like HAL and the Cyclops, and sources of sensory overload, the Star Gate and the Sirens, but also forms of homecoming: Odysseus finally returns to his kingdom and to his waiting wife Penelope while Bowman, now the Star Child, returns to Earth, at least abstractly.[8]

In his book *Kubrick: Inside a Film Artist's Maze*, Thomas Allen Nelson emphasizes Kubrick's more elliptical approach to the narrative, especially when it comes to the director's decisions as to realize his and Arthur Clarke's script.[9] The director uses this approach most effectively in suggesting a sense of the transcendent in terms of an intelligent reality that goes far beyond the current human sphere of perception and intellect. A contrast between the film and Clarke's novel provides some insight since the novel was based on much of the original screenplay materials, including a lengthy prose treatment of the story, those original materials having been loosely based on Clarke's earlier short story "The Sentinel." As Nelson tells us:

> Throughout the novel, Clarke combines these evocations of exploration and wandering amid the lonely expanses of space with an elaborate substructure of explanatory material that ultimately has the effect of subordinating "mystery" to the speculations of science. The film, by contrast, is more open-ended than Clarke's novel, perhaps because Kubrick realized that mystery, whether futuristic or historical, becomes trivialized on the screen once it assumes a definable, objective shape. Consequently, his *2001* is less dependent on narrative exposition than the novel, and more committed to the development of its ideas through the free play of image and sound.[10]

And so, while Kubrick has a definite sense of the positive trajectory of his movie as the depiction of phases in the forward movement of human evolution in which the archetypal instance of *homo sapiens*—namely, Bowman—becomes transformed into a type of "super-human," he provides such a degree of ambiguity in his film that the metaphysical, moral, existential, and spiritual lessons of this evolution are left to the audience. Kubrick's idea of an embryonic Star Child that will eventually return to Earth suggests a vague synthesis of the immanent and the transcendent, the earthly and the other-worldly, the physical and the mental-spiritual. Bowman as the Star Child—loosely analogous to Plato's enlightened and liberated cave dweller in the famous allegory of the Cave in his dialogue

The Republic—is presented in such an abstractly symbolic manner that any vision of "it" returning to earth in some embodied form and initiating a new species is left purely to the viewer's fantasy. It is still an open question, and left to the viewer's imagination, as to how that new species becomes established on earth and what it would mean for conventional humanity to accept or adopt or even reject such an enlightened being.

It might be added by way of a side note that Kubrick's technique of intentional ambiguity has its parallels in Shakespearean drama, particularly in terms of what literary scholar Stephen Greenblatt calls, in his book *Will in the World*, a method of "strategic opacity." [11] Greenblatt makes a convincing case that what has most fascinated readers and audiences about major characters in certain Shakespeare plays, and most especially the character of Hamlet, is the enigma of personality that the playwright has carefully constructed by means of narrative elision. The scholar argues that it was around the time of the Bard's writing of Hamlet, and most probably due to some intensely personal crises that the playwright-poet was facing at the time, including the death of his young son Hamnet, that Shakespeare hit on the idea of evoking a deeper sense of personal interiority in his characters by omitting explanatory devices that would otherwise make certain motives and actions clear to the audience. An illusion of psychological depth was afforded to the character in a way that would summon the imaginative capacities of the audience and perhaps even make a fictional character seem more real in the non-reductive way that complex human beings present themselves in most cases, especially in dramatic situations. In this sense, personal interiority gains a form of irreducibility and ineffability that is suggestive of the general idea of transcendence. [12]

Kubrick likewise chose to omit certain crucial explanatory elements from his movie 2001. Unlike Shakespeare, however, Kubrick's use of "strategic opacity" was not designed to add depth to his human characters, since his characters are at best primitive, as with the prehistoric ape creatures, or impersonal and robotic, as with Bowman and Poole. Rather, what is left out of the film fascinates the audience in terms of any sense of the transcendent realities involved in the story, whether in the form of extraterrestrial intelligence or the deeper nature of the universe itself. Below are some examples of the final choices of narrative elision that Kubrick made in terms of his audiovisual realization of the script that he and Clarke had crafted. First, the director rejected the initial idea—whether that of Clarke or purely his own—to afford more detail and clear functionality to the monolith and, in the "Dawn of Man" segment, "to use the monolith didactically, not mystically, by projecting onto it pictures teaching the apes how to use weapons and kill for meat." [13] Second, Kubrick and Clarke had consulted with astronomer Carl Sagan about their initial challenge in seeking to depict the extraterrestrials on screen. Kubrick took Sagan's advice in choosing not to show them at all. [14] What was not shown would be left up to the audience's imagination. These higher beings, quite possibly consisting of pure mind, energy, or spirit, are manifested only in terms of the mysterious black monoliths that are, in fact, devoid of visual detail.[15] Third, Kubrick eliminated the explanatory voice-over narration that Clarke had originally written for the "Dawn of Man" sequence and also for the "space ballet" sequence, eventually filled with the gorgeous and fitting "Blue Danube" waltz by Johann Strauss, that would follow the four-million-year jump cut from bone tool to spaceship and thereby form a transition between the "Dawn of Man" and the lunar mission. Fourth, Kubrick opted for mostly abstract symbolism in the creation of the Star Gate sequence, relying chiefly on colors and shapes that are interspersed occasionally with close-up reaction shots of Bowman's face and eye. And the very limited use of earthly landscape shots in this sequence are presented in a highly distorted, non-realistic fashion.[16]

Lastly, Kubrick decided to eliminate any clear explanation of HAL's "error" in wrongly detecting the spaceship antenna malfunction. Originally, according to Clarke, there was some attempt to account for HAL's "behavior" by showing that, because he had been programmed to keep the true mission secret from Bowman and Poole, at least until the other astronauts in hibernation had been awakened to complete the mission's goal upon arrival near Jupiter, HAL had begun to malfunction due to the inner conflict between the task of deception or secret-keeping and the computer's more typical task of fact-telling and information-giving. But since Kubrick decided to eliminate that account from the finished movie, we do not know for certain whether HAL's wrongful report of the broken antenna is a pure mistake, some type of psychological test of the astronauts, or part of an elaborate scheme to terminate the lives of the astronauts. Does HAL really suffer from some internal conflict between pre-programmed tasks, not unlike a human's expression of internal conflict? Hamlet comes to mind again. Has HAL been programmed to be so human-like that he begins to develop emotions such as hubris so that, once he does indeed make an error, he must kill all of the astronauts in order to cover up his fallibility? In having been programmed to know about the true nature of the mission since its start, has HAL become envious of the astronauts in their projected encounter with an alien species that will enhance human intelligence? Kubrick leaves the malfunction, or seeming malfunction, a mystery and the viewer is thereby invited to speculate. We do know, however, that once HAL uncovers the astronauts' plan to disconnect him if they restore the antenna and verify that the computer had indeed made a mistake, it is no longer all that puzzling as to why the computer system then attempts to eliminate them. It is done out of a sheer need for mechanical "survival," whether that "instinct" happens to be pre-programmed or not.[17]

Given the film as it stands, the ending of *2001* is ambiguous enough to summon the viewer's own hermeneutic powers and to avoid any neat narrative closure. Optimists and pessimists can interpret as they like, of course. However, in terms of the filmmaker's own "authorial intention," Kubrick did appear to favor a more positive and evolutionary view. Simply put, the more that humans come to know about a form of intelligence and reality that transcends their own, the more that humans become capable of transcending their own current nature. Clarke's own proposed ending of the film, as presented in his more explanatory script-based novel that was developed during the movie's production, had been the depiction of a playful Star Child whose idea of "toying" with the planet before him—Earth—involves the unleashing of multiple megaton bombs that orbit our planet.[18] However, Kubrick rejected that very dark suggestion, not only thinking that such a conclusion would mirror too obviously the apocalyptic finale of his earlier *Dr. Strangelove*, but undoubtedly viewing the Star Child as the primal symbol of a new beginning, the dawn of a new age in which humans will become "super"-human by transcending their previously fixed boundaries of space-time and intelligence.

We know from his interviews that Kubrick was highly enthused about the question of extraterrestrial intelligence and its implications for the intellectual development of the species.[19] He was, to cite his own words, excited about the "grandeur of space and the myriad mysteries of cosmic intelligence."[20] In fact, in rare moments he did not shy away from sharing his own "straightforward" or plot-based reading of the film's ending. As he told one interviewer:

> No, I don't mind discussing it, on the *lowest* level, that is, straightforward explanation of the plot. . . . When the surviving astronaut, Bowman, ultimately reaches Jupiter, this artifact [monolith] sweeps him into a force field or star gate that hurls him on a journey through inner and outer space and finally transports him to another part of the galaxy, where he's placed in a human zoo approximating a hospital terrestrial environment drawn out of his dreams and imagination. In a timeless state, his life passes from middle age to senescence to death. He is reborn, an enhanced being, a star child, an angel, a superman, if you like, and returns to earth to prepare for the next leap forward in man's evolutionary destiny.[21]

Note here that Kubrick speaks positively in terms of "enhanced being," "the next leap forward," and "evolutionary destiny." The very name "Bowman" might suggest the image of an archer whose arrow is directed forward to some desired target or goal. It has also been suggested that the term "bowman" may well refer to Odysseus, who demonstrates his archery skill at the end of Homer's epic from whose title Kubrick's film takes part of its name.[22] Kubrick also speaks intriguingly here of the Star Gate sequence as Bowman's "journey through inner and outer space," which may suggest, in Jungian fashion, that if the astronaut's odyssey, like the odyssey of humanity itself, results in deeper insight into metaphysical reality, that reality is a unity of mind and matter.

Of course, a "reader" of the film certainly does not need to restrict his or her interpretation to clues about the author's intention. An artwork opens up an entire world of interpretation that transcends the parameters of what the author consciously had in mind. However, at the very least, the movie does indeed exhibit a sense of development in terms of humanity's growing insight and self-reflection, even if, along the way, our increasing level of consciousness and self-awareness includes the necessary step of creating a dangerous technology that may possibly destroy us. Later, in 1980, during the production of *The Shining*, Kubrick re-explained his own interpretation of the ending of *2001* with a filmmaker from a Japanese paranormal television series:

> I've tried to avoid doing this [type of explanation] ever since the picture came out. When you just say the ideas they sound foolish, whereas if they're dramatized one feels it, but I'll try. The idea was supposed to be that he is taken in by god-like entities, creatures of pure energy and intelligence with no shape or form. They put him in what I suppose you could describe as a human zoo to study him, and his whole life passes from that point on in that room. And he has no sense of time. It just seems to happen as it does in the film. They choose this room, which is a very inaccurate replica of French architecture (deliberately so, inaccurate) because one was suggesting that they had some idea of something that he might think was pretty, but wasn't quite sure . . . Anyway, when they get finished with him, as happens in so many myths of all cultures in the world, he is transformed into some kind of super being and sent back to Earth, transformed and made into some sort of superman. We have to only guess what happens when he goes back. It is the pattern of a great deal of mythology, and that is what we were trying to suggest.[23]

Kubrick also states in his interview with *Playboy*, concerning the existence of incorporeal life forms in the universe: "I don't really *believe* anything about them; how can I? Mere speculation on the possibility of their existence is sufficiently overwhelming, without attempting to decipher their motives."[24]

Kubrick does tell us in this interview that the basic idea of transcendence lies at the core of the film: "I will say that the God concept is at the heart of *2001*—but not any traditional, anthropomorphic image of God. I don't believe in any of earth's monotheistic religions, but I do believe that one can construct an intriguing *scientific* definition of God. . . ."[25] His concern has more to do with the metaphysical possibilities of the divine rather than with questions of any innate moral qualities such as universal goodness or evil. In this same interview, Kubrick ponders the probable existence of older life-forms with higher intelligence and views these life-forms as possibly "immortal" and machinelike—at the very least, non-biological and so non-anthropocentric—and even non-physical, as "pure energy and spirit":

> Now, the Sun is by no means an old star, and its planets are mere children in cosmic age, so it seems likely that there are billions of planets in the universe not only where intelligent life is on a lower scale than man but other billions where it is approximately equal and others still where it is hundreds of thousands of millions of years in advance of us. When you think of the giant technological strides that man has made in a few millennia—less than a microsecond in the chronology of the universe—can you imagine the evolutionary development that much older life forms have taken? They may have progressed from biological species, which are fragile shells for the mind at best, into immortal machine entities—and then, over innumerable eons, they could emerge from the chrysalis of matter transformed into beings of pure energy and spirit. Their potentialities would be limitless and their intelligence ungraspable by humans.[26]

Even more broadly, 2001 may impel us to consider the possibility of the universe's intelligent design, especially given the implications of the role that a higher power, in the form of extraterrestrial intelligence, plays in the intelligence-cultivating, and yet also violence-escalating, evolution of our species. Once we admit the possibility of the existence of higher intelligence, we are led to ponder further about the sources of *that* intelligence, and so on. At the same time, however, the existence of some form of higher intelligence does not guarantee that the universe *as a whole* is governed by some pan-cosmic source of Logos. Hypothetically, there may well be "happy accidents" of planetary and galactic evolution in the form of singular sources of intelligence. And while the Star Gate sequence depicts Bowman's "journey through inner and outer space," as Kubrick put it, there is nothing in the film that necessarily entails that there is a *universal* source of rationality that pervades or governs *everything*. At most, we can say that the Star Gate experience, as a form of enhanced enlightenment, is some fusion of Bowman's mind, including his personal memory and imagination, and the reality of the higher species that has occasioned the experience. A higher form of intelligence may indicate a form of rational teleology that transcends its own immanent species; but, on the other hand, it may not.

In the end, given Kubrick's own intelligent design, so to speak, some viewers may find the idea of intelligent design to be evoked by the film while others may not. Kubrick's film may also prompt us to ponder what meaning or purpose *we* could give to our own individual lives if there were indeed no cosmic meaning or purpose whatsoever. Perhaps the best that we can do in the moment is to appreciate and make use of what we have simply been given. As Kubrick himself once said: "If man merely sat back and thought about his impending termination, and his terrifying insignificance and aloneness in the cosmos, he would surely go mad, or succumb to a numbing sense of futility. Why, he might ask himself, should he bother to write a great symphony, or strive to make a living, or even to love another, when he is no more than a momentary microbe on a dust mote whirling through the unimaginable immensity of space?"[27] Whether or not the overall "architecture" of the universe follows a rational design, the human existential question remains.

In the foregoing I have indicated several of the directorial choices Kubrick made while adapting the script to screen, especially choices that evoke in the viewer a philosophical need to ponder the idea of transcendence. I have considered the idea of transcendence primarily in terms of extraterrestrial higher intelligence—"gods," as it were—and secondarily in terms of insight into metaphysical reality itself. But there is a related lower-level form of transcendence at play in the film, and this is the idea of humanity's own act of transcending its prior stage of being. This occurs in contemplating the advance from prehistoric ape creature to modern technology-equipped human and, most intriguingly, the advance from current humanity to some future, more enlightened species. The Star Child is a form of transcendence, then, just as current humanity may be viewed retrospectively as transcendent in contrast with earlier forms of biological and mental evolution.

Philosophical questions arise, however, in contemplating technology as a "tool of transcending"—i.e., that which drives this progression from an earlier act of primitive tool-making to the future possibility of advanced civilization, if not going beyond machine technology altogether. In *2001*, the power of technology is presented ambivalently. Human-created machines can operate spaceships, waltz between the planets, and deliver humans to Jupiter and beyond. The film shows us the birth of technology with the invention of the bone tool in prehistoric times, and by means of his four-million-year jump cut, Kubrick draws a clear line of progress between that initial advance of human intelligence and the age of the spaceship. In fact, it is the invention and development of technology that provides the necessary step toward humanity's eventual transformation into a vehicle of higher intelligence. Without the machines to bring us to the moon—thus setting off the "cosmic burglar alarm" and causing the lunar monolith to emit a radio signal in the direction of Jupiter—and without the machines to bring us to Jupiter, Bowman would never become the Star Child. However, it is also human-created technology, in the form of HAL, that almost derails the entire mission. And it is the specter of a purely technological environment that prompts us to ask what we lose when we live in a machine-dominated world. There is an increasing sense of detachment through the replacement of the sensual natural world by the mediation of mechanical artifice.

And so while technology is an essential step in the evolution toward a higher form of being, according to the basic narrative logic of the film, its increasing usage not only breeds violence—the first tool being a weapon, HAL as killer machine, etc.—but it also disconnects us from our earthly, bodily environment and thereby creates a corresponding sense of alienation. In his book *On the Internet*, Hubert Dreyfus refers to this as a feeling of "disembodied presence" that can result, for example, from those who remain "in" cyber-space for vast stretches of time on a daily basis. In *2001*, except for the "Dawn of Man" segment, the human characters never really emerge from their artificial, machine-governed settings. Even when Heywood Floyd and his crew traverse the lunar surface in order to investigate the monolith, or when Bowman and Poole leave the spaceship at different times, they are prisoners of their space suits and helmets. In fact, in contrast with the ape creatures directly touching the monolith earlier in the film, Floyd's hand contact with the lunar monolith is entirely indirect due to the fact that he is wearing a space suit.

In fact, Kubrick really makes the sense of disconnection or detachment a key theme of the movie experience. Kubrick shoots and edits *2001* in such a way that the viewer feels more disconnected than connected, more un-rooted than rooted, and especially in a way that denies identification with a particular individual within a given physical situation. Kubrick takes the viewer on an audiovisual journey in which the personal sense of a fixed location or identity is fleeting because the viewer is almost always on the move, so to speak, across vast stretches of space-time and according to many different perspectives. But the director also summons us to consider the possibilities of an experience in which the role of the natural body—as the active filter of one's individualized experiences and as the fixed point of orientation for one's material existence—is no longer pri-

Figure 10.1. *2001: A Space Odyssey*. Metro-Goldwyn-Mayer (Producer). Stanley Kubrick (Director). *2001: A Space Odyssey*. United Kingdom: 1968.

mary. This is especially the case when our technology has increasingly gained the capacity of delivering a more indirect world, one in which our five senses play a minimized and mostly passive role.

A sense of disembodied presence—of experiencing things in the world without a fixed and continuous physical identity and without a direct, active use of the senses—is also instilled in the viewer during the famous "Waltz of the Spaceships" sequence. From whose different perspectives do we see the various shots and angles of ships in flight? Evidently from the fluctuating standpoints of detached observers who must hover in space like a mind without a body, or at least a mind with a body of no fixed location. The shots are not aligned with the viewpoint of any specific, continuous character. Most of this, of course, occurs subconsciously in the viewer's mind.

In *2001*, Kubrick expands the cinematic possibilities for the audience to experience a seeming escape from the fixity and finitude of the individual human body. The audience's sense of detachment and even dislocation increases as Kubrick intercuts the exterior scenes of white spaceships soaring against the canvas of star-flecked space with interior scenes of Dr. Heywood Floyd asleep in the vehicle that transports him to the wheeling space station. There he will embark on the remainder of his journey to the lunar station Clavius. On Floyd's trip from the space station to the moon so that he can investigate the recent discovery of the lunar monolith, there are further techniques that help to instill a feeling of disconnection in the viewer. There is the reminder of zero gravity as we watch a stewardess deliver a tray of food to the pilots by walking in a circle upside down—at least from the fixed camera's viewpoint—so that she can enter the cockpit in a manner that is oriented to that new location in a different part of the ship. And so as to emphasize the radical change in directionality that is being offered here, Kubrick rotates the camera 180 degrees as the stewardess enters the cockpit and greets the pilots.

The theme of detachment becomes even more pronounced in a narrative manner as the movie progresses. We witness Poole's death while disconnected from the mother ship, Bowman's disconnecting of HAL's "mind," and then Bowman's eventual separation from the mother ship as he is pulled into the Star Gate through the monolithic portal. One might initially view Bowman's departure from the computer-governed *Discovery* and his subsequent experience of the Star Gate as a return to direct and active perception, a return to one's rootedness in the senses of the physical body. However, Bowman can only experience the passing phenomena of the Star Gate by glimpsing them through the glass of his space helmet as well as through the window of his space-pod.

And so Kubrick creates a feeling of disconnection and alienation by means of his manipulation of cinematic space—motion across vast distance, radical change in directionality, lack of conventional fixed perspective, etc.—as well as through a recurring depiction of the artificial mediation of sensory input. He also, however, manipulates cinematic *time* in order to amplify the feeling of detachment or dislocation. He does so in the editing process, in which he worked actively with Ray Lovejoy, the film's chief editor, and evokes in the viewer a sense of temporal discontinuity or disruption. This occurs by means of radical jump cuts between sections of the narrative, with the most radical cut being the now famous four-million-year jump, in a single transition between shots, from prehistoric bone tool to soaring spaceship. There is a less radical jump from the lunar mission sequence to, "18 Months Later," the Jupiter mission sequence. Jump cuts across months or even years are fairly customary in certain types of movies, especially biographies and historical epics. However, the viewer's sense of detachment is amplified less by such rapid jumps in the narrative development and more so by Kubrick's willingness to slow down the pace of certain scenes to a point where the typical viewer is shaken out of her conventional sense of movie-watching. Such examples of "slow cinema" include, for example, the quietly meditative scenes aboard the *Discovery* in which the astronauts go about their time-filling routines, the contemplative scenes with Bowman in the "hospital room" or "astral zoo" toward the end of the film, and, most especially, Bowman's failed attempt to retrieve Poole and his subsequent efforts in boarding the spaceship against HAL's wishes. The brooding suspense of the latter sequence is amplified by Kubrick's highly deliberate pacing as well as the absence of all sound effects, including music, except for the sound of Bowman's heavy breathing.[28]

The theme of disconnection is, like the theme of technology in the film, ultimately ambivalent. On the one hand, the film shows us a type of technology-driven detachment from the natural world that reduces the individual to little more than a passive observer or de-humanized automaton. Such a reduction entails certain psychological, moral, and even spiritual dangers, especially if we recognize the central and active role that the bodily senses play in the activity of being-human. On the other hand, if we are to understand the extraterrestrial beings as non-biological and even non-physical, because they never appear directly, and as manifested within the physical world only in terms of the abstract monoliths, then any transformation from human to super-human—i.e., to a "god-like" state of higher intelligence—would entail a form of disembodiment that is a detachment from the material realm. Therefore, the increasing sense of disconnection from nature that is evidenced most especially in machine-governed spaceship life may be viewed as a form of preparation for the type of genuine disembodiment that occurs in the transformation of Bowman into the abstract Star Child. Disconnection in the form of "disembodied presence" may diminish and even eliminate what we now think of as being truly human—including those emotions and passions that are rooted in our bodily perceptions and responses. But such disconnection may also be viewed as the necessary condition of transcending the human altogether, should that ever prove desirable or inevitable.

NOTES

1. Metro-Goldwyn-Mayer (Producer), Stanley Kubrick (Director), *2001: A Space Odyssey*. United Kingdom: 1968.
2. For the major philosophical ideas of Karl Jaspers, see the following selected works. Karl Jaspers, *Psychologie der Weltanschauungen* (Berlin: J Springer, 1920). Karl Jaspers, *Philosophie*, Vol 1-3 (Berlin: J Springer, 1932). Karl Jaspers, Vernunft und Existenz (Groningen: J. W. Wolters, 1935). Karl Jaspers, Von der Wahrheit (München: Piper, 1947. For a clear introduction to his notion of "the Encompassing" as a form of transcendence, see Karl Jaspers, *Existenzphilosophie* (Berlin: W. de Gruyter & Co., 1956).
3. Rudolf Otto, *Das Heilige, Über das Irrationale in der Idee des Göttlichen und sein Verhältnis zum Rationalen* (München: C. H. Beck, 1963).
4. Hubert Dreyfus, *On the Internet*, Thinking in Action (New York: Routledge, 2001).
5. Jack J. Kessie, "The *Playboy* Interview: Stanley Kubrick," *Playboy*, Vol. 15, No. 9, September 1968, 190.
6. Kessie, "The *Playboy* Interview," 190.
7. Kessie, "The *Playboy* Interview," 92.
8. Arthur C. Clarke once stated: "We set out with the deliberate intention of creating a myth. The Odyssean parallel was in our minds from the beginning, long before the film's title was chosen." Neil M. McAleer, *Arthur C. Clarke: The Authorized Biography* (Chicago: Contemporary Books, 1992), 185.
9. Thomas Allen Nelson, *Kubrick: Inside a Film Artist's Maze* (Indianapolis: Indiana University Press, 2000), 106-107.
10. Nelson, *Kubrick: Inside*, 106-107.
11. Stephen Greenblatt, *Will in the World: How Shakespeare Became Shakespeare* (New York and London: W. W. Norton & Company, 2004).
12. Greenblatt, *Will in the World*, 323-5, 354, 377. On a related note, Ron Rosenbaum explores the idea of "bottomlessness" in terms of experiencing the ineffable and the transcendent in his book *The Shakespeare Wars: Clashing Scholars, Public Fiascoes, Palace Coups* (New York: Random House, 2006). See especially 14-18.
13. Alexander Walker, Sybil Taylor, and Ulrich Ruchti, *Stanley Kubrick, Director: A Visual Analysis* (New York and London: W. W. Norton & Company, 1990), 181.
14. Carl Sagan, *The Cosmic Connection* (Garden City: Anchor Press, 1973), 182. Joe R. Frinzi, *Kubrick's Monolith: The Art and Mystery of 2001: A Space Odyssey* (Jefferson, NC: McFarland & Co. Publishers, 2017), 29.
15. For more on Kubrick's decision-making process about the shape and minimalism of the monolith, see Frinzi, *Kubrick's Monolith*, 31-34.
16. For more on Kubrick's collaboration with Clarke and most especially the differences between the finished film and the original screenplay elements, as evidenced in part by Clarke's novelized version of those elements, see Nelson, *Kubrick: Inside*, 104-109 and 132-33.
17. For more speculation on HAL's seeming malfunction, see Nelson, *Kubrick: Inside a Film Artist's Maze*, 126-28.
18. See Nelson, *Kubric: Inside*, 105
19. Kubrick's personal enthusiasm for these issues and questions is quite evident in his above-mentioned interview with *Playboy*.
20. Kubrick, in response to the New York critics who panned *2001*: "Perhaps there is a certain element of the lumpen literati that is so dogmatically atheist and materialist and earth-bound that it finds the grandeur of space and the myriad mysteries of cosmic intelligence anathema." Kessie, "The *Playboy* Interview," 94.

21. Quoted in Nelson, *Kubrick: Inside*, 133.
22. Frinzi, *Kubrick's Monolith*, 27.
23. The audio-recording of the interview fragment excerpted above is available online, along with a transcription. Stanley Kubric, "Stanley Kubric on the Meaning of the Ending of 2001 in a Rare 1980 Interview," SYFYWIRE, http://www.syfy.com/syfywire/in-lost-interview-stanley-kubrick-explains-the-ending-of-2001-a-space-odyssey, last modified July 5, 2018.
24. Kessie, "The *Playboy* Interview," 94-96.
25. Kessie, "The *Playboy* Interview," 94.
26. Kessie, "The *Playboy* Interview," 94.
27. Kessie, "The *Playboy* Interview," 195.
28. Two valuable books on the topic of cinematic temporality are Yvette Bíro, *Turbulence and Flow in Film: The Rhythmic Design*, trans. Paul Salamon (Bloomington: Indiana University Press, 2008) and Matilda Mroz, *Temporality and Film Analysis* (Edinburgh: Edinburgh University Press, 2013). The former book originated from Bíro's observations of "slow cinema" and expanded into an intricate study of the complex dialectic between the slowness and fastness of film pacing and also in terms of the interconnections between the temporal and the spatial. Mroz, in her first chapter, "Time, in Theory," connects the study of filmic pacing with its philosophical roots (Mroz, *Temporality and Film*, 13-48). She does so especially in terms of Henri Bergson's idea of subject-related and non-quantifiable duration (*la durée*), and Deleuze's influential concepts of the "movement-image" and the "time-image," as elaborated in Gilles Deleuze, *Cinema I, The Movement-Image*, trans. Hugh Tomlinson and Barbara Habberjam (New York: Continuum, 2009), and Gilles Deleuze, *Cinema II, The Time-Image*, trans. Hugh Tomlinson and Barbara Habberjam (New York: Bloomsbury Academic, 2013). Mroz then elaborates on her compelling thesis that temporality should be an essential theme of film scholarship, especially when one recognizes the embodied nature of movie viewing—and particularly in terms of the notion of "haptic visuality." Haptic visuality, referring to the embodied nature of film viewing, is the subject of Laura Marks, *The Skin of the Film: Intercultural Cinema, Embodiment, and the Senses* (Durham: Duke University Press, 2000) as well as Vivian Sobchak, *The Address of the Eye: A Phenomenology of the Film Experience* (Princeton: Princeton University Press, 1992). Aside from numerous articles on the topic of cinematic temporality, other relevant books include Leo Charney, *Empty Moments: Cinema, Modernity, and Drift* (Durham: Duke University Press, 1998), May Ann Doane, *The Emergence of Cinematic Time* (Cambridge: Harvard University Press, 2002), Bliss Cua Lim, *Translating Time: Cinema, the Fantastic, and Temporal Critique* (Durham: Duke University Press, 2009), and the recent anthology, Tiago De Luca and Nuno Barradas Jorge, eds., *Slow Cinema* (Edinburgh: Edinburgh University Press, 2015). Two books that focus on the role of cinematic *moments* within the flux of movie narratives are Tom Brown and James Walters, eds., *Film Moments: Criticism, History, Theory* (British Film Institute, 2010) and Christian Keathley, *Cinephilia and History, or the Wind in the Trees* (Bloomington: Indiana University Press, 2006).

BIBLIOGRAPHY

Bíro, Yvette. *Turbulence and Flow in Film: The Rhythmic Design*. Translated by Paul Salamon. Bloomington: Indiana University Press, 2008.

Brown, Tom and James Walters, eds. *Film Moments: Criticism, History, Theory*. British Film Institute, 2010.

Charney, Leo. *Empty Moments: Cinema, Modernity, and Drift*. Durham: Duke University Press, 1998.

De Luca, Tiago and Nuno Barradas Jorge, eds. *Slow Cinema*. Edinburgh: Edinburgh University Press, 2015.

Deleuze, Gilles. *Cinema I, The Movement-Image*. Translated by Hugh Tomlinson and Barbara Habberjam. New York: Continuum, 2009.
_____. *Cinema II, The Time-Image*. Translated by Hugh Tomlinson and Barbara Habberjam. New York: Bloomsbury Academic, 2013.
Doane, May Ann. *The Emergence of Cinematic Time*. Cambridge: Harvard University Press, 2002.
Dreyfus, Hubert. *On the Internet. Thinking in Action*. New York: Routledge, 2001.
Frinzi, Joe R. *Kubrick's Monolith: The Art and Mystery of 2001: A Space Odyssey*. Jefferson, NC: McFarland & Co. Publishers, 2017.
Greenblatt, Stephen. *Will in the World: How Shakespeare Became Shakespeare*. New York and London: W. W. Norton & Company, 2004.
Jaspers, Karl. *Existenzphilosophie*. Berlin: W. de Gruyter & Co., 1956.
_____. *Psychologie der Weltanschauungen*. Berlin: J Springer, 1920.
_____. *Philosophie*, Vol 1-3. Berlin: J Springer, 1932.
_____. *Vernunft und Existenz*. Groningen: J. W. Wolters, 1935.
_____. *Von der Wahrheit*. München: Piper, 1947.
Keathley, Christian. *Cinephilia and History, or the Wind in the Trees*. Bloomington: Indiana University Press, 2006.
Kessie, Jack J. "The *Playboy* Interview: Stanley Kubrick." *Playboy*, Vol. 15, No. 9, September 1968: 85-96, 158, 180-86, 190-95.
Kubrick, Stanley. "Stanley Kubrick on the Meaning of the Ending of 2001 in a Rare 1980 Interview." SYFYWIRE. Last modified July 5, 2018. http://www.syfy.com/syfywire/in-lost-interview-stanley-kubrick-explains-the-ending-of-2001-a-space-odyssey.
Lim, Bliss Cua. *Translating Time: Cinema, the Fantastic, and Temporal Critique*. Durham: Duke University Press, 2009.
Marks, Laura. *The Skin of the Film: Intercultural Cinema, Embodiment, and the Senses*. Durham: Duke University Press, 2000.
McAleer, Neil M. *Arthur C. Clarke: The Authorized Biography*. Chicago: Contemporary Books, 1992.
Metro-Goldwyn-Mayer (Producer). Stanley Kubrick (Director). *2001: A Space Odyssey*. United Kingdom: 1968.
Mroz, Matilda. *Temporality and Film Analysis*. Edinburgh: Edinburgh University Press, 2013.
Nelson, Thomas Allen. *Kubrick: Inside a Film Artist's Maze*. Indianapolis: Indiana University Press, 2000.
Otto, Rudolf. *Das Heilige, Über das Irrationale in der Idee des Göttlichen und sein Verhältnis zum Rationalen*. München: C. H. Beck, 1963.
Rosenbaum, Ron. *The Shakespeare Wars: Clashing Scholars, Public Fiascoes, Palace Coups*. New York: Random House, 2006.
Sagan, Carl. *The Cosmic Connection*. Garden City: Anchor Press, 1973.
Sobchak, Vivian. *The Address of the Eye: A Phenomenology of the Film Experience*. Princeton: Princeton University Press, 1992.
Walker, Alexander, Sybil Taylor, and Ulrich Ruchti. *Stanley Kubrick, Director: A Visual Analysis*. New York and London: W. W. Norton & Company, 1990.

Index

Arendt, Hannah, 68
Aristotle, 45n41, 88
art mediums, comparison among: film and architecture, 1, 80, 101; film and drama, 1, 101, 124; denouement, 132; Shakespeare, 7, 33, 37, 82, 83, 151, 152. *See also* tragedy; film and music, 1, 81–82, 101, 110, 126; film and narrative, 1, 8, 9, 12, 15, 16–17, 26, 32, 40, 48, 49, 50, 58–60, 61, 64, 79, 81, 82, 104, 121, 125, 129, 138, 139, 147–148, 150, 151–153, 158, 159; *also* myth; film and literature, 1, 110, 124, 129; film and painting, 2, 78, 81–82, 101, 112–114, 117, 124, 130–132; film and photography, 2; film and sculpture, 1, 101
attunement, 6, 7, 10, 40, 49, 124, 126; monastic attunement, 6, 126, 135

Badiou, Alain, 2, 61
Benjamin, Walter, 44n37
Bergson, Henri, 8–9, 78, 82–83, 84n21, 161n28
Bresson, Robert, 92

Cavell, Stanley, 110, 144–145
cipher, 3, 6–7, 10, 11, 12, 18, 30, 32, 33, 36, 37, 43n6, 122, 123, 129–130, 132, 133–135, 135n25, 140, 141, 145n3, 147–148, 149; crown of Jesus, 143–144; El Greco, 130–132; Eucharist, 142–143, 144; *fumie*, 122, 126, 128–130, 132; monolith, 147, 149–150, 151–152, 153, 156, 157, 158, 159, 160n15; ostriches, 38–39, 42; Quaker Oats, 37, 39; Star Child, 147, 149, 150, 153, 156, 159; Star Gate, 147, 150, 152, 153, 155, 158; tatami mat, 7, 93; vase, 7, 94, 95. *See also* death, skull
Cronenberg, David, 2, 4, 7, 8, 47–61

Danto, Arthur, 1
death, 7, 8, 25, 70, 72, 89, 105, 122, 126–127, 133, 145n3, 149, 152; annihilation of human race, 148–149, 153; dance of death, 111, 114; death of art, 1; execution of Joan of Arc, 137, 142–143, 144, 144–145; not real, 66–67, 69, 73; skull, 143
Deleuze, Gilles, 2, 8, 65, 71, 100, 161n28
Derrida, Jacques, 3, 48
Descartes, René, 19
Dostoevsky, Fyodor, 133
dream sequence, 3, 7, 15–26; hypnagogia, 3, 15, 19, 20, 21, 22, 23; hypnopompia, 3, 20
Dreyer, Carl Theodor, 2, 5, 92, 137–145, 145n3
Dreyfus, Hubert, 148, 157

ecstatic, 3, 44n37, 123, 127, 133; ecstatic leap, 21; ecstatic time, 81
Endo, Shusaku, 121–123, 124, 126, 128–130

face, 5, 7, 10, 11, 124, 130–131, 143; close-up shot, 137–139, 139, 141–142, 142, 143; face of God, 10, 122, 131, 131–132, 135; face of the world, 10, 135; mask of madness, 7, 37, 40; Winkie's diner, 24–26; unmasking, 23
Fellini, Federico, 2, 5, 9, 10, 100–101, 111–117, 118n16
film noir, 109
Fromm, Erich, 79, 82

Index

groundlessness, 4, 6, 8, 11, 41, 42, 61, 74n15, 125, 160n12; body, detachment from, 157–159, 161n28; nature, detachment from, 148, 156–157, 159; *kenosis*, 133; temporal detachment, 158–159

Hegel, G.W.F., 87–88, 106, 108
Heidegger, Martin, 2, 8, 26, 48, 63–64, 68, 71, 74n19, 127; being-in-the-world, 12, 144. See also immanence, thinking
Henry, Michel, 2, 5, 8, 77–83, 84n15, 84n21
Heraclitus, 124, 134n5
Herzog, Werner, 2, 4, 7, 32, 32–42, 44n37, 45n39, 45n42
Homer, 31–32, 41, 42, 45n44, 150, 153, 160n8
horizon, phenomenological, 4, 5, 9, 10, 35, 39, 40, 64–65, 72, 90, 91–92, 145n3
horror, 2, 109
Husserl, Edmund, 2, 5, 9, 82, 87–92

immanence, 5, 65, 81, 93, 99, 101, 124–125, 131, 133; and transcendence, 3, 5, 8, 9, 11, 77–78, 83, 84n22, 91; contra transcendence, 92, 95, 105, 109, 125, 132–133, 140, 141; immanent temporality, 81; thinking, 64, 68–69

Jaspers, Karl, 2, 6, 7, 9, 22–23, 29–30, 32–33, 35–36, 37, 38, 40, 41, 42, 43n6, 44n33, 45n38, 45n39, 47–48, 56, 61, 71–72, 77, 83, 84n22, 87, 90, 91–92, 95, 135n25, 137, 138, 140, 143, 147, 160n2. See also cipher
Jung, Carl, 113, 154

Kandinsky, Wassily, 81, 82, 84n15
Kant, Immanuel, 3, 87, 91, 106
Kierkegaard, Søren, 2, 5, 9, 63, 68, 100–109, 113, 117. See also time; repetition
Kubric, Stanley, 2, 3, 11, 147–161, 160n15, 160n17, 160n19, 160n20, 161n23

Lynch, David, 2, 3, 4, 7, 15–26

Malick, Terrence, 2, 3, 4, 5, 8, 63–73, 73n5, 74n9, 74n10, 74n17, 74n18
Malle, Louis, 8, 83
Merleau-Ponty, Maurice, 2, 6, 20, 121, 123–126, 131, 133–135
mise-en-scène, 38
mood, phenomenological, 5, 11, 127, 133, 138
mono no aware, 6, 9, 94–95
mu, 9, 95
myth, 4, 7, 12, 30, 32, 33, 34, 35, 37, 39, 40, 65, 68, 70, 154, 160n8. See also Homer; tragedy

Nicholas of Cusa, 131–132
Nietzsche, Friedrich, 2, 12, 133, 135n32, 149

Otto, Rudolph, 147
Ozu, Yasujiro, 2, 6, 92, 93–95; still lives, 6, 9, 93–94, 95

Plato, 31, 88; Cave allegory, 3, 68–69, 150–151; Recollection, 9, 101–104, 105, 106–107, 110

rhythm, 3, 5, 6, 8–9, 10, 11, 15, 123–124, 126, 130–131, 132, 133–135, 137–145, 145n3, 161n28
Ricoeur, Paul, 32
Richie, Donald, 93, 94, 95

sacred, 9, 39, 70, 122
Sartre, Jean-Paul, 2, 18, 19, 23, 26, 34–35, 40
Schelling, F.W.J., 68, 74n15
Schopenhauer, Arthur, 81
Schrader, Paul, 9, 87, 92–93, 95
Scorsese, Martin, 2, 10, 121–135, 135n31
shibui, 9, 93–94
silence, 10, 11, 16, 31, 56, 64, 68, 69, 73, 83, 138–139; caesura, 127, 132, 133; ineffable, 92, 121–135, 138, 140, 141, 147, 151, 160n12
symbolism. See cipher

Tarkovsky, Andrei, 1

television, 5, 8, 59, 77–78, 79–80
time, 5, 10, 81, 88, 101, 102, 105, 106, 126, 137, 161n28; *kinesis*, 99–100, 106, 109; mystery film, 109, 112, 115–116; quest film, 109, 112, 115; repetition, 5, 9, 10, 58, 59, 82, 100–117. *See also* ecstatic; ecstatic time; immanence; immanent temporality; groundlessness; temporal detachment
tragedy, 11, 29, 31–32, 32–33, 34, 35–36, 37, 38, 40, 41, 42, 44n33, 45n38, 152; Greek tragedy, 4, 7, 29–30, 33–34, 35, 37–39, 40, 43n22, 44n37. *See also* Homer
transcendence, types of: evolutionary, 156–157; human, 153, 155, 161; transcendent anxiety, 26; self, 10, 111, 117, 137, 143; transcendental style, 6, 9, 87, 92–93
Transcendence and Film project, 1, 2, 11–12

Verhoeven, Paul, 8–9, 82

Weil, Simone, 31, 43n9
Wittgenstein, 63, 68

Zen, 5, 93, 94–95

About the Contributors

John B. Brough is Professor of Philosophy Emeritus from Georgetown University. His expertise is in phenomenology, philosophy of art, and modern philosophy. His work on Husserlian phenomenology includes translations of Husserl's *Phantasy, Image Consciousness, and Memory (1898-1925)* (2005) and *On the Phenomenology of Consciousness of Internal Time* (1992). Brough is the author of *The Many Faces of Time* (2011), *Philosophical Knowledge (1893-1917)* (1980), and *Art and Artworld: Some Ideas for a Husserlian Aesthetic* (1978).

Allan Casebier currently lectures for the Department of Philosophy at the University of Miami. He is also Professor Emeritus from the University of Southern California where he taught at the Bryan Singer Division of Cinema & Media Studies. His books include *Film and Phenomenology: Toward a Realist Theory of Cinematic Representation* (2009), *A New Theory in the Philosophy and History of Three Twentieth-Century Styles in Art: Modernism, Postmodernism, And Surrealism* (2006), *Social Responsibilities of the Mass Media* (1978), and *Film Appreciation* (1976).

Herbert Golder is Professor of Classical Studies at Boston University and Editor-in-Chief of *Arion: A Journal of Humanities and the Classics*. He has written extensively on Greek drama and on related classical and modern subjects, as well as translated and adapted Greek drama for the stage. He also served as General Editor of *The Greek Tragedy in New Translations* series published by Oxford University Press. His work in film includes, most notably, a collaboration with legendary filmmaker Werner Herzog on ten films, features, and documentaries. Golder's most recent film, *Ballad of a Righteous Merchant* (2017), explores that collaboration with Herzog.

David P. Nichols is Associate Professor of Philosophy at Saginaw Valley State University, where he teaches existentialism, Greek philosophy, and religious studies. He completed his PhD in Philosophy of Religion at Boston University. He is the former President of the Karl Jaspers Society of North America. His research interests center on philosophy of art and tragic visions of human existence. This includes various articles on Greek tragedy and the appropriation of tragic themes in continental philosophy. He is the editor of *Van Gogh among the Philosophers: Painting, Thinking, Being* (2017).

K. Malcolm Richards is Associate Professor and Chair of the low-residency MFA program at the Pennsylvania Academy of the Fine Arts. He is an artist, experimental musician, critic, curator, art historian, and theoretician specializing in the work of Jacques Derrida. His other areas of expertise include nineteenth century art and aesthetics, contemporary art, French theory, and film history. His publications include *Derrida Reframed: A Guide for the Visual Arts Student* (2008) and "Eve's Dropping/Eavesdropping," in *The Writings of Michael Fried*, edited by Jill Beaulieu, Mary Roberts, and Toni Ross (2000).

Frédéric Seyler is Associate Professor of Philosophy at DePaul University. He specializes in phenomenology and German idealism, especially Fichte and Michel Henry. Seyler is also the author of *Fichtes' "Anweisung zum seligen Leben": Ein Kommentar zur Religionslehre von 1806* (2014), *Eine Ethik der Affektivität: Die Lebensphänomenologie Michel Henrys* (2010), and *Barbarie ou culture: L'éthique de l'affectivité dans la phénoménologie de Michel Henry* (2010). Seyler has co-translated Fichte's *Doctrine of Religion* (2012). He is also the coeditor for both *The Michel Henry Reader (Studies in Phenomenology and Existential Philosophy)* (2019) and *Sein, Existenz, Leben: Michel Henry und Martin Heidegger* (2013).

Kevin L. Stoehr is Associate Professor of Humanities at Boston University. He is the author of *Nihilism in Film and TV: From Citizen Kane to The Sopranos* (2006), the coauthor of *Ride, Boldly Ride: The Evolution of the American Western* (2012), the coeditor of *John Ford in Focus: Essays on the Filmmaker's Life and Work* (2007), and the editor of *Film and Knowledge: Essays on the Integration of Images and Ideas* (2002). He is currently at work on projects related to the filmmaker King Vidor.

Dylan Trigg has held several prestigious research and teaching posts, and most recently, the FWF Lise Meitner Fellow for the Department of Philosophy at University of Vienna. His research concerns phenomenology and existentialism, philosophies of subjectivity and embodiment, aesthetics and philosophies of art, and nineteenth-century German philosophy. His books include *Topophobia: a Phenomenology of Anxiety* (2016), *The Thing: A Phenomenology of Horror* (2014), *The Memory of Place: A Phenomenology of the Uncanny* (2012), and *The Aesthetics of Decay: Nothingness, Nostalgia and the Absence of Reason* (2006). He is the coeditor for *Unconsciousness Between Phenomenology and Psychoanalysis* (2017).

Joseph Westfall is Associate Professor of Philosophy at the University of Houston-Downtown. He is the author of *The Kierkegaardian Author* (2007) as well as numerous essays on Kierkegaard, continental philosophy, authorship, and the arts. He is the editor of *The Continental Philosophy of Film Reader* (2018) and *Authorship and Authority in Kierkegaard's Writings* (2018), and coeditor of *Foucault and Nietzsche: A Critical Encounter* (2018).

Jason M. Wirth is Professor of Philosophy at Seattle University, and works and teaches in the areas of continental philosophy, Buddhist philosophy, aesthetics, environmental philosophy, and Africana philosophy. His recent books include *Nietzsche and Other Buddhas: Philosophy after Comparative Philosophy* (2019), *Mountains, Rivers, and the Great Earth: Reading Gary Snyder and Dōgen in an Age of Ecological Crisis* (2017), *Commiserating with Devastated Things* (2015), and *Schelling's Practice of the Wild* (2015). He is the associate editor and book review editor of the journal *Comparative and Continental Philosophy*. He is currently completing a manuscript on the cinema of Terrence Malick.

www.ingramcontent.com/pod-product-compliance
Lightning Source LLC
Chambersburg PA
CBHW061716300426
44115CB00014B/2716